Edited by Nick Pulford

Contributors

Richard Birch
Matt Gardner
David Jennings
Paul Kealy

Richard Lowther
Kevin Morley
Dave Orton
Graeme Rodway

Stefan Searle
Tom Segal
Craig Thake
Nick Watts

Designed by David Dew

Cover artwork by Duncan Olner

Published in 2024 by Pitch Publishing on behalf of Racing Post, 9 Donnington Park, 85 Birdham Road, Chichester, West Sussex, PO20 7AJ. www.pitchpublishing.co.uk info@pitchpublishing.co.uk.

Pitch Publishing specifies that post-press changes may occur to any information given in this publication. A CIP catalogue record for this book is available from the British Library.

ISBN 978-1839501449

Printed by Short Run Press

WELCOME to the Racing Post Cheltenham Festival Guide – and once again we can look forward to four fabulous days of jump racing, headlined by a couple of superstars who could put this year's meeting in the memory banks for many seasons to come.

From Britain comes Constitution Hill, who already holds the best figure recorded in the Champion Hurdle in more than 30 years since Racing Post Ratings started. This time, if pressed more closely by last year's nine-length runner-up State Man, Nicky Henderson's brilliant hurdler could take even higher rank among the all-time greats.

From Ireland there is Willie Mullins' Galopin Des Champs, who also recorded an exceptional RPR in winning last year's Gold Cup. Only the phenomenal Kauto Star and Sprinter Sacre have bettered his figure at any distance in the past 15 years.

Already, then, we are in the presence of greatness and others – notably El Fabiolo in the Champion Chase – may take the opportunity to move into that realm at this festival.

Everyone will be looking, too, for the emerging stars from the novice ranks, currently headed by the likes of Ballyburn, Sir Gino and Fact To File.

In the annual quest for winners, we hope this 208-page guide will provide valuable insight and advice.

The first half of the book features the views of tipsters and bookmakers, Racing Post Ratings, analysis of the key formlines, the lowdown on the Irish challenge and trainer pointers.

In the second half of the book, Racing Post top tipster Paul Kealy provides his race-by-race guide with forthright opinions and profiles of more than 100 of the top horses, along with key trends from Kevin Morley.

We wish you a successful festival – and let's hope it's one to savour.

NICK PULFORD, EDITOR

VIEWS FROM THE SPECIALISTS
4

The Racing Post's top tipsters and form experts, along with the major bookies, pick their fancies and debate the big issues

RACE-BY-RACE GUIDE
114

In-depth form guide to the main contenders by Racing Post top tipster Paul Kealy, with all the key trends

THE SPECIALISTS

The Racing Post's team
of experts reveal their
festival fancies and the
major bookmakers discuss
the big issues in our Q&A

Let's have a Good Time

Richard Birch

WHILE most people were salivating over the might of Galopin Des Champs, El Fabiolo and State Man at the Dublin Racing Festival, it was a performance in a handicap that excited me most in terms of a future punt.

Good Time Jonny, a Cheltenham Festival regular, may have been beaten 27 lengths into fifth behind Heart Wood in the Leopardstown Handicap Chase at 18-1, but he shaped with infinitely more promise than the losing distance suggests.

The nine-year-old has made the mid-March trip to Cheltenham three times. He finished well beaten in the Champion Bumper (2020) and Albert Bartlett Novices' Hurdle (2022) but made it third time lucky last year when comfortably landing the 23-runner Pertemps Network Final.

The importance of festival form can sometimes be overstated but it's never a negative and Good Time Jonny has clearly been meticulously laid out for the Fulke

Good Time Jonny: set for another big run in a festival handicap

Walwyn Kim Muir Handicap Chase by ace plotter Tony Martin.

The fact that Derek O'Connor partnered him two starts ago over a wholly inadequate two miles at Naas reinforces the likelihood of the Kim Muir being the target over the Ultima Handicap Chase.

Good Time Jonny was having just his fifth start over fences at Leopardstown and remains open to considerable improvement. He's also thoroughly unexposed at trips in excess of three miles and makes considerable appeal.

Corbetts Cross also boasts festival form, having been sent off a heavily backed 9-4 favourite for the Albert Bartlett Novices' Hurdle last year.

He was in second place – and holding every chance of landing the gamble – when he jinked right and ran out at the final flight.

The winner Stay Away Fay has made up into a smart novice chaser this term and was beaten only three and a half lengths in Cheltenham's Grade 2 Cotswold Chase behind Capodanno and The Real Whacker. He boasts an official rating of 159 over fences.

Corbetts Cross has also taken extremely well to chasing, winning on soft ground at Fairyhouse in December prior to running a career-best when second to Grangeclare West over Leopardstown's 3m½f in a Grade 1 later that month.

He has always been considered a horse with plenty of class who will stay extreme distances and the 3m6f of the National Hunt Novices' Chase promises to suit him well.

His Fairyhouse fall just five weeks before Cheltenham was far from the ideal preparation, but Emmet Mullins can be relied upon to have him spot on for the big day.

The Kim Bailey-trained **Chianti Classico** also contested the Albert Bartlett last March. Odds of 66-1 reflected his chance and he was pulled up after the second-last.

Prior to Cheltenham, he had won a Market Rasen bumper and three races over hurdles at Chepstow, Market Rasen and Wincanton to stamp himself a young horse going places.

Following wind surgery over the summer, Chianti Classico has thrived as a novice chaser this season, winning novice handicaps at Chepstow and Ascot before finishing second to Flegmatik at Kempton.

His stable was chronically out of form at the time, so that Kempton performance under the steadier of 11st 10lb should be marked up.

Chianti Classico's sole run in a point-to-point saw him beat Stumptown by two and a half lengths at Tipperary. Stumptown is now officially rated 147 over fences after landing a valuable 3m1½f handicap chase at Cheltenham on New Year's Day, and Chianto Classico looks tailor-made for the demands of the Ultima Handicap Chase.

There promises to be more mileage in his mark of 143 and connections have made no secret of the regard in which this exciting seven-year-old is held.

Jonjo O'Neill was also trumpeting the claims of **Springwell Bay** after the lightly raced son of Kayf Tara had won a 2m5f handicap hurdle at Cheltenham's Paddy Power meeting in November by a length and a quarter from Gyenyame.

"My dream plan is to get him to the Stayers' Hurdle," the trainer said.

That dream may have to wait until 2025 as Springwell Bay's current mark of 143 makes him a highly attractive proposition for the Pertemps Network Final.

The vast majority of recent winners have been rated between 138 and 148 and O'Neill boasts a wonderful record in the race, having landed it four times with Danny Connors (1991), Inching Closer (2003), Creon (2004) and Holywell (2013).

Springwell Bay is a most likeable horse with plenty of pace who also stays three miles well. His high cruising speed suggests big-field handicaps will bring further improvement.

Indeed, he produced a career-best under 12st in a 14-runner qualifier for the Pertemps Final when second to Curley Finger at Musselburgh.

Winner of five of his ten starts to date, he can enjoy his finest hour by landing the three-mile Premier handicap.

Introducing the NEW VH Advantage

SUPERIOR NECK PROTECTION / REINFORCED CHEST AND SPINAL AIRBAGS

SPECIALIST IN AIR TECHNOLOGY / DEDICATED UK SERVICE CENTRE / CE NF S72 - 800 2022

www.hitairuk.co.uk | facebook: HitAirUK | instagram: @hitairukofficial | 07500 962 397

Cor! Let's bet on Cross

David Jennings

CORBETTS CROSS is the best bet of the Cheltenham Festival and I'm happy to take the 4-1 currently available for the National Hunt Novices' Chase.

That's his only entry now after being scratched from the Turners and Brown Advisory, so we know where he's going and I have a strong suspicion he'll outclass his rivals – even hot favourite Embassy Gardens, who ran a shocker in last year's Albert Bartlett.

Corbetts Cross was still on the tail of Stay Away Fay when crashing through the wing of the final hurdle in that Albert Bartlett, and his chasing career hasn't exactly been smooth sailing either. He's been sent off at 1-4, 11-10, 13-8 and 2-1 for his four outings over fences and the funny thing is that his only win came at the biggest price.

But there's no shame in twice being beaten by Grangeclare West, who was favourite for the Brown Advisory before meeting with a setback. Corbetts Cross was given plenty to do

Corbetts Cross (right): top bet for the National Hunt Novices' Chase

when they met in a Grade 1 at Leopardstown at Christmas and still breezed ten lengths clear of Flooring Porter, who is generally a 7-1 shot for the National Hunt Chase.

A little four-runner event around Fairyhouse was supposed to be a confidence-booster for Corbetts Cross last time and it was all going fine until Run Wild Fred cannoned into him at the third-last and he fell.

His jumping isn't electric but he can pop away over 3m6f at Cheltenham in what's likely to be a small field and I'll be disappointed if he's beaten barring accidents like the one at Fairyhouse.

Also on the opening day, I like the look of **Amirite** in the Ultima Handicap Chase at 25-1. Ireland has a shocking record in the race but this Henry de Bromhead-trained eight-year-old could end the drought.

He was given a sighter of the Old course at Cheltenham in October and travelled powerfully through a 3m1f handicap chase won by stablemate Whacker Clan. His saddle slipped there and he finished only fourth, but the way he moved through the race suggests he's capable of landing a good prize off his mark.

Amirite again caught the eye in the Paddy Power Chase at Leopardstown over Christmas. The ground went against him there, but he was beaten only 11 and a half lengths in fifth and I have a feeling he'll be a good deal better than the bare form of that on better ground.

Gordon Elliott is the most successful trainer in the 19-year history of the Boodles Juvenile Handicap Hurdle thanks to Flaxen Flare (2013), Veneer Of Charm (2018), Aramax (2020) and Jazzy Matty (2023) and **Ndawwi** could add his name to the roll of honour this year.

Ndawwi was a classy 93-rated performer on the Flat for Andrew Balding, good enough to take his place in the Lingfield Derby Trial and the Queen's Vase at Royal Ascot, and he has shown steady improvement in three starts over hurdles.

There was a real swagger about the way he won a maiden hurdle at Naas in January and the official margin of two and a half lengths doesn't even begin to do his superiority justice. He got an RPR of 128 for that and was handed a British mark of 134 when given an entry at Kelso recently.

A mark of 134 will mean Ndawwi has plenty of weight in the Boodles (last year's topweight McTigue had a rating of 142) but he could have the class to cope with it and it wouldn't surprise me if he turned out to be a Graded performer over hurdles. I liked the way he jumped up the straight at Naas and put the race to bed quickly.

It looks like Ballyburn is Supreme-bound and that could leave the door open for stablemate **Ile Atlantique** to take the Baring Bingham.

He did much of the donkey work in the Lawlor's of Naas Novice Hurdle and that allowed stablemate Readin Tommy Wrong to pounce late, but he'll surely take a lead at the festival and that could make the difference.

Some say **Teahupoo** *(above)* had his opportunity in last year's Stayers' Hurdle and didn't take it, but he's only seven and is worth another chance.

This time he comes straight from the Hatton's Grace Hurdle at Fairyhouse in early December. The edge hasn't been taken off him like it was in the Galmoy at Gowran Park last season and that could prove the big difference as we know by now he's best fresh.

The final selection is **Ferns Lock** in the Hunters' Chase. He was a sight for sore eye at Thurles in his prep and I fancy him strongly to do the business for David Christie and Barry O'Neill.

Crambo a star stayer

Graeme Rodway

GORDON ELLIOTT trains the first two in the ante-post market for the Stayers' Hurdle and both are owned by Robcour. As a result, it's probably unlikely that both Irish Point and Teahupoo will run and it's Irish Point who is expected to move aside and go to Aintree, where he won last season.

Teahupoo is a top-class hurdler but his best form has definitely come over shorter than three miles and he traded at 1.7 in running to win this race last year only to falter on the run-in and get outstayed by Sire Du Berlais.

That makes me think he isn't a strong stayer at the distance.

With question marks over his stamina, this is a good race for a bet and the one to be on is **Crambo**. There's no doubt about him staying the trip and nothing will be finishing faster.

Crambo has improved significantly this season and should probably be coming here with three wins in a row to his name because he ran the final furlong 1.32 seconds quicker than Slate Lane when third at Haydock in November. He would have won in another half-furlong.

To put that into perspective, 1.32 seconds

Crambo (near side): Long Walk win confirmed he's on a rapid upward curve

equates to around six lengths on good to soft going, which it was at Haydock, and that is an extraordinary amount of ground to make up over such a short distance. Crambo's last furlong was the fastest in his race and the quickest on the card.

Crambo confirmed he's on a rapid upward curve when beating Paisley Park in the Grade 1 Long Walk Hurdle at Ascot in December and not many have been able to outbattle that rival after jumping the last alongside him in recent years. Stamina is evidently Crambo's strength.

That was an 18lb improvement on his previous best Racing Post Rating and there should be plenty more progress to come on what will be only his third outing over further than 2m4f.

The stiff uphill finish at Cheltenham also promises to bring out the best in Crambo and Fergal O'Brien is superb at getting his horses right after a long break, so an 82-day absence is a plus.

The Supreme Novices' Hurdle opens the meeting and Ballyburn, who showed his class when running out the most impressive winner on either day at the Dublin Racing Festival, is now a short price. However, the Baring Bingham is also being considered, so he isn't certain to run.

One who looks sure to run here is **Jeriko Du Reponet**, who has this as his only entry in the novice hurdles all week, and trainer Nicky Henderson hasn't mentioned a different target.

Jeriko Du Reponet started the season with a tall reputation and was flawless on his first two runs over hurdles at Newbury, twice winning without needing to be fully asked for his effort.

He was underwhelming when having his prep run for the festival in Grade 2 company at Doncaster in January, scoring by only a length and a quarter, but he was going away at the finish and probably wasn't suited by the slow early gallop, which led to a frantic late sprint.

Granted a stronger pace in the festival opener, Jeriko Du Reponet looks certain to post an improved performance and Henderson has won two of the last four runnings of this Grade 1.

Marine Nationale and Gaelic Warrior both put in dismal efforts at the Dublin Racing Festival and the market for the Arkle now has an open feel. The Irish contenders don't look that strong and this could go to the best British performer, **JPR One**, who has improved for fences.

He should have won three of his four starts since going chasing as he was clear when falling at the last in a trial for this race over course and distance in November. He clearly acts at the track.

JPR One was below form when third in a Grade 1 at Sandown next time, but maybe the heavy going was against him that day and a bad mistake at the second-last didn't help.

He put that firmly behind him when landing a Grade 2 on Winter Million weekend at Lingfield in January, when improving his RPR by 8lb, and further progress is likely.

My final selection is **Grey Dawning** *(above)* in the Brown Advisory. He should be coming here unbeaten in his last three runs because he would probably have beaten Ginny's Destiny at Cheltenham two starts ago but for a bad mistake two out, and that rival has won subsequently.

The step up to 3m at Warwick last time brought further improvement from Grey Dawning when he slammed Apple Away by 14 lengths in a good time and there looks to be more to come.

Elementary for Watson

Nick Watts

THE Champion Hurdle appears to be a closed shop, and to a slightly lesser extent so do the Champion Chase and Gold Cup, so for the most part we must look beyond the big championship races for attractive options.

One is the Willie Mullins-trained **Lecky Watson**, who could have the Albert Bartlett on his radar and is a generally available 12-1.

His run in the Champion Bumper at last year's festival was excellent, finishing fourth and close to such horses as Fact To File, Captain Teague and It's For Me. Since going hurdling, he won on his return at Thurles over 2m7f in November before being placed in two Graded races over the shorter trip of 2m4f.

Both of those runs were excellent, particularly two starts ago at Navan, where he finished half a length behind the classy Slade Steel. That showed he's probably not quite up to a crack at the Baring Bingham, but he's still unexposed over staying distances and

Lecky Watson: looks well suited to the Albert Bartlett test

his winning run at Thurles suggested that's where he needs to go.

He pulled far too hard there and did plenty wrong, but still pulled the race out of the fire, and he can go well in the Albert Bartlett if he switches off in the likely big field.

The Stayers' Hurdle has been unpredictable in recent years. We had a 33-1 winner last season, a 50-1 winner in 2020, and even Flooring Porter was a relatively unfancied 12-1 for his first victory two years ago.

However, in the hope that some order is restored this year, I'm going for ante-post favourite **Teahupoo** to step up two places on last year's close third behind Sire Du Berlais and Dashel Drasher.

Compared to some in this field, he's a spring chicken at the age of seven and he seems to be getting better year on year. He's starting to make the Hatton's Grace Hurdle his own, having won the Fairyhouse Grade 1 for the last two years, and while the decision to keep him off the track after his latest win in early December hasn't pleased the purists, in his case it was the right thing to do.

He goes well fresh. His two Grade 1 wins have come after absences of 219 and 220 days, so going to Cheltenham off a gap of 102 days should work to his advantage.

He almost did it last year – a couple of sloppy jumps and a messy finish where he had to be switched turned what might have been a win into a narrow defeat. Hopefully this year he can put that right.

Mullins will probably win a hatful again and his streak is likely to start in the first race on Tuesday, the Supreme, where he can pick between Ballyburn and **Mystical Power**.

Both are obvious contenders, but will they run against each other? That doesn't appear likely and I would hazard a guess that Ballyburn will go in the Baring Bingham and Mystical Power in the Supreme.

I'm hoping that's the case as I was most impressed by the way Mystical Power won the Moscow Flyer at Punchestown last time out. It might not have been the strongest running of the Grade 2, but Mystical Power was having his first run for 167 days and was very light on experience going into it.

That rawness showed through the race and he remains a work in progress, but the talent is most definitely there. Being by Galileo out of Annie Power doesn't automatically mean he's going to be a superstar, but the signs are promising after three starts and apparently he does nothing at home – which I take as a positive that he saves it for the racetrack.

Don't be surprised if he comes off the bridle at Cheltenham, but don't be surprised either if he finishes off his race strongly once he gets organised.

The Arkle, which follows immediately after the Supreme, has been thrown wide open after Marine Nationale's defeat at the Dublin Racing Festival.

Il Etait Temps has thrust himself to the forefront after taking to fences much better than most expected. However, his Cheltenham record is undistinguished – two fifth places from two starts – and his Mullins stablemate **Facile Vega** is way ahead in that respect.

Facile Vega won the Champion Bumper in 2022 and was a good second to Marine Nationale in the Supreme last year. In my view, he has been unfairly maligned, probably on account of his illustrious lineage as a son of Quevega, but he has won eight of his 12 starts, four in Grade 1 company.

Last time out he bounced back from a dreadful run at Christmas to finish on the heels of Il Etait Temps in the Irish Arkle at the Dublin Racing Festival. Judging from that race, a more forceful ride might benefit him over two miles.

He jumps well and stays further, so he has the attributes to stretch his opponents. At Leopardstown Paul Townend was content to sit in second behind Found A Fifty and Facile Vega got done for a bit of toe after the last.

He wasn't beaten far, however, and more positive tactics could see him in a different light. He has drifted out to a decent price for the Arkle at around 8-1 and I think he'll finish in the frame at least. With a bit of luck, he might well win it.

Tuesday, March 12

1.30 Sky Bet Supreme Novices' Hurdle ITV/RTV
2.10 My Pension Expert Arkle Novices' Chase ITV/RTV
2.50 Ultima Handicap Chase ITV/RTV
3.30 Unibet Champion Hurdle ITV/RTV
4.10 Close Brothers Mares' Hurdle ITV/RTV
4.50 Boodles Juvenile Handicap Hurdle RTV
5.30 National Hunt Novices' Chase RTV

Wednesday, March 13

1.30 Baring Bingham Novices' Hurdle ITV/RTV
2.10 Brown Advisory Novices' Chase ITV/RTV
2.50 Coral Cup Handicap Hurdle ITV/RTV
3.30 Betway Queen Mother Champion Chase ITV/RTV
4.10 Glenfarclas Cross Country Chase ITV/RTV
4.50 Grand Annual Handicap Chase RTV
5.30 Weatherbys Champion Bumper RTV

Thursday, March 14

1.30 Turners Novices' Chase ITV/RTV
2.10 Pertemps Network Final Handicap Hurdle ITV/RTV
2.50 Ryanair Chase ITV/RTV
3.30 Paddy Power Stayers' Hurdle ITV/RTV
4.10 TrustATrader Plate Handicap Chase ITV/RTV
4.50 Ryanair Mares' Novices' Hurdle RTV
5.30 Fulke Walwyn Kim Muir Handicap Chase RTV

Friday, March 15

1.30 JCB Triumph Hurdle ITV/RTV
2.10 County Handicap Hurdle ITV/RTV
2.50 Albert Bartlett Novices' Hurdle ITV/RTV
3.30 Boodles Cheltenham Gold Cup ITV/RTV
4.10 St James's Place Hunters' Chase ITV/RTV
4.50 Mrs Paddy Power Mares' Chase RTV
5.30 Martin Pipe Conditional Jockeys' H'cap Hurdle RTV

ED CHAMBERLIN will lead the ITV coverage again this year, supported by Sir Anthony McCoy, Ruby Walsh, Megan Nicholls, Mick Fitzgerald, Alice Plunkett, Oli Bell, Rishi Persad, Matt Chapman, Luke Harvey, Richard Hoiles, Kevin Blake, Brough Scott and Chris Hughes.

Once again there will be a 90-minute Opening Show programme on ITV4 each morning. The preview show will run from 8.30am to 10am.

ITV's live racing show featuring the first five races each day is scheduled to run from 1pm to 4.30pm.

Racing TV will show all 28 festival races live and there will be a live preview show from Cheltenham every morning until racing starts.

DONATE TODAY

To donate £5, text ROR2 to 70970
To donate £10, text ROR2 to 70191

Help retired racehorses find new purpose and loving homes

We offer retraining, rehoming, and welfare programmes for retired racehorses to ensure they have a dignified and fulfilling life after they stop racing

RoR Retraining of Racehorses®

01488 648998   **DONATE**®   ror.org.uk

'His price is simply too big'

Who do you fancy for the Gold Cup?

Richard Birch Galopin Des Champs had the look of a potential multiple Gold Cup winner the moment he went 12 lengths clear in the 2022 Turner Novices' Chase prior to falling at the final fence. He ticked off the first one with an awesome seven-length success 12 months ago and looks a class above his rivals. L'Homme Presse offers the best each-way value against him.

David Jennings It's a better Gold Cup than last year with Fastorslow, Gerri Colombe and Shishkin in there, but there can only be one winner if Galopin Des Champs is in his Savills Chase form. Perhaps Gerri Colombe is the value from an each-way perspective. He's had a light campaign and 3m2½f around the

New course at Cheltenham is a different kettle of fish to 3m at Leopardstown. He should get much closer to the favourite.

Graeme Rodway Galopin Des Champs is going to be difficult to beat and it's possible to argue that he should be shorter than his current price. He has put some blips firmly behind him on his last two starts at Leopardstown, has loads of Cheltenham form and should win. If you'd rather back something at bigger odds, Protektorat could run into a place.

Nick Watts I think Galopin Des Champs will win again and it could be a re-run of the Irish Gold Cup with Fastorslow his biggest danger. If there was to be a surprise result, Corach Rambler could be the one to provide it. He's a two-time festival winner who'll devour the hill.

Martin Brassil with his Gold Cup challenger Fastorslow

Who's your pick for the Champion Hurdle?

Richard Birch We don't see Constitution Hill very often, but every time we do it's a special occasion. There isn't a two-miler around who can get him off the bridle at the second-last and make him work hard. State Man has looked top class this winter but he was thrashed nine lengths by the champion last year.

David Jennings It might be closer but it's hard to envisage the result being any different from last year. Constitution Hill is a freak and any of his performances, apart from the Aintree Hurdle one, ought to suffice. State Man is the only realistic danger.

Graeme Rodway Constitution Hill is a class apart and it's a shame that his biggest danger, Lossiemouth, is heading to the Mares' Hurdle instead. With her out of the way, Constitution Hill has only State Man to beat again and he made short work of him last year. It might be closer but I still expect Constitution Hill to win. Luccia is the most interesting outsider.

Nick Watts Constitution Hill will probably win. But he has been campaigned a bit negatively for me and I'd love to see State Man give him a proper race. It's down to him to provide meaningful opposition as there's nothing else.

What do you make of the Champion Chase?

Richard Birch It's hard to see El Fabiolo being beaten. He slammed Jonbon by five and a half lengths in the Arkle last year and looks to have improved since. Edwardstone's odds were slashed after his Newbury win but he has never filled me with any confidence.

David Jennings El Fabiolo appears to be getting better and has already proved he has more natural ability than Jonbon. Arkle winners have a terrific record in the following year's Champion Chase and he can be another to complete the double.

Graeme Rodway El Fabiolo still appears to be improving and will probably beat Jonbon by

Home By The Lee: a much bigger price for the Stayers' Hurdle this year

further than he did in last year's Arkle. Jonbon is still the biggest danger but I wouldn't be surprised if Edwardstone runs a big race. He looked good at Newbury last time and is back in top form.

Nick Watts I strongly fancied El Fabiolo until Edwardstone's win in the Game Spirit. I still do fancy him but if Edwardstone jumps fluently off the front there'll be no margin of error for El Fabiolo. Still, the favourite will win if he gets it right at the fences.

What's your view on the Stayers' Hurdle?

Richard Birch It looks wide-open. Perhaps

it's my heart – rather than my head – telling me that Paisley Park is overpriced at 16-1, so the bet is Home By The Lee at 25-1. Sent off 9-1 last year, he never fully recovered from a bad mistake at the sixth flight, but was beaten only three and three-quarter lengths in fifth. His price is simply too big.

David Jennings Teahupoo has his knockers, but he's only seven and already has five RPRs of 163 or more on his CV. He wasn't beaten far in the race last year when his Galmoy exertions on bottomless ground may have taken the edge off him. He's fresher this time and that could make the difference.

Graeme Rodway Crambo is one of the bets

of the week. I backed Teahupoo in last year's race and I don't think he stayed the trip up the hill. There won't be any worries on that score for Crambo, who flew home for third at Haydock in November and outbattled Paisley Park in the Long Walk at Ascot. The stiffer test of stamina on the New course looks certain to bring further progress.

Nick Watts I like the way Gordon Elliott has left Teahupoo off since he won the Hatton's Grace at Fairyhouse in December. A quick glance through his record shows he goes very well fresh and he came mighty close to winning this race last season. Asterion Forlonge is a big price but could hit the frame.

Shishkin: back on track for the Gold Cup with his prep win in the Denman

'I think he can put it up to the favourite'

Who do you fancy for the Gold Cup?

Bet365 Pat Cooney Galopin Des Champs still looks to be improving based on his two most recent races, so I expect him to retain his title. If the ground isn't too testing, Shishkin may well be the only other runner still on the bridle turning in, but the guaranteed stamina of the favourite should decide the outcome.

Betfair Barry Orr It's Galopin Des Champs' race to lose but I really can't see Shishkin out of the first three. We all know he can be a bit moody but he retains a lot of ability and has some guts in a fight. His win in the Denman Chase was very encouraging and the trip on better ground will play to his strengths.

BoyleSports Alan Reilly Galopin Des Champs was hugely impressive at Leopardstown again and comprehensively reversed form with Fastorslow. The pace of the Gold Cup should enable Shishkin to remain interested throughout and I wouldn't rule out L'Homme Presse if it comes up very soft on this return to his preference for a left-handed track.

Coral Andrew Lobo Galopin Des Champs didn't impress everyone last time and I was a little underwhelmed. I'm happy to chance Gerri Colombe, who has long looked a thorough stayer and seemed to peak in the spring last year. No doubt Gordon Elliott will have this second-season chaser spot on for the big day.

Ladbrokes John Priddey I was still a critic of Galopin Des Champs at the start of the season but positive tactics have improved his jumping,

which was the only real chink of light for the opposition. I'm a convert now and his short price is justified.

Paddy Power **Paul Binfield** I'd imagine bookies will be keen to lay Galopin Des Champs at odds-on but he's been awesome on his last two starts and I think he's a certainty. I know Fastorslow has beaten him twice but both those reversals came at Punchestown. Galopin was far too good for him in the Irish Gold Cup and is brilliant at Cheltenham, winning twice and being 12 lengths ahead when falling at the last in his other run there.

Tote **Jamie Hart** I'm going with two whose latest efforts may have been undervalued. Bravemansgame's inability to win when cruising in the Charlie Hall Chase dominated the post-race conversations, but Gentlemansgame showed great stamina and speed that day and looks the type to improve again. L'Homme Presse's rusty jumping raised a few question marks on his return at Lingfield, but when asked for maximum effort he delivered in spades. Even at Ascot he plugged on behind a course specialist in Pic D'Orhy as though the Cheltenham hill would suit him perfectly. I'll combine both with Galopin Des Champs in Exactas and Trifectas.

William Hill **Jamie McBride** If Galopin Des Champs turns up in the same form as last year or Leopardstown at Christmas, he'll be extremely hard to beat. I can see Gerri Colombe relishing this test and running a career-best but whether that's good enough to beat the favourite remains to be seen.

Who's your pick for the Champion Hurdle?

Bet365 **Pat Cooney** State Man may well be better this season but I just can't see him reversing the form with Constitution Hill. On the day there's bound to be 'betting without the big two' and I'll focus on those who come from off the pace.

Betfair **Barry Orr** We haven't seen anything

Bravemansgame with Harry Cobden and (inset) en route to winning the 2022 King George

that could remotely suggest defeat for Constitution Hill. It's a race to savour and hopefully witness brilliance.

BoyleSports Alan Reilly I find it impossible to see State Man getting any closer to the favourite. Lossiemouth was hugely impressive on Trials day and would be an interesting alternative in receipt of the mares' allowance. However, all indications are that she'll go for the Mares' Hurdle, where she'll present punters with another would-be banker.

Coral Andrew Lobo They're playing for places behind Constitution Hill. Maybe Luccia can nick third if she takes her chance.

Ladbrokes John Priddey State Man hasn't missed a beat and has won three Grade 1s without fuss, whereas Constitution Hill has had one race and a whole load of excuses. I know this is borderline sacrilege, but does an improved State Man have more than a 25 per cent chance of beating a rusty Constitution Hill? I think he does.

Paddy Power Paul Binfield It's a brave man who takes on Constitution Hill, although at his price he'd probably be more one for the accas. State Man is unlucky that he's around at the same time as him as he's clearly the best in Ireland and was four lengths clear of the third in last year's race. Perhaps he's value if you think it only takes one mistake from Constitution Hill, but the favourite has justified the mighty hype so far.

Tote Jamie Hart We'll be lucky if four runners line up, so State Man each-way could be very good value while there are still three places being paid ante-post for this.

William Hill Jamie McBride Paul Townend seems adamant State Man wasn't at his best in last year's race, so he could well close the gap on Constitution Hill, but it's still a stretch to imagine the reigning champ not following up. Irish Point could make the frame if running here instead of the Stayers' Hurdle.

What do you make of the Champion Chase?

Bet365 Pat Cooney We know El Fabiolo is

five and a half lengths better than Jonbon on last year's Arkle, so it looks a done deal here again. While it was good to see a new version of Edwardstone at Newbury last time, I'd prefer Captain Guinness to fill third place.

Betfair Barry Orr I'm looking at an each-way alternative for a bit of value and Captain Guinness is the one I'm leaning towards with his good festival record. He was just hunted around last time at Leopardstown and should be primed for a big run in March.

El Fabiolo: on course for a rematch with old rival Jonbon

BoyleSports Alan Reilly It's hard to oppose El Fabiolo. He held Jonbon comprehensively in the Arkle and has done everything asked of him in both runs this season.

Coral Andrew Lobo Jonbon was looking like he could be a big danger until his recent blip. It's hard now to see past the favourite, but I still wouldn't be that surprised if Jonbon gave him a race.

Ladbrokes John Priddey El Fabiolo is clear on form but that's well factored into his price. Plenty of standout two-milers have been undone by the fine margins over the years and I think Jonbon is far from out of it. We haven't seen the best of him.

Paddy Power Paul Binfield El Fabiolo isn't always the most fluent jumper and I was blown away by Edwardstone's victory at Newbury, where in contrast he jumped so well. If he goes to the front again and jumps like that, he could just make El Fabiolo vulnerable to a mistake or two.

Tote Jamie Hart Dysart Dynamo set a decent pace in last year's Arkle and Jonbon probably set up the race for El Fabiolo by sticking fairly closely to it. Things will be different this year with no obvious leader. No horse should be able to get back from the kind of mistake Jonbon made four out in the Clarence House, so I can forgive him that defeat. The value looks to be with him.

William Hill Jamie McBride El Fabiolo is clearly the one to beat but if Jonbon can jump better than on Trials day and if Edwardstone can back up his Game Spirit performance, it has the potential to be one of the races of the meeting.

What's your view on the Stayers' Hurdle?

Bet365 Pat Cooney Anything's possible in this race nowadays after Lisnagar Oscar winning at 50-1 in 2020 and Sire De Berlais at 33-1 last year. I'll go for 2019 winner Paisley Park to raise the roof with an emotional win. His form this season doesn't read like a 12-year-old on the decline.

Betfair Barry Orr Gordon Elliott and owners Robcour have showed great restraint in sticking to their plan and not running Teahupoo again after winning the Hatton's Grace. He was a good third last year and has a remarkable record fresh. He should take all the beating.

BoyleSports Alan Reilly I think it's one of the front two owned by Robcour. The race becomes competitive only if they take each other on, which looks unlikely. The progressive Irish Point stayed well at Leopardstown, while Teahupoo will be a fresh horse not having run since winning the Hatton's Grace again. The rest are much of a muchness and have been beating each other all season.

Coral Andrew Lobo Nothing stands out on form, so I'd be looking for a big-priced one on the day. Maybe one of the handicappers can improve into a place.

Ladbrokes John Priddey It's probably the best puzzle of all the championship races. I like Irish Point most among the single-figure prices – he's the only one I could see progressing to dominate the division. As an each-way bet, why not Sire Du Berlais? The whole case against him is "he's 12" but the division is no stronger than last season and we don't know for sure he has regressed.

Paddy Power Paul Binfield This hasn't been the easiest for punters recently but I'm opting for Crambo, who has improved dramatically this season. I appreciate he was no match for Irish Point at Aintree last season but his improvement, combined with a completely different track, makes this a new ball game. He won a competitive Long Walk and was the best horse at the weights at Haydock before that.

Tote Jamie Hart I can't see Teahupoo and Irish Point taking each other on, so I'd be wary of backing either before the day. I'll go for Long Walk Hurdle winner Crambo to establish himself as the new leader in the staying hurdle division.

William Hill Jamie McBride Monkfish was good in the Galmoy Hurdle and can go close here if he's in the same form. At a big price Janidil would be an interesting runner if pointed here.

The Art of Ashes

12th - 15th March 2024
9am to 1pm

THE OX
RACE WEEK BRUNCH

The Breakfast of Champions

BOOK YOUR TABLE AT
THEOXCHELTENHAM.COM
OR SCAN THE CODE

10 CAMBRAY PLACE, CHELTENHAM, GL50 1JS
TELEPHONE 01242 234 779

'He looked outstanding when winning last time'

Who do you fancy for the novice hurdles?

Richard Birch Willie Mullins has an abundance of riches over the four days and can kick off the meeting by saddling Ballyburn to land the Supreme. He was most impressive at Leopardstown and has that ideal blend of speed and stamina. Stablemates Ile Atlantique and Dancing City appeal for the Baring Bingham and Albert Bartlett respectively. Nicky Henderson's Sir Gino can prevent a Closutton clean sweep by taking the Triumph.

David Jennings It's hard to look beyond Ballyburn in the Supreme, although Firefox has already beaten him and is an each-way alternative. Some say Ile Atlantique has a soft centre, but I'm not so sure and I'd fancy him to take Readin Tommy Wrong in a rematch in the Baring Bingham. I've liked My Trump Card for the Albert Bartlett for quite a while but he needs to jump better, so Captain Teague gets the vote there. Sir Gino looks flawless in the Triumph.

Graeme Rodway There are some really promising novice hurdlers this year, but which races they'll go for is anyone's guess. Jeriko Du Reponet appears to have only one target and makes plenty of appeal in the Supreme, while Captain Teague, Brighterdaysahead and Gidleigh Park are others to look out for. Ballyburn is hugely exciting too, but will be short wherever he goes.

Nick Watts I hope Mystical Power runs in the Supreme and Ballyburn in the Baring Bingham rather than the other way round. Sir Gino looks immense in the Triumph. The Albert Bartlett is wide open and Lecky Watson could go well if pointed in that direction – he ran well behind Slade Steel over shorter in December.

Ballyburn: ideal blend of speed and stamina

NATIONAL HORSERACING MUSEUM

MORE THAN JUST A MUSEUM...!

The museum occupies a 5-acre site in the heart of Newmarket and provides a wonderful day out for all ages.

Using the latest interactive and audio-visual displays you can find out about the history of horseracing, enjoy some of the country's best examples of sporting art, meet former racehorses and even have a go on our racehorse simulator!

National Horseracing Museum
Palace Street, Newmarket, Suffolk, CB8 8EP

@NHRMuseum

www.nhrm.co.uk

Il Etait Temps (right) beats Found A Fifty in the Irish Arkle

Which novice chasers stand out?

Richard Birch I like Il Etait Temps in the Arkle, with the Joe Tizzard-trained JPR One capable of making the first three at fair odds. Fact To File stands out in the Brown Advisory or Turners – whichever race Mullins decides to run him in. Never has one stable dominated the build-up to a Cheltenham Festival as much as this one – and it's not healthy.

David Jennings Marine Nationale's blowout at the Dublin Racing Festival has opened up the Arkle but he still looks by far the most talented in the likely field, so maybe he's worth another chance at 5-2. I don't know whether I'd back him at that but I don't want to back any of the others either. Fact To File looks a bit special and will take some stopping in

the Turners, while I like Stay Away Fay in the Brown Advisory. He's tough.

Graeme Rodway JPR One is a lively outsider in the Arkle. He's often ignored as he was an average hurdler, but he didn't have many runs over hurdles and is much better over fences. It could be a good year for the British in the novice chase division because Grey Dawning looked an outstanding prospect when winning at Warwick last time and can land the Brown Advisory.

Nick Watts Out of the three novice races, Fact To File would be my strongest selection to win the Turners. He's a sound jumper and more than fast enough for the shorter race. Grey Dawning could keep the Brown Advisory at home, while in the Arkle I haven't given up on Facile Vega.

'He keeps improving and will be right up there'

Slade Steel (left): big chance in the Baring Bingham

Who do you fancy for the novice hurdles?

Bet365 Pat Cooney Ballyburn in the Supreme and Sir Gino in the Triumph are both machines. Slade Steel was no match for Ballyburn over 2m but the Baring Bingham trip is ideal for him. I'd oppose anything at single figures in the Albert Bartlett – it's the hardest race to find the winner at the whole meeting.

Betfair Barry Orr The Irish will make sure Ballyburn goes off very short in the Supreme but King Of

Kingsfield will get a lot closer to him this time and has a good each-way chance. In the Baring Bingham I like Captain Teague, who'll be fresh after a hard race when winning the Challow. Shanagh Bob won the Albert Bartlett trial before Christmas and will go close in the main event.

BoyleSports Alan Reilly It's all about which race Ballyburn runs in and he'll be a very warm order wherever he lines up. It's hard to look beyond Sir Gino in the Triumph and he's another problematic banker for us bookies.

Coral Andrew Lobo We weren't keen on Jeriko Du Reponet when he was Supreme favourite earlier in the season and took a fair bit, but he could end up being the forgotten one if Ballyburn runs there. The Baring Bingham looks open. Slade Steel was well beaten at the Dublin Racing Festival and I'd be looking for an unexposed one like Billericay Dickie. He was impressive in his only start for Willie Mullins and represents a powerful owner who wouldn't have many social runners – if he runs on the day I'd take the hint. Sir Gino is a banker for many in the Triumph but I'm not sure what he beat last time and you'd have to take him on at odds-on.

Ladbrokes John Priddey Ballyburn's form is the strongest and the DRF race he won is such a key trial, but he's stoutly bred and you wonder if he's just the best of a poor year. Is there not something faster around? At big prices I think Tellherthename (Supreme), Predators Gold (Baring Bingham), Great Pepper (Albert Bartlett) and Storm Heart (Triumph) will give you some fun.

Paddy Power Paul Binfield Ballyburn will take some beating in the Supreme, while Slade Steel was no match for him at the Dublin Racing Festival but stayed on relentlessly and could be the one for the Baring Bingham. Captain Teague rewarded favourite backers in the Challow Hurdle and I think he'll be better over 3m in the Albert Bartlett, while Salvator Mundi at double-figure odds in the Triumph is intriguing given his form behind Sir Gino in France.

Tote Jamie Hart Ballyburn looks a good favourite in the Supreme, having blown a decent field apart in the Grade 1 two-miler at the Dublin Racing Festival. Don't back him now, though. He'll be bigger on the day. Handstands only holds an entry for the Baring Bingham, and that's half the battle when looking for value by betting early. He's unbeaten, keeps improving and will be right up there. The Albert Bartlett often goes to an outsider who just clicks in the hurly-burly of the big field and Stellar Story could fit the bill. He jumped awkwardly at Leopardstown in the six-runner 2m6f Grade 1 but has a better record in double-figure fields and is worth keeping onside. The only one I can see getting past Sir Gino in the Triumph is old rival Salvator Mundi. Now's the time to snap up a big price on him.

William Hill Jamie McBride It looks like Ballyburn is being pointed towards the Supreme and he'll be hard to beat, as will Sir Gino in the Triumph. If Mystical Power is switched to the Ballymore to avoid Ballyburn, I'd be keen on him. I can see him improving for a step up in trip.

Which novice chasers stand out?

Bet365 Pat Cooney Found A Fifty has solid form for the Arkle and I've now jumped off the Marine Nationale bandwagon after his recent poor run. Paul Nicholls could win the Brown Advisory with Stay Away Fay, who did well against more experienced chasers last time, and the Turners with Ginny's Destiny – I've liked all his three wins around Cheltenham.

Betfair Barry Orr Triumph Hurdle winner Quilixios is my fancy in the Arkle. A drop back to 2m saw him to best effect at Naas last time when he jumped great. I'm a massive Stay Away Fay fan – I loved his run in the Cotswold and I'm on him for the Brown Advisory. It's hard to see past Fact To File if he rocks up in the Turners.

BoyleSports Alan Reilly Ginny's Destiny in the Turners is one of my best bets of the week. Apart from a slight error two out, he was always

Sir Gino: hot favourite for the Triumph

Fact To File: strong claims for Turners or Brown Advisory

travelling like the winner on Trials day and was otherwise very fluent.

Coral Andrew Lobo The Arkle looks very open now but I can't get too excited by Il Etait Temps at a short price. It looked like the DRF was his big day. Fact To File looks a banker in whichever race he runs in given his impressive time in just a two-runner race last time.

Ladbrokes John Priddey The Arkle is very open now. Willie Mullins seems to have always regarded Facile Vega ahead of Il Etait Temps, so I'd keep the faith in him. The stopwatch suggests Fact To File is extremely good and he'll be rock solid whichever race he goes for – I hope it's the Brown Advisory to make way for another Ginny's Destiny exhibition in the Turners.

Paddy Power Paul Binfield I like Il Etait Temps' price in the Arkle compared to Marine Nationale as over the years I've relied upon the form book rather than reasons why one

horse might turn the form around with another next time. Monty's Star relished the step up to three miles at Punchestown last time and I think he'll be better at Cheltenham. Ginny's Destiny makes plenty of appeal in the Turners as a three-time course winner at around 2m4f.

Tote Jamie Hart The Arkle looks wide open but Marine Nationale can bounce back and make a mockery of the 5-2. Fact To File should be the right fit for the Turners given his travelling speed was on a par with El Fabiolo at the DRF, and Monty's Star can go one better than Monalee and Minella Indo for the same connections by winning the Brown Advisory with his lightning jumping.

William Hill Jamie McBride I'm a big fan of Fact To File and he'll be hard to beat whichever race he contests. The Arkle has an open look to it after Marine Nationale's Leopardstown flop and I could see Master Chewy running well at a big price.

JOIN A SYNDICATE

—— • ——

ENJOY THE THRILL OF OWNING A RACEHORSE BUT FOR A FRACTION OF THE COST

—— • ——

Shares start from just £39

Scan to find a syndicate
or racing club

'He comes from the key race and looks well treated'

What's your best festival bet?

Bet365 Pat Cooney Dysart Enos in the Mares' Novices' Hurdle. I'd fancy her at level weights but she's been skilfully placed by Fergal O'Brien to avoid carrying a penalty for a Class 1 or 2 win and will be getting 5lb from many of her rivals.

Betfair Barry Orr The undefeated Brighterdaysahead looks special and a drop back to 2m1f in the Mares' Novices' Hurdle won't be a problem. There aren't many who count in the race and she's nap material for me at current odds of 3-1.

BoyleSports Alan Reilly Ginny's Destiny in the Turners Novices' Chase is one of my best bets of the week. Apart from a slight error two out, he was always travelling like the winner on Trials day and was otherwise very fluent. It's all about the ground for Banbridge in the Ryanair – he has an outstanding chance on a good surface.

Coral Andrew Lobo Crebilly has caught the eye with the way he's travelled through his three novice chases, winning the last of them cosily at Exeter, and he's qualified for a handicap at the festival.

Ladbrokes John Priddey Crebilly for the Plate. He comes from the key Ginny's Destiny/Grey Dawning race and looks well treated if he can produce a clear round.

Paddy Power Paul Binfield She's not the greatest price in the world but I'd be surprised if anything beat Dinoblue in the Mrs Paddy Power Mares' Chase. She jumped brilliantly at Leopardstown at Christmas and won't come up against anything of El Fabiolo's calibre in a race confined to her own sex.

Tote Jamie Hart Sa Fureur was entered in a British handicap chase and was given a mark of 143. If he runs off that in the Grand Annual, he should win.

William Hill Jamie McBride The Yellow Clay can win an open-looking Champion Bumper. He was a big eyecatcher at the Dublin Racing Festival and the form through Redemption Day is comparable with others who are half his price.

Dysart Enos (right): well weighted

Do you know your payload before you drive to an event?

It is very easy to overload a 3500kg horsebox, and even a 7500kg one, as most people don't take into account passengers, tack, water, hay, and these add to the payload considerably.

For example, an empty 3500kg horsebox normally weighs about 2500kg, leaving 1000kg for the driver and passenger, horse, tack, etc. Many of these horseboxes are stalled for two horses, and that can be a big problem. If you are overloaded and have an accident, your insurance will be invalidated and you could be facing a number of offences, both overloading and licence ones. In recent years, the DVSA has found that more than 80% of LCV's stopped on the roadside on suspicion of overloading, are in fact overweight.

Why Uprating

You have a limited payload capacity and wish to carry an extra horse or equipment. You don't want to buy a newer, bigger horsebox so you can save money by converting your current vehicle. You want to avoid a large fine by DVSA.

What to do if you are overloaded.

The first thing is to weigh your horsebox FULLY LOADED with your horse(s), tack, water, food, and passengers so that you know where you stand. Remember to weigh each axle individually as you may find that whilst you may be under the Gross Vehicle Weight, you have actually overloaded the rear axle. This is very common in lightweight horseboxes. Fortunately SvTech can help, and is keen to promote its uprating service for lightweight horseboxes (3500kg), whereby the horsebox can gain an extra 200-300kg in payload. This provides vital payload capability when carrying an extra horse and/ or tack and offers peace of mind for the owner.

SvTech has carried out extensive work and testing on lightweight models and has covered uprates for most lightweight vehicles. It is worth noting that some uprates require modifications or changes to the vehicle's braking, tyres and/or suspension, for which SvTech provides a simple purpose-built suspension assister kit. This will take between 1-2 hours for you to fit. Your horsebox will then go for a formal inspection to bring it into the 'Goods' category, and, depending on the vehicle's age, may also require fitment of a speed limiter, for which there are one or two options.

Most importantly, vehicles registered after May 2002 must be fitted with manufacturer's ABS, if going above 3500kg.

We can start the ball rolling by asking customers to fill in an enquiry form and send it back with photos of the Horsebox plate, the weight ticket and Registration Document.

Champs looks golden

Matt Gardner

GOLD CUP

The Cheltenham Gold Cup has gone to Ireland in eight of the last ten years and Galopin Des Champs has another great chance to extend their superiority.

Galopin Des Champs' ascent to the top of the chasing tree has been quite rapid. He ran away with last year's race to become a Gold Cup winner at the age of seven, a relatively uncommon feat this century, and recorded a Racing Post Rating of 184, the best figure posted in the race since Kauto Star in 2009.

There have been missteps along the way too. He fell when set to collect in the Turners as a novice and was beaten twice by Fastorslow last year. His jumping held him back on two of those three occasions and again it wasn't too fluent in the Irish Gold Cup last time, even though he beat Fastorslow comfortably. His jumping is probably the one thing his opponents can cling to, as on form he's a standout candidate.

The rival with the strongest form claims is Shishkin, who has developed into something of a maverick in recent years. His Champion Chase flop two years ago and refusal to race on his reappearance this season have damaged his previously robust profile built on an unbeaten two-year run that stretched from a novice hurdle win in 2020 to the Clarence House in 2022 and included the Supreme and the Arkle at the festival.

Shishkin has looked more like his old self of late, however, and set himself up nicely for the Gold Cup with a straightforward success in the Denman Chase. His best form gives him a shout with Galopin Des Champs and, should he put it all together, there's a suspicion he may be able to pull out a career-best performance.

Bravemansgame finished runner-up last

Galopin Des Champs works at home under Adam Connolly

year but hasn't looked quite the same horse this season, and a more convincing second British challenger is L'Homme Presse. He appeared to retain all of the ability that brought him victory in the Brown Advisory Novices' Chase in 2022 when making a winning return from more than a year off in the Fleur De Lys Chase at Lingfield, and he's always left the impression that the Gold Cup trip will suit.

Fastorslow will probably need Galopin Des Champs to be below par if he's to lower his colours for a third time and Gerri Colombe also has a significant gap to close, although there may be greater cause for optimism in his case.

He finished second in last year's Brown Advisory, shaping as if the Gold Cup trip would be right up his street, before going on to win the Mildmay at Aintree at the end of his novice campaign and the Champion Chase at Down Royal on his reappearance this season. Hopes were high that he could challenge Galopin Des Champs in the Savills Chase, only for him to disappoint, but he remains an unexposed second-season chaser who could improve if he peaks in the spring.

GOLD CUP

This year's top rated	RPR
Galopin Des Champs	184
Shishkin	179
Bravemansgame	177
Fastorslow	175
Ahoy Senor	174
Hewick (right)	173
Conflated	171
L'Homme Presse	170
Protektorat	169
Gerri Colombe	168

How the past ten winners rated

Year	Winner	Win RPR	Pre-race RPR
2023	Galopin Des Champs	184	177
2022	A Plus Tard	183	180
2021	Minella Indo	179	170
2020	Al Boum Photo	172	178
2019	Al Boum Photo	178	171
2018	Native River	177	174
2017	Sizing John	171	168
2016	Don Cossack	182	181
2015	Coneygree	178	168
2014	Lord Windermere	168	157

10yr winning average Racing Post Rating: 177

Man could push up Hill

Matt Gardner

CHAMPION HURDLE

State Man has met with defeat only three times in his career – on his racecourse debut in France, on his Irish debut (fell when likely to win) and against Constitution Hill in last year's Champion Hurdle.

That last defeat is clearly the most relevant, not least as it was a nine-length drubbing despite State Man running creditably on the figures. His 166 in that race slots in exactly at the midpoint of his RPRs after winning his first open Grade 1 at the Punchestown festival in 2022, with the remarkably consistent range being 162 to 170.

It's fair to say State Man is an improved performer since Cheltenham last year. His RPR of 170 for his latest win in the Irish Champion

Hurdle was a career-best by 2lb and he's by far the most credible opposition to Constitution Hill. Even that improved effort leaves him with half a stone to find, however, and that's before we factor in what heights the reigning champ may still be capable of reaching.

Constitution Hill has completed two simple assignments since Cheltenham last year, winning the Aintree Hurdle and the Christmas Hurdle without needing to come within 10lb of his Champion Hurdle performance.

His RPR of 177 was the best figure recorded in the Champion

Constitution Hill: last year's RPR of 177 was the best ever in the Champion Hurdle

Hurdle in the history of Racing Post Ratings, which is saying something considering it wasn't run at a particularly strong pace and he left the firm impression he could have scored by even further.

The highest-rated hurdler historically on RPRs is Istabraq, who ran to 181 when winning at Punchestown in 1999. That's the target figure for Constitution Hill in the greatness stakes and an improved State Man may just be the opponent to draw it out of him.

The likes of Zanahiyr and Not So Sleepy have been here before and are likely playing for third at best, although even that might be out of reach if connections of Lossiemouth do an about-turn and run her here instead of in the Mares' Hurdle.

Last year's Triumph Hurdle winner would have more to find on form than the clamour in the aftermath of her International Hurdle victory would suggest. That performance was more style than substance but her presence would add a degree of intrigue that, outside of the top two, is lacking in the division.

CHAMPION HURDLE

This year's top rated		RPR
Constitution Hill		177
State Man		170
Lossiemouth		162*
Pied Piper *(right)*		161
Zanahiyr		161
Echoes In Rain		160*
Love Envoi		160*
Not So Sleepy	*Includes	160
Irish Point	7lb mares'	158
Fils D'Oudairies	allowance	157

How the past ten winners rated

Year	Winner	Win RPR	Pre-race RPR
2023	Constitution Hill	177	176
2022	Honeysuckle	159	166
2021	Honeysuckle	165	163
2020	Epatante	162	158
2019	Espoir D'Allen	171	164
2018	Buveur D'Air	165	171
2017	Buveur D'Air	170	159
2016	Annie Power	162	164
2015	Faugheen	170	169
2014	Jezki	171	167

10yr winning average Racing Post Rating: 171

Last year's winning novices set to step up

Jonbon: tough task against old rival El Fabiolo

Matt Gardner

CHAMPION CHASE

The Champion Chase is rarely competitive in terms of numbers, with a double-figure field just three times in the last ten years, but excels in terms of quality. Wednesday's feature has the second-best winning performance on average among the championship races after the Gold Cup.

This year's race is all about El Fabiolo and Jonbon, which will be a repeat of their novice clash from last year's Arkle. El Fabiolo emerged on top comfortably that day, beating Jonbon by five and a half lengths, and he's done little since to dispel the notion that he's the top two-mile chaser around.

If there's a chink in El Fabiolo's armour it is perhaps his jumping. He's never failed to complete but isn't always the most fluent at his fences, albeit while largely avoiding significant errors. That facet of his game is unlikely to come under much more pressure than we've previously seen, given the general calibre of the likely opposition, and he's very much the one to beat. We're probably still to see the best of him.

Jonbon is second in the ante-post betting, a position deserved on form if perhaps not quite to the extent that the market implies. He's always had a big reputation and has looked good in winning plenty of races against lesser opposition, but he's been found wanting on the two occasions he's come up against stiffer tasks, against Constitution Hill in the Supreme in 2022 and El Fabiolo in the Arkle.

Jonbon arrives here on something of a retrieval mission, having been beaten by the veteran Elixir De Nutz in the Clarence House after an error-strewn display, although he's better judged on his overall body of work rather than that one disappointment.

Ferny Hollow, who looked an outstanding prospect as a novice in 2021, might be a more enticing option at more than five times the ante-post price, if a riskier one given his fragility.

RYANAIR CHASE

Thursday's feature chase is more competitive for the absence of Allaho, who misses Cheltenham for the second year running through injury, but lacks a standout performer as a result.

Boasting the best form is Stage Star, who blows rather hot and cold but looks good when on song, as when winning the Turners last year and the Paddy Power Gold Cup on his reappearance this season, despite a near catastrophic final-fence error.

If Stage Star has an off day, waiting in the wings are Banbridge and Envoi Allen.

Banbridge has generally come up short at the top level and the Manifesto Novices' Chase he won at Aintree last season was a weak running of that Grade 1, but he's a likeable individual who's likely to run his race as long as conditions (best away from soft ground) are favourable.

Envoi Allen landed this prize last year but that performance rated below what it usually takes to win the Ryanair and he'll probably have to find a bit more this time.

Protektorat would be of interest if he turned up here. He's run in the Gold Cup for the last two years but ought to be just as effective dropping back in trip and has performed with credit this season, finishing third in a handicap off a mark of 165 in December before finding only L'Homme Presse too good at Lingfield last time. In some ways, this may present a slightly easier task than either of those races.

CHAMPION CHASE

This year's top rated		RPR
El Fabiolo		179
Edwardstone *(right)*		171
Jonbon		171
Ferny Hollow		168
Gentleman De Mee		167
Captain Guinness		165
Editeur Du Gite		164
Funambule Sivola	*Includes*	162
Maskada	*7lb mares'*	162*
Elixir De Nutz	*allowance*	160

How the past ten winners rated

Year	Winner	Win RPR	Pre-race RPR
2023	Energumene	179	177
2022	Energumene	177	179
2021	Put The Kettle On	162	160
2020	Politologue	173	173
2019	Altior	173	183
2018	Altior	183	177
2017	Special Tiara	170	170
2016	Sprinter Sacre	176	173
2015	Dodging Bullets	169	173
2014	Sire De Grugy	173	174

10yr winning average Racing Post Rating: 175

RYANAIR CHASE

This year's top rated	RPR
Stage Star	171
Banbridge	169
Pic D'Orhy	169
Protektorat *(right)*	169
Janidil	168
Envoi Allen	167
Capodanno	164
Fugitif	162
Minella Drama	161
Appreciate It	160
French Dynamite	160

10yr winning average Racing Post Rating: 173

Ground key for Teahupoo

Matt Gardner

STAYERS' HURDLE

Teahupoo and Irish Point dominate the market for the Stayers' Hurdle, an unusual scenario given that they're owned and trained by the same connections.

There was talk earlier in the season that Irish Point might be saved for Aintree, but it's hard to escape the conclusion that this is the ideal race for both horses. More recent indications are that both will run and it would be refreshing if connections went ahead with the clash instead of keeping them apart.

There's an age difference of just one year between them but this will be Teahupoo's third run at the festival whereas Irish Point has the feel of the new kid on the block about him.

Teahupoo's previous visits have resulted in varying levels of performance. He was last in the Champion Hurdle in 2022 but a far more respectable third in this race last year.

The excuse given by connections for Teahupoo's lacklustre effort in 2022 was that he needed easier ground than the official soft, which on the times was riding more like good. That theory is borne out by his overall record, with his best efforts coming when the ground is soft or heavy.

That was the case when Teahupoo beat Impaire Et Passe in the Hatton's Grace in December and connections decided to keep him fresh for Cheltenham thereafter, which is potentially a shrewd decision as his record after an absence of three months or more stands at 4-4.

If conditions are testing Teahupoo will be the one to beat but ground more like good to soft could see him come up a little short of his best, which would open the door for several others.

Irish Point is the obvious alternative as an unexposed hurdler both overall and at this trip. He was impressive in Leopardstown's Christmas Hurdle on his first start over a staying trip, beating Asterion Forlonge by an easy 11 lengths.

That steadily run race tested speed more than stamina, however, and he still has the staying question to answer even if he heads here with the potential to improve again.

Monkfish *(left)* presents a different conundrum. He won't fail for stamina, being both an Albert Bartlett and a Brown Advisory winner, and if anything his chance will be enhanced if the ground comes up testing. What has to be proved is his wellbeing, having raced just four times since his last visit to the festival three years ago. His comeback win in the Galmoy Hurdle suggested he retains most of his ability but he needs to go the right way from that.

Dashel Drasher and Flooring Porter in theory represent more solid propositions, although the former hasn't been at his best this season, despite winning Newbury's Long Distance Hurdle in December, while Flooring Porter, should he run here, will be reverting to hurdles after an unconvincing stint as a novice chaser.

A more interesting option is Crambo, who has improved for the step up to three miles this season and edged out Paisley Park in the Long Walk at Ascot last time. He needs to progress again but that's a distinct possibility, having fewer miles on the clock than most of his likely rivals.

Teahupoo: testing conditions would be to his advantage

STAYERS' HURDLE

This year's top rated	RPR
Teahupoo	168
Flooring Porter *(right)*	166
Sire Du Berlais	166
Blazing Khal	164
Dashel Drasher	163
Home By The Lee	163
Monkfish	160
Asterion Forlonge	159
Crambo	159
Irish Point	159
Paisley Park	159

How the past ten winners rated

Year	Winner	Win RPR	Pre-race RPR
2023	Sire Du Berlais	164	162
2022	Flooring Porter	166	169
2021	Flooring Porter	168	167
2020	Lisnagar Oscar	159	151
2019	Paisley Park	168	172
2018	Penhill	162	158
2017	Nichols Canyon	164	166
2016	Thistlecrack	176	172
2015	Cole Harden	168	158
2014	More Of That	172	161

10yr winning average Racing Post Rating: 167

Plenty with chances in intriguing division

Matt Gardner

NOVICE CHASERS

For much of the season the Arkle looked the most clear-cut of the festival novice chases to solve. Marine Nationale, last year's sparkling Supreme Novices' Hurdle winner, was the standout, an opinion strengthened by his impressive debut over fences.

That changed, however, when Marine Nationale disappointed behind Il Etait Temps in the Irish Arkle at the Dublin

Marine Nationale: worthy of another chance in the Arkle

PREMIER EQUINE
ENGLAND

Turnout Rugs   Stable Rugs   Cooler Rugs   Horse Boots

Saddle pads   Saddles   Therapy

PROUD SUPPLIERS TO THE RACING COMMUNITY

To apply for a trainer's trade account, please contact:
sales@premierequine.co.uk | Order Line 01469 532279
www.premierequine.co.uk

Racing Festival. That necessitated a small rethink of his chasing debut – with the benefit of hindsight, it was a thin race and the form hasn't worked out.

It's possible to make excuses for Marine Nationale's disappointing run, not least as he made a significant mistake late in the race, and on the whole he remains an exciting prospect. He's certainly worthy of another chance in an Arkle that might not be the deepest we've seen.

Il Etait Temps matched the pick of his hurdles form in winning the Irish Arkle. That's both to his credit but also a limitation, as he's finished fifth in both the Triumph and Marine Nationale's Supreme at the festival, which suggests he might not have all that much more to come.

Facile Vega, Il Etait Temps' stablemate, also came up short in the Supreme last year and is yet to build on a bright start over fences this term.

Found A Fifty has the form to play a part but perhaps not the potential and he may be more likely to contest the Turners in any case.

More exciting prospects include Hunters Yarn, who's already made up into a better chaser than hurdler despite being less than foot-perfect at his fences, and Iroko, last year's Martin Pipe winner, who made an impressive debut over fences in November. He suffered an injury after that but has returned to training much faster than anticipated and has scope for plenty of improvement.

The Turners has been something of the ugly duckling of the three Grade 1 novices in recent years, taking the least winning on average. The gap between it and the Arkle and Brown Advisory widens further when discounting 2015 winner Vautour, whose performance stands out on the recent roll of honour.

This year it looks the obvious port of call for Fact To File, one of the season's leading novices. His jumping looks assured and he's likely to prove hard to beat, although the likeable and rapidly progressive Ginny's Destiny, who has plenty of Cheltenham experience, may give him more to think about than the ante-post market suggests.

Britain's best chance may lie in the Brown Advisory, with both Grey Dawning and Stay Away Fay boasting appealing profiles for the race.

Grey Dawning saw out a well-run race on testing ground really strongly at Warwick in January and Stay Away Fay, last season's Albert Bartlett winner, has also made a bright transition to fences. He came up short in open company in the Cotswold Chase last time but is another who ought to be well suited to the demands of the Brown Advisory.

Found A Fifty: has the form but perhaps not the potential

NOVICE CHASERS	
Top rated	**RPR**
Il Est Francais	168
Fact To File	164
Grey Dawning	162
Stay Away Fay	162
Ginny's Destiny	161
Gaelic Warrior	160
Nickle Back	159
Grangeclare West	158
Hercule Du Seuil	157
Il Etait Temps	156
Marine Nationale	156
Arkle 10yr av	**168**
Turners 10yr av	**164**
Brown 10yr av	**167**

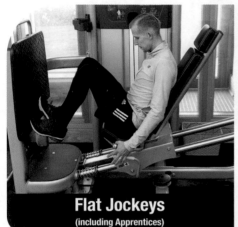
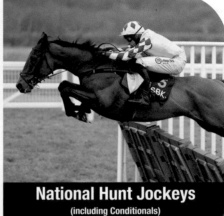

Mullins has strong pack to shuffle

Matt Gardner

NOVICE HURDLERS

Generally speaking the novice hurdle that has taken the least winning historically is the Albert Bartlett. Not only does it boast the lowest average winning Racing Post Rating of the three races over the last ten years but, since its inception in 2005, no horse has broken the 160 barrier, with Black Jack Ketchum coming closest on 159 in 2006.

That may well be the case again, not least as it's the one race where this season's leading novice hurdler, Ballyburn, isn't entered. At this stage it's still up in the air whether the Supreme or the Baring Bingham will be the target selected by Willie

Firefox: the only horse to have beaten Ballyburn

VISIT CHELTENHAM
THE FESTIVAL TOWN

A celebration of all things Cheltenham

EVENTS & FESTIVALS

PLACES TO EAT

THINGS TO DO

STAND OUT SHOPPING

www.visitcheltenham.com

Mullins, but what is clear is that he has the form and potential to take plenty of beating in either.

The ante-post markets are anticipating that Ballyburn will contest the Supreme. He would head there on the back of an impressive win at the Dublin Racing Festival, where he finished seven lengths in front of Slade Steel, who in turn pulled clear of several other promising sorts.

That success was certainly more impressive than what Jeriko Du Reponet, previously his main market rival for the Supreme, produced in a Doncaster Grade 2 last time.

To Jeriko Du Reponet's credit, that was a muddling race run at a steady pace and the additional experience, having previously won a pair of weaker events, will serve him well. It's hard to escape the conclusion that he's priced more on potential than form, however.

Another possible rival is Firefox, who beat Ballyburn in a Fairyhouse maiden hurdle in December. He had the benefit of match fitness then and has disappointed over a longer trip since, but he was impressive that day and looks worth another chance.

Between Readin Tommy Wrong, Ile Atlantique and Mystical Power, Mullins is also likely to win the Baring Bingham.

Readin Tommy Wrong beat Ile Atlantique in a Naas Grade 1 last time, seeming to knuckle down a bit better than his stablemate as they pulled clear, but the most compelling of the Mullins squad is Mystical Power.

Annie Power's first foal has improved in chunks on each start, impressing on just his second run over hurdles in a Punchestown Grade 2 last time. He's open to plenty more improvement and is an exciting prospect, even if he'll be conceding experience to most of his rivals.

Mullins' chances of a clean sweep in the festival novice hurdles look solid, as he also has a strong hand in the Albert Bartlett. High Class Hero has gained plenty of experience over hurdles in compiling an unbeaten run, but others perhaps boast more potential, chief among them being stablemate Dancing City.

Dancing City has won two of his three starts over hurdles, including when usurping his better-fancied stablemate Predators Gold in a Grade 1 at Leopardstown last time. The step up to three miles seems sure to suit and he sets the standard.

Others to consider include the Paul Nicholls-trained Captain Teague, who won the Challow Hurdle and appeals as being likely to relish this trip, and Nicky Henderson's Shanagh Bob, who won the Albert Bartlett course trial in December. That race was rather muddling and it is likely he has more improvement to come.

The standout candidate in the Triumph Hurdle is Sir Gino, who has looked an exciting prospect for Henderson in his two outings this season, winning the trial for this race in particularly impressive fashion last time.

Burdett Road, previously well fancied for the Triumph, was ten lengths behind Sir Gino that day and, although it's anticipated he'll come on for that run, it seems unlikely he'll be able to turn the tables, not least as Sir Gino looks open to considerable improvement.

The leading Irish-trained contender on form is Kargese, although plenty went her way in a Grade 1 at Leopardstown last time and she might be vulnerable to improvers, who could include stablemate Storm Heart. He finished second to Kargese in that race but is likely to be well suited by the stamina test that the Triumph generally provides.

NOVICE HURDLERS	
Top rated	RPR
Ballyburn	158
Caldwell Potter	152
Dancing City	152
Predators Gold	150
Readin Tommy Wrong	149
Slade Steel	148
Anotherway	147
High Class Hero	147
Ile Atlantique	146
Supreme 10yr av	**161**
Ballymore 10yr av	**157**
A Bartlett 10yr av	**154**

JUVENILE HURDLERS	
Top rated	RPR
Sir Gino	143
Kargese	*139
Storm Heart	138
Bunting	137
Majborough	137
Kala Conti	*136
Ethical Diamond	134
Burdett Road	130
Nurburgring	130
*Includes 7lb fillies' allowance	
Triumph 10yr av 150	

World Horse Welfare is the only equine welfare charity that actively supports the responsible involvement of horses in sport.

With racehorse welfare under the spotlight like never before, we provide independent advice to British racing to help them meet the high expectations of everyone in the sport and outside of it.

Please give £3 a month to help support our work.

Scan the QR code to donate today.

www.worldhorsewelfare.org
Registered charity no. 206658 and SC038384

Anne Colvin House, Snetterton, Norfolk, NR16 2LR, UK

Registered with
FUNDRAISING
REGULATOR

BROWN ADVISORY NOVICES' CHASE

Grey Dawning (advised at 9-1)
The best staying novice hurdlers last season were trained in Britain and they normally make the best novice chasers in the following campaign, so this is one race that might not be booked for export.

The suggestion is Grey Dawning after he surely put up the staying novice chase performance of the season when winning at Warwick in January. He gave Grade 1-winning hurdler Apple Away 10lb and a 14-length beating, with the 150-rated Broadway Boy a further 18 lengths away. It was a big step up on his previous form and that was because the race turned into a huge stamina test. It suited Grey Dawning perfectly.

The more you study his form, the better it looks, and he should really have won at Cheltenham the time before when making a bad mistake two out. Once again he showed impressive depths of stamina to pick up after that error and he was closing down a good horse fast come the line.

RYANAIR CHASE

Fil Dor (advised at 14-1)
A young up-and-comer could improve past the horses we already know everything about in the Ryanair. The bar that an improver has to reach is not actually that high. Yes, Banbridge might be that star

Fil Dor: could be a big improver in the Ryanair

horse, but on form he's not there yet and the youngest horse still left in, Fil Dor, is worth considering as well.

He has festival form, having been second in the Triumph, and might just be a big improver as the form of his two runs over 2m this season looks good. The only two to beat him this winter are El Fabiolo and Dinoblue, who are both short-priced favourites to win at Cheltenham, and on both occasions he strongly suggested he needs to go up in trip.

ARKLE NOVICES' CHASE

My Mate Mozzie (advised at 25-1 each-way)
My Mate Mozzie is going to be ridden to make the frame and, in a race where I expect only a handful of runners, has every chance of doing so.

He isn't the easiest to win with but has most definitely improved for the application of a tongue-tie.

Two starts ago, in an admittedly weak race over course and distance, he jumped really well to come out on top in a canter, and then he did really well

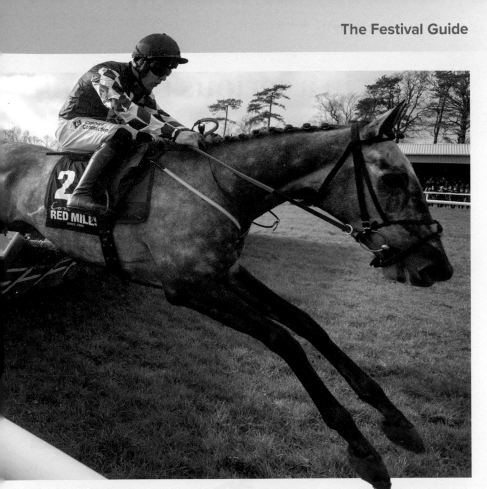

to run on into second at Leopardstown last time, splitting Found A Fifty and Facile Vega, given he was ridden way off the pace in a race that didn't have a strong gallop.

I have no doubt My Mate Mozzie is more talented than Gabynako, who finished second in the Arkle for Gavin Cromwell, and the trainer has a great record when targeting one at a big race.

CHAMPION HURDLE
State Man (advised at 4-1)
Without Constitution Hill, I reckon many would be hailing State Man as one of the best of all time and expecting him to win two or three Champion Hurdles.

When watching the 2023 Champion Hurdle again, the one thing that struck me was how negative Paul Townend was on State Man, holding him up out the back on the outside and giving Constitution Hill plenty of easy lengths.

In no way is it possible to think he could have beaten the winner, but State Man was never put under any serious pressure throughout the whole race, and he will surely get a lot closer if ridden differently this time.

Trying to match strides with Constitution Hill may be the quickest way to get any horse beaten, but the Willie Mullins team are going to have to try something different and I'm pretty sure State Man is at least half a dozen lengths better than he showed last year.

If Constitution Hill makes a mistake, or is a little bit below his best, that would put State Man right on the premises.

'He put in a serious round of jumping'

CHELTENHAM'S Trials day is the last chance for a prep run on the track before the festival and it has proved a decent stepping stone, although its impact is somewhat limited by not having the same breadth of races as Leopardstown's Dublin Racing Festival the following weekend.

In the past decade, 13 of the 59 Trials day winners to attempt a festival follow-up have been successful at a healthy 22 per cent strike-rate. The most recent to double up was Stage Star,

who went on from victory in the novice handicap chase on Trials day last year to land the Grade 1 Turners Novices' Chase at the festival.

The only other winner at last year's festival who had run on Trials day was Energumene, who was third in the Clarence House Chase (transferred from Ascot to the Cheltenham card, as it was again this year) and then won the Queen Mother Champion Chase.

In all, six of last year's 28 festival winners (21%) had run at Cheltenham that season, including four last time out.

Perhaps more significantly, 15 of the 28 winners had

competed previously at the festival and two others had run at the course.

Of those 17 winners, 14 had won or finished second on at least one previous visit to Cheltenham. Considering many younger horses – especially those trained in Ireland – have had limited opportunity to run at Cheltenham, the value of course experience is plain.

Tipsters and bookmakers pick some eyecatchers from Trials day . . .

Richard Birch Sir Gino burst the Burdett Road bubble and emerged as very

RECORD OF TRIALS DAY WINNERS AT THE CHELTENHAM FESTIVAL

Based on last ten runnings of the meeting

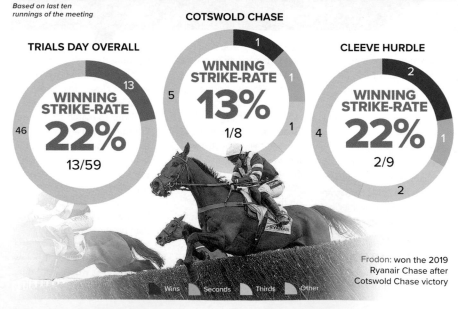

TRIALS DAY OVERALL

13
46
WINNING STRIKE-RATE
22%
13/59

COTSWOLD CHASE

1
5
1
1
WINNING STRIKE-RATE
13%
1/8

CLEEVE HURDLE

2
4
1
2
WINNING STRIKE-RATE
22%
2/9

Wins Seconds Thirds Other

Frodon: won the 2019 Ryanair Chase after Cotswold Chase victory much the one to beat in the Triumph when strolling home by ten lengths.

David Jennings Stay Away Fay. Plenty were disappointed that he didn't win the Cotswold Chase, but I wasn't one of them. A lot went wrong in the race and he was still bang there coming up the hill. He's tough, tries hard and will take some stopping in the Brown Advisory.

Graeme Rodway Excelero is from the Jane Williams stable, which does well with juveniles, and was a good fourth behind Sir Gino in the Triumph Trial. A mark of 124 would have got Excelero into last year's Fred Winter, so I'll be looking for his name in the entries.

Nick Watts Richard Bandey's Theatre Man was a strong-staying second behind Ginny's Destiny in the novice handicap chase and could be interesting if he goes for the Ultima.

Bet365 Pat Cooney Fugitif was noted staying on well in the Clarence House. The step up in trip to the Ryanair Chase should really suit and he may be worth an each-way interest at a price.

Betfair Barry Orr For a novice having only his third start over fences, Stay Away Fay put in a serious round of jumping in the Cotswold against some seasoned campaigners and he'll revert to novice company in the Brown Advisory.

Lossiemouth: impressive win on Trials day

BoyleSports Alan Reilly Ginny's Destiny and Lossiemouth were the standouts.

Coral Andrew Lobo Excelero ran a good race for Jane Williams behind Sir Gino on just his second run and is bound to come on again. He could be one to follow if allowed to take his chance in the Triumph or Fred Winter should he qualify.

Ladbrokes John Priddey Lossiemouth looks a different species to the rest of the mares and it's as if the Mares' Hurdle is already in the bag.

William Hill Jamie McBride Ahoy Senor showed sparkle in the Cotswold Chase, where he was giving weight all round and had tack problems. I could see him running well at a big price in an open Ryanair.

GOLD CUP

KEY FORM RACE

Galopin Des Champs faced something of an acid test in the **Savills Chase** having lost his next two outings after landing last season's Gold Cup. He answered every question with an imperious display, easily seeing off main market rival Gerri Colombe by 23 lengths.

The switch to more positive tactics made a big difference and he looked much happier over his fences.

It matched his career-best Racing Post Rating in the Gold Cup and the form is red hot, with third-placed stablemate Capodanno winning the Grade 2 Cotswold Chase at Cheltenham next time out.

SOLID PERFORMER

Fastorslow was runner-up to Corach Rambler in handicap company at last year's festival but Martin Brassil's eight-year-old elevated his form to the top level when winning Grade 1s on his next two runs, with a below-par Galopin Des Champs behind both times.

He was unable to confirm that form in the Irish Gold Cup in February but still gave his old rival a fright up the home straight. Although he has plenty of gears, he shouldn't have an issue with the stiffer test of the Gold Cup.

DARK HORSE

It might seem a stretch to put **L'Homme Presse** in this category, but the 2022 Brown Advisory winner is still somewhat unexposed as a top-level staying chaser.

There was much to admire about his comeback win in the Fleur de Lys Chase at Lingfield in January. He was well on top and second-placed Protektorat – a fine benchmark – gave the form substance behind Shishkin in the Grade 2 Denman Chase next time.

Although L'Homme Presse was no match for front-running Pic D'Orhy in the Grade 1 Ascot Chase in February, that was an inadequate test and he's much happier on left-handed circuits.

VERDICT

Having shown his true colours again in his last two runs, **Galopin Des Champs** has outstanding claims of back-to-back Gold Cup wins. He'll be sent off at skinny odds, though, and the classy **L'Homme Presse**, who has won both outings at Cheltenham, appeals as a solid each-way alternative.

DAVE ORTON

Presse has solid each-way claims

L'Homme Presse: set for first crack at Gold Cup

Constitution has absolute authority

*Constitution Hill and
Nico de Boinville*

CHAMPION HURDLE

KEY FORM RACE

Constitution Hill went off at 4-11 in last year's **Champion Hurdle**, travelled strongly behind the leader and went on to beat State Man by an easy nine lengths, with the race in the bag as soon as Nico de Boinville asked him to go through the gears on the home turn. Anything but a similar outcome this year is hard to envisage.

SOLID PERFORMER

State Man has run a dozen times for Willie Mullins, falling on his debut but winning ten of the 11 since, eight of them Grade 1s, with the sole defeat coming in last year's Champion Hurdle. Sure, he's beaten a total of only 29 horses in his Grade 1 victories and 14 of them have been his stablemates, but he's an ultra-reliable, top-tier hurdler who deserves to add a Champion Hurdle at Cheltenham to his CV. With Constitution Hill around, though, he probably won't.

DARK HORSE

While Nicky Henderson basks in glory as Constitution Hill cruises home from State Man, he can train his binoculars on his other contender **First Street**, who is capable of claiming third at a big price. He was beaten less than 11 lengths by Constitution Hill in the Christmas Hurdle at Kempton and is a reliable performer who should be running on at the end.

VERDICT

Constitution Hill, who'll be having just his second race in 11 months when he lines up on the opening afternoon, is long odds-on to retain his Champion Hurdle crown. There's just one chink in his armour – even though he's a superb jumper in the main, there's always the chance he'll get one wrong and end up on the floor. That's something Nicky Henderson will be only too aware of as his 2017 and 2018 winner Buveur D'Air did just that when going for the hat-trick. Realistically, though, Constitution Hill proved much too strong for State Man in last year's race and the outcome will surely be the same again.

RICHARD LOWTHER

CHAMPION CHASE
KEY FORM RACE
On his first outing in open company at the top level, the brilliant El Fabiolo confirmed himself a great two-mile chaser with a bloodless victory over high-class stablemate Dinoblue in the **Dublin Chase** at Leopardstown in February. That made it six in a row since embarking on life as a chaser and, despite again being less than fluent at times over the fences, it was a pretty effortless career-best display that left him cherry ripe for another trip to Cheltenham.

SOLID PERFORMER
Although he fluffed his lines when pipped by Elixir De Nutz in the rescheduled Grade 1 Clarence House Chase at Cheltenham in January, **Jonbon** is hard to crab on his form in his first season outside novice company. He actually did extremely well to finish as close as a neck behind that day after a couple of howlers and his previous win in the Grade 1 Tingle Creek at Sandown, when beating old rival Edwardstone, is top-class form.

DARK HORSE
The wheels have rather come off last year's runner-up **Captain Guinness** after his second straight reappearance win in the Grade 2 Fortria Chase at Navan in November. He was pulled up with an irregular heartbeat at Leopardstown's Christmas meeting and never landed a blow behind El Fabiolo back there at the Dublin Racing Festival. However, that was a recovery mission and if capable of returning to his Navan form, when he thrashed the smart mare Riviere D'Etel, the Henry de Bromhead-trained nine-year-old could well surprise a few with the return to Cheltenham much more his bag.

VERDICT
Put simply, a clear round should be enough for **El Fabiolo** to extend his unbeaten record as a chaser and see off old rival Jonbon, with ante-post odds of around 1-2 at the time of writing perfectly reasonable. He's bona fide banker material. **Captain Guinness** could make the podium again.
DAVE ORTON

Bona fide banker

El Fabiolo: six out of six over fences

Irish Point on the rise

STAYERS' HURDLE

KEY FORM RACE

Irish Point announced himself as a major contender with victory in the Grade 1 **Christmas Hurdle** at Leopardstown, drawing right away after the last to beat Asterion Forlonge by an easy 11 lengths. He saw out the trip really well, albeit in a race not run at a searching gallop, and is eminently capable of improving on the bare form. His trainer Gordon Elliott, of course, won last year's race with Sire Du Berlais.

SOLID PERFORMER

Horses don't come much more solid than **Paisley Park**, who's been beaten a head or less into second by Dashel Drasher, Crambo and Noble Yeats in his three races this season. It's a testament to his toughness that Emma Lavelle's veteran is still a major player five years on from his Stayers' win and, while it would be a huge feat if he could wrest back the crown at the age of 12, he won't be too far away.

DARK HORSE

Dashel Drasher isn't exactly dark, but he's one who could well outrun his odds. Jeremy Scott's 11-year-old was runner-up to Sire Du Berlais last year (albeit the stewards temporarily took second from him) and has continued to show high-class form this season. Hard as nails, he led over the last in the Cleeve Hurdle on his latest start, succumbing only on the run-in, and can be guaranteed to give his all. A wet Cheltenham would increase his chance.

Irish Point: capable of more improvement

SCULPTURE TO WEAR

by Rosemary Hetherington

Est. 1990

STAYERS' HURDLE VERDICT

A difficult race to call but **Irish Point**, with improvement almost guaranteed, makes more appeal than the other market leader, Teahupoo. Fergal O'Brien's Long Walk Hurdle winner Crambo is also on the upgrade, while the evergreen Paisley Park (*above*) and Dashel Drasher are still capable of big performances.
RICHARD LOWTHER

Banbridge form is outstanding

RYANAIR CHASE
KEY FORM RACE

Banbridge picked up where he left off in Grade 1 company at Aintree's Grand National meeting last year with an electrifying comeback win in the **Silviniaco Conti Chase** at Kempton in January. It was

Banbridge: electrifying comeback success

MOORCROFT

Equine Rehabilitation Centre
Charity No: 1076278

At the centre in West Sussex, we help many horses to return to soundness and then a better life. We have many years of real experience at rehabilitation, and we now help many other breeds too who need help after surgery, time off or lameness issues. If you are worried about your horse and feel you need help, please call us or come and see us. We are a charity set up to help when horses are in need, and we keep our costs affordable by fundraising and with the support of many who value what we do.

www.moorcroftracehorse.org.uk

Huntingrove Stud, Slinfold, West Sussex RH13 0RB Tel:07929 666408

Hitman: last year's third is an each-way shout again

a clear career-best on ground that was right up his street and the form is outstanding, with classy flat-track specialist Pic D'Orhy also posting a peak effort under a penalty in second and then going on to land the Ascot Chase. The runner-up was himself 17 lengths clear of another Irish raider, Janidil, runner-up to Allaho in the 2022 Ryanair Chase, and subsequent Game Spirit winner Edwardstone was left trailing in fourth.

SOLID PERFORMER

Envoi Allen has been kept mad fresh since giving high-class Gerri Colombe a real fright at Down Royal in November in the Grade 1 Champion Chase, a race he landed in 2022. He performed to the same level there that brought him victory in last season's Ryanair, which was his third festival success and eighth at Grade 1 level. He'll line up with rock-solid claims of a repeat win.

DARK HORSE

There are numerous candidates in this category, with last year's third Hitman high up the list having returned to near his best behind old rival Shishkin in the Grade 2 Denman Chase at Newbury in February. However, at twice the odds (100-1 at the time of writing) none fits the bill as enticingly as **French Dynamite**, who was one place off Hitman when running a screamer in last year's Ryanair Chase. He's been kept fresh by trainer Mouse Morris, no stranger to festival success, and is well up to making the frame providing the ground isn't too deep.

VERDICT

With Allaho once more on the sidelines, this has been a muddling division again this season. **Banbridge** missed the festival last term due to unsuitably deep ground, but he's an outstanding traveller and would be hard to stop if taking part this time. Both **Hitman** and **French Dynamite**, third and fourth last year, are each-way possibilities at big odds providing the heavens don't open.

DAVE ORTON

RACING POST

HORSES
IN TRAINING 2024
550 TRAINERS 20,000 HORSES
Plus 150 pages of facts, figures and contacts

THE INDISPENSABLE TOOL FOR EVERY RACING ENTHUSIAST

Horses in Training is an institution in racing – an indispensable tool for every racing enthusiast.

Written in an easy-to-follow style, it is an encyclopaedia of invaluable information on the horses each trainer has in their care, with almost 20,000 horses and around 550 trainers. The book lists alphabetically the British, Irish and French trainers, their horses, the owner and breeder of every horse, foaling dates of two-year-olds and the trainer's address and phone numbers.

Fully indexed and numbering 720 pages, it includes more than 150 pages of key statistics, covering everything from big-race winners to trainer tables, fixtures and racecourse information. The book is expertly edited by Graham Dench, a *Racing Post* senior reporter and former form book editor.

NOVICE CHASERS 2M-2M4F

KEY FORM RACE

The market for the **Irish Arkle** strongly suggested last year's Supreme Novices' Hurdle winner Marine Nationale would extend his unbeaten record and make it 2-2 as a chaser, having hosed up on his debut over fences at Leopardstown's Christmas meeting. However, he was a massive flop, running too freely and jumping deliberately under more patient tactics, which opened the door for Il Etait Temps – only fifth in last year's Supreme – to come through and prove best of Willie Mullins' trio.

Sporting a first-time tongue-tie, Il Etait Temps narrowly fought off the consistent Found A Fifty, who had won a Grade 1 at the course on his previous outing, and stablemate Facile Vega returned to near his best in third, so it has to rate the leading trial for this year's Arkle.

SOLID PERFORMER

Since being turned over by a rejuvenated American Mike on his chasing and seasonal debut at Navan, **Fact To File** has massively impressed in two outings at Leopardstown. His Grade 1 win over a hugely disappointing Gaelic Warrior came in a shambolic match race at the Dublin Racing Festival. However, he travelled like a top-class chaser and there's surely a lot more to come from last year's Champion Bumper runner-up over whichever distance is preferred by Mullins.

DARK HORSE

Iroko was thought to be out for the campaign due to a foot injury after a seamless start to life over fences in a small-field novice chase at Warwick in November. However, connections have got the six-year-old back in top condition and he'd be a real unknown quantity if he makes it to the festival for the Turners, which now seems likely. He's a strong stayer over the intermediate trip and loves Cheltenham, having landed the Martin Pipe Handicap Hurdle at last year's festival.

VERDICT

The Arkle became wide open after Marine

Fact To File takes pole position

Nationale's shock defeat at the Dublin Racing Festival and, although he's failed to spark in two festival appearances, it's hard to knock Irish Arkle winner **Il Etait Temps**. He surely has more to offer over the minimum trip as a chaser. Mullins should be much more confident of landing the Turners with **Fact To File**, who would rate near banker material if he turns up there.

DAVE ORTON

Fact To File: looks a top-class chaser

Grey Dawning set for big home run

NOVICE CHASERS 3M+

KEY FORM RACE

Grey Dawning gained compensation for an unlucky defeat by the progressive Ginny's Destiny at Cheltenham when he slammed his rivals in the Grade 2 **Hampton Novices' Chase** at Warwick in January, having been stepped back up to 3m. His jumping was impressive and the form is hard to ignore. The mare Apple Away – a Grade 1 novice hurdle winner – was beaten 14 lengths in second and third-placed Broadway Boy had won his previous two starts at Cheltenham in decent fashion.

SOLID PERFORMER

Embassy Gardens could hardly have been more impressive in making it 2-2 as a novice chaser. An easy victory at Punchestown in December was followed by a smooth Grade 3 success at Naas in January. That was a personal-best, with 152-rated Letsbeclearaboutit 18 lengths behind in third, and he's open to a good deal of progress as a staying chaser for Willie Mullins.

DARK HORSE

There's every chance Henry de Bromhead's lightly raced **Monty's Star** has a lot more to offer. Although pulled up in last year's Albert Bartlett, he was a useful novice hurdler and was waiting to jump fences. There was a lot to like about the way he readily reversed form with old rival Three Card Brag when recording a personal-best on his second chase outing back over 3m at Punchestown in December.

VERDICT

Dan Skelton's fast-improving **Grey Dawning** is well up to producing a home win in the Brown Advisory, which could cut up significantly. **Embassy Gardens** would rate a confident wager for his mighty operation if he goes for the demanding National Hunt Chase.

DAVE ORTON

Grey Dawning and (inset) Embassy Gardens both have leading chances

Ballyburn a Supreme talent

NOVICE HURDLERS 2M-2M1F
KEY FORM RACE

Ballyburn heads the ante-post markets for the Supreme and the Baring Bingham and will take a huge amount of beating whichever race he runs in. The feeling is that, following his victory in the 2m Grade 1 **Tattersalls Ireland 50th Derby Sale Novice Hurdle** at the Dublin Racing Festival, he'll be aimed at the shorter option in March. It was a commanding performance at Leopardstown. The time was quicker than State Man recorded later in the afternoon and the form looks sound, with runner-up Slade Steel a leading contender for the Baring Bingham.

SOLID PERFORMER

Sir Gino will be a banker for many in the Triumph Hurdle and rightly so given how dominant he proved in his trial at Cheltenham in late January. Nicky Henderson's powerfully built youngster surged clear of market rival Burdett Road after the last and it's difficult to imagine anything stopping him on Gold Cup day. Unlike many Triumph Hurdle types, he has the physical scope to make a big impact in years to come.

DARK HORSE

Joyeuse, who shares her name with one of Frankel's half-sisters, is an interesting one for the Mares' Novices' Hurdle. The grey won her only race in France, a 1m4f bumper in October 2022, before being snapped up by JP McManus and switched to Nicky Henderson. Her dam is a half-sister to their Champion Hurdle winner Epatante, which might explain the thinking behind the purchase. She beat geldings on her successful hurdles debut at Taunton in January, form which has been boosted, and has a sporting chance of continuing the British run of success in the Grade 2.

VERDICT

Ballyburn should start favourite backers on a winning note in the Supreme if Willie Mullins gives him the green light for that race. It's difficult to envisage anything other than a comfortable victory for **Sir Gino** in the Triumph Hurdle and his stablemate **Joyeuse** is an interesting each-way shout for the mares' novice.
RICHARD LOWTHER

Sir Gino: dominant in his trial for the Triumph

Atlantique appeals

Ile Atlantique: capable of big run in the Baring Bingham

NOVICE HURDLERS 2M5F-3M

KEY FORM RACE

Willie Mullins has any number of entries to juggle, including the first three home in the Grade 1 **Lawlor's of Naas Novice Hurdle** at Naas in January. Readin Tommy Wrong, the outsider of the whole field, prevailed in gritty style from Ile Atlantique and Lecky Watson, and he's near the head of the market for both the Baring Bingham over 2m5f and the 3m Albert Bartlett. Mullins had the 1-2-3 in the shorter race at last year's festival and his interpretation of the Lawlor's of Naas form will affect the make-up of both contests this time. Fourth in the Naas race was Firefox, who beat Ballyburn at Fairyhouse when both were debuting over hurdles.

SOLID PERFORMER

Gidleigh Park is unbeaten in four races – a bumper and three hurdles – and looks sure to go well in his chosen Cheltenham assignment. Harry Fry's six-year-old had to work to land a Grade 2 on Cheltenham's Trials day, but the race turned into a sprint, which was no good for him at all. A stronger gallop would suit this imposing individual in the Baring Bingham and he'd have no problem staying the trip in the Albert Bartlett.

DARK HORSE

One who fits the bill is **Chigorin**, whose only Grade 1 festival entry is in the Albert Bartlett. Trained by Henry de Bromhead, he hasn't surfaced since winning at Fairyhouse before Christmas, when he stayed on strongly up the run-in to win going away. Willie Mullins' O'Moore Park was the beaten favourite in third but has won since to bolster the form. Chigorin is a son of Shantou, also the sire of last year's Albert Bartlett winner Stay Away Fay.

VERDICT

Willie Mullins has a strong hand in the Baring Bingham and it may be **Ile Atlantique**, owned by Brighton & Hove Albion chairman Tony Bloom, who emerges on top. He's proven at the highest level and unexposed at the trip, while his trainer has hinted at a change of tactics at Cheltenham. The improving **Gidleigh Park** appeals in the Albert Bartlett and **Chigorin** has the stamina to give a bold showing at a big price.

RICHARD LOWTHER

Ballyburn (red cap) leads Slade Steel (left) in the Grade 1 2m novice hurdle

'She keeps producing excellent runs in hot handicap hurdles'

THE Dublin Racing Festival had a significant impact at Cheltenham last year, with eight of the 18 Irish winners (44%) having run at the Leopardstown weekend the previous month. There were also 18 Cheltenham winners for Ireland in 2022 but a reduced number of five (28%) had run at the DRF.

In both years the figure was higher when considering only hurdles and the bumper. The 14 races in those categories account for half the Cheltenham programme and Ireland won eight last year, with half of those winners (50%) having run at the DRF. In 2022 Ireland won ten and four (40%) had run at the DRF.

Tipsters and bookmakers pick some eyecatchers from the Dublin Racing Festival . . .

Richard Birch Good Time Jonny looked like he was being carefully mapped out for the Fulke Walwyn Kim Muir Chase when fifth of 25 behind Heart Wood in the Grade 3 Leopardstown Handicap Chase. He'll be spot on for Cheltenham.

David Jennings Majborough is the obvious one but I'll go for You Oughta Know. He'd have hated the ground in the Grade 2 bumper but stayed well and looks like he'll relish the hill on better ground in the Champion Bumper.

Graeme Rodway Zenta won a Grade 1 juvenile hurdle at Aintree last year and shaped like she could have another big race in her when third on her handicap bow in a 2m Listed event. She's in both the Mares' Hurdle and Chase, but I reckon her big target might be one of the handicap hurdles.

Nick Watts King Of Kingsfield was beaten 14 lengths by Ballyburn, which showed he isn't a Supreme horse. However, a big field in the County Hurdle might be perfect for him and I'd be very interested in him if he ran in that.

Bet365 Pat Cooney I thought the bumper on the

Saturday was the strongest Cheltenham pointer we've seen all season. The runner-up You Oughta Know ran really well and, although Willie Mullins has several leading contenders for the Champion Bumper, I'm sure he'll go well.

Betfair Barry Orr Heart Wood was impressive on his handicap debut in a competitive chase. It'll be interesting to see what mark the British handicapper gives him but he'd appeal if he goes for the Plate.

Coral Andrew Lobo Fact To File's time in what ended up a one-horse race was impressive and he looks a genuine Grade 1 horse.

Ladbrokes John Priddey Gaoth Chuil *(right)* looks sure to go close in the Pertemps and keeps producing excellent runs in hot handicap hurdles, including when second to Maxxum at the DRF. She travels so well that I suspect we haven't seen the best of her in deep ground over the winter.

Paddy Power Paul Binfield Slade Steel may well have come up against a monster in Ballyburn. The pair of them had the Grade 1 2m novice hurdle to themselves a long way out and a bit of extra distance in the Baring Bingham will suit Slade Steel down to the ground.

Tote Jamie Hart Good Time Jonny ran well over too short a trip and has to be a good thing in the Kim Muir.

William Hill Jamie McBride Ethical Diamond, sixth in the Grade 1 Spring Juvenile Hurdle, could be worth supporting at big prices each-way and in betting without Sir Gino on the Triumph.

Mullins leads the way – with plenty of back-up

A SIGN of things to come? Willie Mullins dominated the Dublin Racing Festival on February 3-4 in unprecedented fashion, winning all eight Grade 1 races plus a Grade 2 to boot. Now it's full steam ahead to the Cheltenham Festival, where many will expect him to match or surpass his 2022 record of ten winners.

The DRF was a remarkable show of force by the 17-time champion trainer. Not only did he take all the big prizes back to Closutton, Mullins had three one-twos (and even the first four in the Spring Juvenile Hurdle) and didn't need all his big fancies to perform at their best. Three of his favourites were beaten but still he turned up the winner in those races at odds of 16-1, 7-2 and 6-4.

His rival trainers could barely get near him. To emphasise the exceptional quality and strength in depth of his team, Mullins had 15 finishers in the first three in the DRF Grade 1s, against just seven for all other yards. With such an array of talent at his disposal, the Closutton master stands in a supremely powerful position heading towards Cheltenham.

Looking at 23 festival races – and leaving out five handicaps where the market was yet to form fully – Mullins had 12 favourites after the DRF. Next best with two apiece were Gordon Elliott, his great Irish rival, and Nicky Henderson, his great British rival.

Overall, Ireland had the favourite in 19

of the 23 races – other trainers with market leaders at that stage were Barry Connell, Gavin Cromwell, Emmet Mullins, Joseph O'Brien and David Christie.

Mullins' three hottest favourites – Galopin Des Champs, El Fabiolo and Lossiemouth – all have 'been there, done that' badges from last year's festival.

Galopin Des Champs has a strong chance of back-to-back Gold Cups after reasserting his supremacy with decisive wins in the Savills Chase and Irish Gold Cup. His Racing Post Rating of 184 from last year's Gold Cup and the Savills gives him a clear edge, with none of his rivals having got beyond the 170s over a staying trip.

Many have stepped up from Arkle victory as a novice to take the Champion Chase crown and El Fabiolo looks well on

Galopin Des Champs: clear edge on RPRs for his Gold Cup defence

WILLIE MULLINS v BRITAIN AT THE CHELTENHAM FESTIVAL

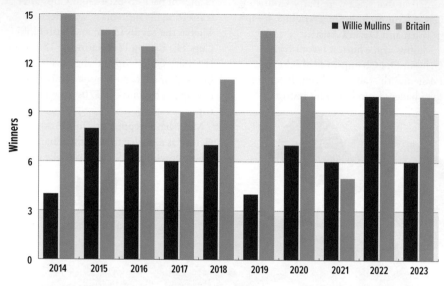

course to join them after being untroubled again in the Dublin Chase at the DRF. That merely tightened his position against old British rival Jonbon, who had been beaten the previous weekend in the Clarence House Chase at Cheltenham.

Lossiemouth is also in the Mullins big three after her impressive victory on her belated reappearance in the International Hurdle on Cheltenham's Trials day. Some would like to see last year's Triumph Hurdle winner pitted against Constitution Hill in the Champion Hurdle, but the Mares' Hurdle looks hers for the taking.

As for the Champion, Mullins will stand ready to take advantage of any slip by Constitution Hill with the excellent State Man but reversing last year's nine-length defeat looks unlikely unless Nicky Henderson's superstar underperforms by something like half a stone.

Thursday's two feature Grade 1s also present Mullins with difficulty. He lacks a

standout for the Stayers' Hurdle and has been left short for the Ryanair Chase after Allaho was ruled out again with injury.

Elliott holds the strongest hand in the Stayers' with Robcour-owned duo Teahupoo and Irish Point, both kept out of the fray after Grade 1 wins before Christmas over Closutton rivals.

It will be interesting to see if that approach makes the difference for Teahupoo, a close third to veteran stablemate Sire Du Berlais in the Stayers' last year after going off 9-4 favourite. Elliott's view is that the seven-year-old is best fresh, hence the decision not to run him again after a second consecutive victory in the Hatton's Grace Hurdle at Fairyhouse in December.

Teahupoo has the pace for that 2m4½f contest and he seemed to prove his stamina when landing the 3m½f Galmoy Hurdle in last season's festival prep, although possibly that took the edge off him for Cheltenham.

Speed allied to staying power is a potent combination and, with a 100 per cent win record from seven runs after a break of 50-plus days, Teahupoo has been given every chance of stepping up for the win this year.

The year-younger Irish Point has a similar profile, having won the 2m4f novice Grade 1 at Aintree last season and then showed his staying prowess by taking the 2m7½f Christmas Hurdle on heavy ground at Leopardstown in December.

He has yet to get into the 160s on Racing Post Ratings, however, and that gives him a significant amount to find with Teahupoo. Improvement can be anticipated from Irish Point, of course, but Teahupoo has the better form in the book.

The age stats are certainly with the Elliott pair. Sire Du Berlais took the Stayers' at the age of 11 but most of the winners in the past decade were six or seven. Only a couple of the other main contenders are in that bracket.

Irish stables have won seven of the past eight runnings of the Ryanair, albeit mainly through Mullins, and hold a strong hand again. Envoi Allen, last year's winner for Henry de Bromhead, is set to return

but he has been headed in the ante-post market by Joseph O'Brien's Banbridge.

There are a number of positives for Banbridge. He is largely a two-and-a-half-mile specialist (unlike many of his leading opponents), is a Cheltenham winner both as a hurdler at the festival and later over fences, and is still improving after recording his best RPR of 169 in his Grade 2 victory over Pic D'Orhy at Kempton in January.

Elliott's pair Conflated and Fil Dor and the Mullins-trained Appreciate It don't offer such compelling form credentials and the biggest threat to Banbridge could be fellow second-season novice Stage Star, representing British champion trainer Paul Nicholls.

The novice divisions are where the Irish trainers, especially Mullins, are likely to streak ahead of the home team. Nearly all the favourites belong to the raiding party, with only the Nicky Henderson-trained Sir Gino in the Triumph Hurdle looking a strong candidate to hold back the Irish tide.

Mullins' novice hurdlers feature Ballyburn, Mystical Power, Tullyhill, High Class Hero and Readin Tommy Wrong

Teahupoo (far side) beats Impaire Et Passe in the Hatton's Grace Hurdle

WHERE IRELAND HAS DONE BEST (AND WORST) IN THE PAST DECADE

	2014	2015	2016	2017	2018	2019	2020	2021	2022	2023
TUESDAY										
Supreme Novices' Hurdle	●	●		●		●				●
Arkle Novices' Chase		●	●		●	●	●			●
Ultima Handicap Chase		●	●		●	●	●			●
Champion Hurdle	●	●						●		●
Mares' Hurdle	●	●					●	●		●
Juvenile Handicap Hurdle					●	●	●	●		●
National Hunt Novices' Chase		●		●	●			●	●	●
WEDNESDAY										
Baring Bingham Novices' Hurdle	●	●	●		●		●		●	
Brown Advisory Novices' Chase		●			●					
Coral Cup Handicap Hurdle			●	●			●		●	●
Queen Mother Champion Chase				●					●	
Cross Country Chase		●	●	●	●	●			●	●
Grand Annual Handicap Chase	●						●			●
Champion Bumper	●			●	●	●		●	●	●
THURSDAY										
Turners Novices' Chase		●	●	●			●		●	
Pertemps Handicap Hurdle			●	●	●		●	●		●
Ryanair Chase			●	●	●		●	●		●
Stayers' Hurdle			●	●	●			●		●
Plate Handicap Chase			●	●	●		●	●		●
Mares' Novices' Hurdle *(eight runnings)*			●	●	●	●	●	●		●
Kim Muir Handicap Chase	●						●	●		●
FRIDAY										
Triumph Hurdle	●		●		●		●		●	●
County Handicap Hurdle	●	●		●			●	●	●	
Albert Bartlett Novices' Hurdle	●		●		●		●	●	●	●
Cheltenham Gold Cup	●	●	●		●		●	●	●	●
Hunters' Chase	●	●	●				●			
Mares' Chase *(three runnings)*								●	●	●
Martin Pipe Handicap Hurdle	●	●		●	●	●		●	●	●

Impervious (right) wins last year's Mares' Chase, maintaining Ireland's 100 per cent record

IRISH INJURED JOCKEYS WOULD LIKE TO
THANK ALL OUR SUPPORTERS WITHIN
THE INDUSTRY AND FROM THE PUBLIC
WHOSE GENEROSITY ENABLES US TO
PROVIDE OUR SERVICES

Despite what our name suggests we deal with much more than injured jockeys.

- We are here to help riders with personal crises whether medical, financial or psychological.
- We have a support team who provide a prompt professional response to potential beneficiaries.
- In conjunction with HRI/Equuip we have implemented a Financial Literacy course for riders.
- We also have schemes for payment of bursaries to assist jockeys upskill/study for alternative careers when riders finish racing.

All our funding comes from fundraising and donations. Our aim is to make a difference to the lives and welfare of jockeys past and present, and their families by effective use of these funds.

IRISH INJURED JOCKEYS, CURRAGH HOUSE, RACE,
DUBLIN ROAD, KILDARE , CO. KILDARE
T: + 353 (0) 45 533011
W: WWW.IRISHINJUREDJOCKEYS.COM

among a host of possibilities also including DRF Grade 1 winners Dancing City and the juvenile Kargese, probably the biggest threat to Sir Gino in the Triumph.

Ballyburn will be the Mullins banker for many after his seven-length victory over De Bromhead's Slade Steel in the Grade 1 2m novice hurdle at the DRF. Interestingly, that was almost identical to the distance between the pair when they were first and third in a bumper at the Punchestown festival last spring, and in between them that day was Mullins' Dancing City, beaten six lengths by his stablemate.

That bumper form looks extremely strong now, with Dancing City also a Grade 1 winner at the DRF in the 2m6½f novice hurdle. Going up against Ballyburn in a 2m bumper was clearly a difficult task, given his strong staying performance at Leopardstown to beat better-fancied stablemate Predators Gold, and he looks ready to step up in trip again in the Albert Bartlett Novices' Hurdle.

Mullins also has Readin Tommy Wrong and High Class Hero as leading chances for the Friday three-miler, although he seems likely to drop at least one of them into the Baring Bingham Novices' Hurdle over 2m5f. Readin Tommy Wrong, winner of the Grade 1 Lawlor's of Naas over 2m4f in January and yet to go beyond that trip under rules, looks best suited to the intermediate trip.

Nobody knows better than Mullins, but his top contenders for the three novices look to be Ballyburn (Supreme), Readin Tommy Wrong (Baring Bingham) and Dancing City (Albert Bartlett).

He is possibly most vulnerable in the Baring Bingham, where he could also throw in the highly promising Grade 2 2m winner Mystical Power.

Slade Steel could be a strong challenger

there for De Bromhead. His only defeats have been over 2m against Ballyburn and he was a 2m4f Grade 2 winner at Navan before Christmas, as well as a 3m point winner.

Sir Gino is seen as a British banker in the Triumph but Mullins has the most likely alternatives if that one doesn't deliver. Kargese, Storm Heart, Majborough and Bunting filled the first four places in the Spring Juvenile Hurdle at the DRF and all represent different owners, so it is likely at least two or three will line up at Cheltenham.

Last year the Mullins first two from the Spring took the same places in the Triumph, but in reverse order, and there would be a good chance of something similar but for Sir Gino.

Over fences the Mullins novice squad is headed by Fact To File, who ultimately had a stroll round under-performing stablemate Gaelic Warrior at the DRF but did it so easily that he took top rank among the British and Irish in the division with an RPR of 164.

Admittedly it was hard to say we learned anything new about him there, but he had run to an RPR of 160 the time before, also over Leopardstown's 2m5½f, and is a solid as well as high-class contender. The Turners looks the obvious choice for him but the Brown Advisory option is open too.

Gaelic Warrior had looked a class act in his Limerick Grade 1 win over Christmas but his poor run at the DRF puts a major question mark against him. Further weakening of the Mullins team came a few days after the DRF when Grangeclare West, who had been as short as 3-1 for the Brown Advisory Novices' Chase, was ruled out for the season through injury.

Potentially that could prompt some juggling by Mullins. Embassy Gardens had

looked well set for the National Hunt Novices' Chase after his Grade 3 victory over 3m1f at Naas in January but it's possible he could be switched to the Brown Advisory. "He looks a natural for one of the staying novice chases at Cheltenham and nearer the time we'll decide which one," Mullins said at Naas.

With second favourite Corbetts Cross having fallen last time out at Fairyhouse, Embassy Gardens looks in a strong position at the head of the NH Chase market if that is the chosen target. Mullins' main fancy for this race tends to run well with recent form figures of 11UF1 when priced at 9-2 or below.

Marine Nationale, last year's Supreme Novices' Hurdle winner for Barry Connell, had looked set to be an Irish banker again in the Arkle, but he was another to run poorly at the DRF. He was beaten more than ten lengths in fifth in the Irish Arkle as Mullins' Il Etait Temps won by a neck from the Elliott-trained Found A Fifty.

In an open Arkle, Marine Nationale held his position at the head of the market but the top contenders are closely matched on RPRs. The favourite lacks experience over fences and, if that becomes a key factor in a battle, Found A Fifty could have the edge at decent odds. Having been dropped in trip, he might be suited by a strong pace over the testing Cheltenham track and can turn the tables on the diminutive Il Etait Temps.

Ireland's advantage over Britain is nearly always extended by the dominance of the raiding party in the Champion Bumper, Cross Country Chase and the three mares' races. Last year Ireland took four out of five, losing out only in the Mares' Novices' Hurdle but still providing the second and third there.

Mullins and Elliott dominate the

Champion Bumper betting again, having won six of the last seven runnings between them. Jalon D'Oudairies, "a proper horse" according to Elliott, should go well in an open contest. He was put away after beating Redemption Day (an excellent yardstick who was then third in the Grade 2 bumper at the DRF) at Leopardstown's Christmas meeting.

Elliott is definitely the one to beat in the Cross Country, having dominated since it changed from a handicap to a conditions race in 2016. With previous experience so important, it is difficult to get away from

Embassy Gardens: strong fancy for the National Hunt Novices' Chase

Delta Work in his hat-trick bid even with stablemate Galvin (last year's runner-up) and Henry de Bromhead's 2021 Gold Cup wnner Minella Indo in opposition.

A clean sweep of the mares' races is highly possible, and they could all go to Mullins. He has two hot favourites in Lossiemouth (Hurdle) and Dinoblue (Chase) and another strong chance with Jade De Grugy in the novice hurdle.

With Mullins leading the way, and with handicap successes sure to boost the total, Ireland's festival supremacy looks sure to go on.

■ PICK OF THE BUNCH

Embassy Gardens Strong fancy for the National Hunt Novices' Chase

Slade Steel Good chance in the Baring Bingham Novices' Hurdle

Fact To File Excellent credentials for the Turners Novices' Chase if he heads there

Teahupoo Keeping him fresh could make the difference in the Stayers' Hurdle

Banbridge Plenty of positives on his side in the Ryanair Chase

Dancing City Might turn up at a decent price in the Albert Bartlett

Century looms into view

WILLIE MULLINS has been leading trainer at the festival for five years in a row – and ten times in all – and now stands on the brink of becoming the first to hit a century at jump racing's showpiece meeting.

Six winners last year took him to 94 and a repeat showing would put him in three figures. Having had at least half a dozen winners at each of the past four festivals, including a record ten in 2022, he has every chance of reaching that remarkable milestone this year.

The 17-time Irish champion trainer has exceeded five winners at eight of the past nine festivals (he dipped slightly to four in 2019) and now leads Nicky Henderson by 21 in the all-time list.

A notable change in recent years is that the final day has become a Mullins strong point, whereas his cornerstone used to be the opening day in his years of dominating the Champion Hurdle and Mares' Hurdle.

His final-day figures since 2020 are four, two, five and two and the bigger totals in two of those years were decisive in securing the leading trainer award. They also reflect a shift towards more chase winners in recent years, with Mullins taking the Gold Cup for the third time in five years when Galopin Des

Champs triumphed last year.

Chases (16 wins) just outweigh hurdles (14) on the Mullins roll of honour at the past five festivals, and at a higher strike-rate (16 per cent against eight per cent). Traditionally the stable's main strength in Grade 1 races was over hurdles, particularly over 2m, but Mullins has won 20 Grade 1 chases in the past nine years.

His most fancied runner is well worth noting in the four non-handicaps for novice chasers (Arkle, National Hunt, Brown Advisory and Turners). He won two of those again last year with El Fabiolo (11-10f in the Arkle) and Gaillard Du Mesnil (10-11f in the NH Chase).

The market is a strong

pointer to Mullins' successes. Five of last year's six winners went off favourite and the other (Impaire Et Passe in the Ballymore Novices' Hurdle) was a close second favourite. At the four festivals since 2020, 16 of his 30 winners were favourite and eight were second favourite, cementing a trend established in 2014-2018 (the only break from the norm was in 2019).

One area where Mullins missed out last year was in handicap hurdles, but in general this has been a strength. He has had 11 handicap hurdle winners since 2010 (six at double-figure odds) and excluding the Juvenile Handicap Hurdle, which he has never won, his strike-rate in that period is 11-128 (+17.75pts). The key targets have been the County Hurdle (6-48, +40.25pts) and Martin Pipe Conditional Jockeys' Hurdle (4-29, +6.5pts).

He remains the one to beat in races restricted to mares, having won nine out of 16 in the Mares' Hurdle, five of the eight runnings of the Mares' Novices' Hurdle and two of the three runnings of the Mares' Chase, and is strong in the Champion Bumper, where 11 of his 12 winners were five-year-olds (and six of those had won their sole outing prior to arriving at Cheltenham).

FESTIVAL WINNERS BY RACE TYPE

- ■ Hurdles **51**
- ■ Chases **31**
- ■ Bumpers **12**

1995
YEAR OF FIRST WINNER AT CHELTENHAM

33
CHELTENHAM FESTIVAL WINNERS IN THE LAST FIVE YEARS – 11% STRIKE-RATE

94
CHELTENHAM FESTIVAL WINNERS

MOST SUCCESSFUL RACES

Champion Bumper
■■■■■■■■■■■■■

Mares' Hurdle
■■■■■■■■■

Supreme Novices'
■■■■■■■

Baring Bingham Novices' Hurdle
■■■■■■

County Hurdle
■■■■■■

Arkle Chase
■■■■■

Brown Advisory Novices' Chase
■■■■■

Mares' Novices' Hurdle
■■■■■

Ryanair Chase
■■■■■

Champion Hurdle
■■■■

Martin Pipe Hurdle
■■■■

National Hunt Chase
■■■■

Triumph Hurdle
■■■■

Turners Novices' Chase
■■■■

2023 KEY STAT

FIVE OF MULLINS' SIX WINNERS WERE SENT OFF FAVOURITE

Master of the mighty Hill

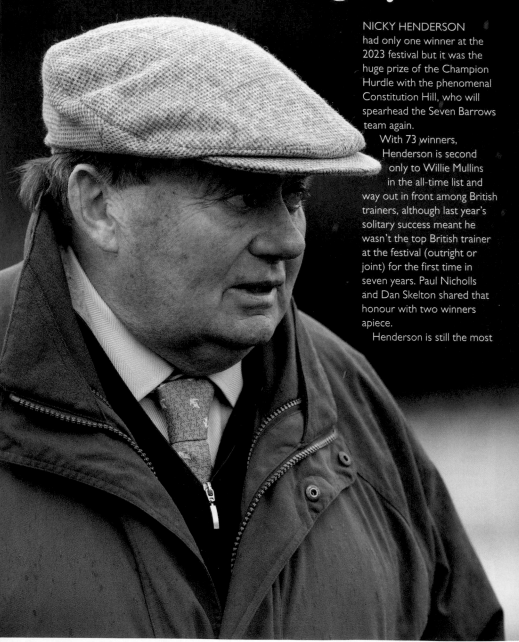

NICKY HENDERSON had only one winner at the 2023 festival but it was the huge prize of the Champion Hurdle with the phenomenal Constitution Hill, who will spearhead the Seven Barrows team again.

With 73 winners, Henderson is second only to Willie Mullins in the all-time list and way out in front among British trainers, although last year's solitary success meant he wasn't the top British trainer at the festival (outright or joint) for the first time in seven years. Paul Nicholls and Dan Skelton shared that honour with two winners apiece.

Henderson is still the most

NICKY HENDERSON FESTIVAL WINNERS BY RACE TYPE

- G1 hurdles **26**
- G1 chases **22**
- Non G1 chases **16**
- Non G1 hurdles **9**

MOST SUCCESSFUL RACES

Champion Hurdle
■■■■■■■■■

Arkle Chase
■■■■■■■

Triumph Hurdle
■■■■■■■

Champion Chase
■■■■■■

Supreme Novices'
■■■■■

Plate Handicap Chase
■■■■

Brown Advisory Novices' Chase
■■■■

Coral Cup
■■■■

Cathcart Chase*
■■■■

Kim Muir
■■■

* No longer held

73
CHELTENHAM FESTIVAL WINNERS

1985
YEAR OF FIRST WINNER AT CHELTENHAM

13
CHELTENHAM FESTIVAL WINNERS IN THE LAST FIVE YEARS – 10% STRIKE-RATE

assured source of quality among the home team, having had at least two Grade 1 winners at seven festivals in a row up to 2022 and then another with Constitution Hill last year. Overall he has an excellent record of delivering with the hot ones in Grade 1 races. In the past decade he has sent out 19 favourites in that category and ten have won, returning a level-stakes profit of 3.83pts.

It has been a different story in handicaps. Only one of his ten favourites in the past decade was successful (Dame De Compagnie at 5-1 in the 2020 Coral Cup).

Even so, Henderson's handicap runners are always worth a look, especially at longer odds. Eleven of his 14 handicap winners since 2005 were returned at 12-1 or bigger, while the same number came over trips of at least 2m4f.

Last year he went close in the Pertemps Final Handicap Hurdle (Mill Green third at 22-1, having filled the same position at 33-1 in 2022) and the Martin Pipe Handicap Hurdle (No Ordinary Joe second at 14-1).

Besides Constitution Hill, he has leading Grade 1 prospects this year with red-hot Triumph Hurdle favourite Sir Gino, Jeriko Du Reponet (Supreme Novices' Hurdle), Jonbon (Champion Chase) and Shishkin (Gold Cup).

Handicap possibles include hurdlers Iberico Lord, Lucky Place, Under Control and Impose Toi and chaser Haddex Des Obeaux. He is always well stocked for mares and Joyeuse looks his best prospect in the novice hurdle in that division.

2023 KEY STAT

66% OF HENDERSON'S FESTIVAL HURDLE WINS HAVE BEEN AT 2M FOLLOWING CONSTITUTION HILL'S CHAMPION TRIUMPH

Plenty of big contenders

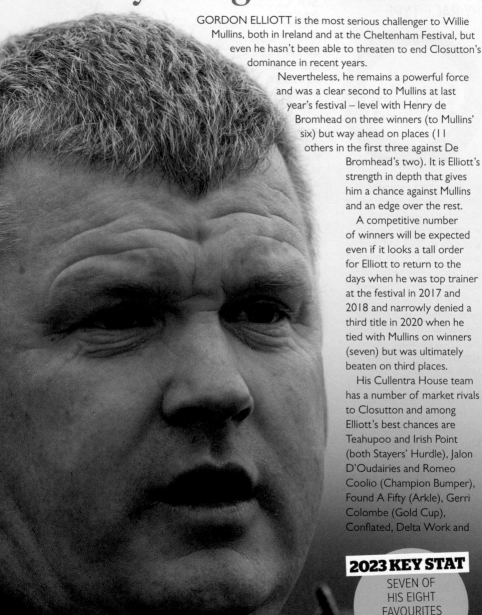

GORDON ELLIOTT is the most serious challenger to Willie Mullins, both in Ireland and at the Cheltenham Festival, but even he hasn't been able to threaten to end Closutton's dominance in recent years.

Nevertheless, he remains a powerful force and was a clear second to Mullins at last year's festival – level with Henry de Bromhead on three winners (to Mullins' six) but way ahead on places (11 others in the first three against De Bromhead's two). It is Elliott's strength in depth that gives him a chance against Mullins and an edge over the rest.

A competitive number of winners will be expected even if it looks a tall order for Elliott to return to the days when he was top trainer at the festival in 2017 and 2018 and narrowly denied a third title in 2020 when he tied with Mullins on winners (seven) but was ultimately beaten on third places.

His Cullentra House team has a number of market rivals to Closutton and among Elliott's best chances are Teahupoo and Irish Point (both Stayers' Hurdle), Jalon D'Oudairies and Romeo Coolio (Champion Bumper), Found A Fifty (Arkle), Gerri Colombe (Gold Cup), Conflated, Delta Work and

2023 KEY STAT

SEVEN OF HIS EIGHT FAVOURITES WERE BEATEN

37

CHELTENHAM FESTIVAL WINNERS

2011

FIRST CHELTENHAM WINNER

15

CHELTENHAM FESTIVAL WINNERS IN THE LAST FIVE YEARS – 7% STRIKE-RATE

MOST SUCCESSFUL RACES

Cross Country Chase
■■■■■

Juvenile Hcap Hurdle
■■■■

National Hunt Chase
■■■■

Coral Cup
■■■

Pertemps Network Final
■■■

Baring Bingham Hurdle
■■

Champion Bumper
■■

Kim Muir Hcap Chase
■■

Martin Pipe Hcap Hdle
■■

Triumph Hurdle
■■

Turners Novices' Chase
■■

GORDON ELLIOTT FESTIVAL WINNERS BY RACE TYPE

■ Grade 1 **12**
■ Non Grade 1 **25**

FESTIVAL WINNERS BY RACE DISTANCE

■ Below 2m4f **10**
■ 2m4f-3m **15**
■ Above 3m **12**

Galvin (all Cross Country Chase), Brighterdaysahead (Mares' Novices' Hurdle), Halka Du Tabert (Mares' Chase), Minella Crooner (Pertemps Final) and Wodhooh (Juvenile Handicap Hurdle).

The three races he won last year were the Stayers' Hurdle, Cross Country and Juvenile Handicap Hurdle and they might give him a solid foundation for his challenge again this time.

The Cross Country is Elliott's most successful festival race and it is no coincidence that it is one of the longest contests on the programme. Twelve of his 16 chase wins have come at distances in excess of 3m, in the Cross Country (five),

National Hunt Chase (four), Kim Muir (two) and Gold Cup – albeit seven of them were provided by multiple festival scorers Cause Of Causes and Tiger Roll.

Some of Elliott's 19 successes over hurdles also emphasise the stable's accent on stamina, with wins in the Pertemps (three), Coral Cup (three), Baring Bingham Novices' Hurdle (two), Martin Pipe Handicap Hurdle (two) and Stayers' Hurdle (one) coming at distances of 2m4f-plus. In the Martin Pipe he has had two winners, three seconds and two thirds from 33 runners.

He also has a notably good record with juvenile hurdlers,

having won the division's handicap hurdle four times and the Triumph Hurdle twice. Six of his 35 runners in those races since 2013 have won (at odds of 25-1, 10-1, 33-1, 9-1, 15-2 and 18-1).

The market has not always been that good at identifying Elliott's winning chances, with only ten of his 41 festival favourites having been successful, and over the years it has been profitable to back his runners in races where he had only one representative. That has produced fewer winners in the last couple of years but plenty of big-priced placed runners.

Festival Grade 1 force again

PAUL NICHOLLS FESTIVAL WINNERS BY RACE TYPE

- G1 chases **19**
- G1 hurdles **10**
- Non G1 chases **9**
- Non G1 hurdles **10**

PAUL NICHOLLS returned to the top as leading British trainer at the festival last year, finishing level with his former assistant Dan Skelton on two winners but beating him on places (four to none).

Two winners is a far cry from Nicholls' festival glory days when he was leading trainer six times, most recently with five winners in 2009, but it was a significant bounce-back from his blanks in 2021 and 2022 (his last before those had been in 2002).

Most encouraging of all is that Nicholls is a force again in the festival Grade 1s. Both wins last year came at that level with Stage Star in the Turners Novices' Chase and Stay Away Fay in the Albert Bartlett Novices' Hurdle.

His Grade 1 resurgence started with the 2019 victories of Frodon in the Ryanair Chase and Topofthegame in the RSA (now Brown Advisory) Novices' Chase, followed by Politologue in the 2020 Queen Mother Champion Chase.

This year his main strength appears to be in the novice chase division. Stay Away Fay looks likely to bid for more festival success in the Brown Advisory and course-and-distance winner Ginny's Destiny is a leading contender for the Turners.

The senior chasing ranks at Manor Farm Stables include Stage Star (Ryanair Chase) and Gold Cup outsider

MOST SUCCESSFUL RACES

Champion Chase
██████
County Hurdle
████
Gold Cup
████
Grand Annual
████
Hunters' Chase
████
Stayers' Hurdle
████
Boodles Hcap Hurdle
███
Brown Advisory Nov Chase
███
Ryanair Chase
███

Bravemansgame, runner-up to Galopin Des Champs last year but with a bit more to find on form this season.

Other possible chances lie with Captain Teague (Albert Bartlett), Liari (Triumph) and Teeshan (Champion Bumper).

Prior to his recent Grade 1 winners, Nicholls had become reliant mainly on handicaps to keep the scoreboard ticking and his runners are worth checking. From 2013 to 2018, eight of his 11 winners came in that sphere, including two apiece in the County Hurdle, Grand Annual Chase and Martin Pipe Handicap Hurdle.

The key to finding a Nicholls handicap winner at the festival, especially over hurdles, is to identify a young, lightly raced type yet to be exposed to the handicapper.

48
CHELTENHAM FESTIVAL WINNERS

1999
YEAR OF FIRST WINNER AT CHELTENHAM

5
CHELTENHAM FESTIVAL WINNERS IN THE LAST FIVE YEARS – 6% STRIKE-RATE

2023 KEY STAT

STAY AWAY FAY WAS HIS FIRST G1 HURDLES WINNER AT THE FESTIVAL SINCE 2012

Eight of his ten handicap hurdle winners were aged four or five, and nine of his 15 handicap winners overall have carried between 10st 10lb and 11st 1lb (two of the three above that weight were in the Martin Pipe).

It is worth noting that Nicholls has won the County Hurdle and the Grand Annual Chase four times apiece – both are over 2m, and that is another factor to take into account.

Profitable to level stakes

2023 KEY STAT

TWO MORE G1
WINNERS MADE IT
10/35 AT THAT LEVEL
IN THE PAST THREE
YEARS

STARS such as Honeysuckle have established Henry de Bromhead as one of the big five trainers at the festival – and indeed he ranks second only to Willie Mullins over the past five years.

Last year's festival pretty much mirrored the overall picture since 2019. Mullins was clear in front, with double the next best total, while De Bromhead was locked together with Gordon Elliott – three winners apiece in this case.

While it is fair to say Elliott would almost certainly be just ahead in second place overall since 2019 (rather than one behind De Bromhead's 16 winners) if he hadn't missed the 2021 festival through suspension, it has been a remarkable rise to the top table for De Bromhead's Knockeen operation.

As an illustration, while De Bromhead and Elliott are close together in terms of winners, the Knockeen trainer has more than double the strike-rate (15 per cent against seven per cent).

The most notable point is that De Bromhead has an impressive 42.03pts profit to level stakes with all runners at the past five festivals. A loss is the norm, especially for trainers with a high number of runners, and Nicky Henderson is a distant next best among the top five on -9.31pts.

De Bromhead's 16 winners over the past five years have

21
CHELTENHAM FESTIVAL WINNERS

2010
YEAR OF FIRST WINNER AT CHELTENHAM

16
CHELTENHAM FESTIVAL WINNERS IN THE LAST FIVE YEARS – 15% STRIKE-RATE

been evenly split between chases and hurdles and there is a similar pattern with his profit figures (+22.20 in chases and +19.83 in hurdles).

Last year he had three winners from 27 runners for a strike-rate of 11 per cent and another profit of 6.75pts. That was largely due to Maskada's 22-1 success in the Grand Annual Handicap Chase, backed up by Grade 1 wins in the Mares' Hurdle with Honeysuckle and the Ryanair Chase with Envoi Allen.

He has had at least one winner at each of the past seven festivals and his total is up to 21, with the quality of

DE BROMHEAD FESTIVAL WINNERS BY RACE TYPE

- Hurdles **8**
- Chases **13**

MOST SUCCESSFUL RACES

Champion Chase
■■■
Arkle Chase
■■
Champion Hurdle
■■
Gold Cup
■■
Mares' Hurdle
■■
Ryanair Chase
■■

his string evident in the fact that 16 of those wins have been in Grade 1 contests.

The good news with De Bromhead's stronger fancies is that he usually does best with runners at 10-1 or lower. Twelve of his last 13 winners were in that category, making it 17 out of 21 overall.

Overall, at 10-1 or lower, De Bromhead has had 17 winners, 12 seconds and six thirds from 65 runners since 2010 (26%, +29.53pts).

Dan Skelton in the winner's enclosure after Langer Dan's Coral Cup victory

High hopes with Dawning

A RUN of three festival blanks in a row was broken in no uncertain terms last year when Dan Skelton recorded a handicap hurdle double from his dozen runners.

Faivoir gave him a fourth success in the County, his favourite festival race, and Langer Dan gained a deserved victory in the Coral Cup, having been second (to Galopin Des Champs) in the 2021 Martin Pipe Handicap Hurdle and brought down the following year. Faivoir also stepped up on a previous festival effort, having been 11th in the County 12 months earlier.

At 9-1, Langer Dan became the third of Skelton's five handicap hurdle winners to go off 12-1 or lower and, from a total of 27 handicap runners in that price bracket, he has also had a 13-2 runner-up and three thirds at 6-1, 7-1 and 15-2.

Faivoir, though, was a 33-1 winner of the County (as was Mohaayed in the 2018 race) and the beaten favourite was stablemate Pembroke, who was 17th at 7-2.

Looking further into what the market reveals, Skelton has had only 23 festival runners priced under 10-1 and yet most have run well

(winners at 8-1 and 9-1 and 11 others in the first four).

Perhaps his best chance in a Grade 1 will lie with novice chaser Grey Dawning. Runner-up to Ginny's Destiny over 2m4½f at Cheltenham in December and then an impressive Grade 2 3m winner at Warwick, he looks a decent prospect for the Brown Advisory.

Langer Dan might well return for the Coral Cup and other possibles include Nurse Susan (Pertemps Final), Galia Des Liteaux (Mares' Chase), Latenightpass (Cross Country) and Let It Rain (Champion Bumper).

GAVIN CROMWELL ranks alongside Dan Skelton as next best after the big five in the trainer standings over the past five festivals with four winners from just 25 runners (16%).

The County Meath trainer (*right*) has the rare distinction of a level-stakes profit from all runners in that period, with his +25pts ranking second only to Henry de Bromhead among those in the upper echelon.

All of Cromwell's winners have been over hurdles – and they have all been big ones. His breakthrough came with Espoir D'Allen in the 2019 Champion Hurdle, Flooring Porter won back-to-back Stayers' Hurdles in 2021 and 2022 and Vanillier took the 2021 Albert Bartlett Novices' Hurdle.

Top-level threat

With just under half of his 25 runners having been in Grade 1 races, he has a 33 per cent strike-rate at that level with a 38pts profit. He has also had a second, third and two fourths in Grade 1s and it is clear Cromwell's top-level runners merit close consideration.

This year could bring a breakthrough winner over fences. Flooring Porter looks set to go for the National Hunt Novices' Chase and Doncaster Listed winner Limerick Lace has good prospects in the Mares' Chase, along with Brides Hill.

Given that three of the yard's festival wins have been at double-figure odds (from 12-1 to 16-1), Cromwell could have each-way prospects with My Mate Mozzie and Letsbeclearaboutit (Grand Annual) and Inotheyurthinkin (Plate) if they head there.

OUTSIDE the big five, **Joseph O'Brien** is the most likely trainer to have a finisher in the first three.

Fifteen of his 61 runners at the past five festivals have made the places at a strike-rate of 25 per cent, with three wins.

It is also worth noting that technically O'Brien had a festival winner in 2016 when he oversaw Ivanovich Gorbatov's preparation for the Triumph Hurdle, although his first official successes did not come until 2019 with Band Of Outlaws in the Boodles Juvenile Handicap Hurdle and Early Doors in the Martin Pipe Handicap Hurdle.

Last year he drew a blank from eight runners, however. The only one priced below 10-1 was Home By The Lee (9-1), who did best of his team in fifth in the Stayers' Hurdle.

This year's big hope is Banbridge (Ryanair Chase), a Grade 1 winner with strong course form. The stable is often well stocked with younger horses and the latest crop includes promising juvenile hurdlers Lark In The Mornin and Nurburgring and Champion Bumper hope Samyr.

Thursday a big one for O'Brien

VENETIA WILLIAMS has registered only two festival winners in the past decade but both were in 2022 and signalled her re-emergence as a major force. Third was the best she could manage last year with 33-1 shot Pink Legend in the Mares' Chase but she did not have a particularly strong team, with most of her 14 runners priced at 40-1 or above. Not that big prices are necessarily a barrier to success – Chambard was a 40-1 winner of the Fulke Walwyn Kim Muir Handicap Chase in 2022 (she also had 66-1 Didero Vallis in third). In the past five years her form figures with her small number of runners under 10-1 are P313 and Gold Cup hope L'Homme Presse may well go off in that bracket.

MARTIN BRASSIL has solid results from a small group, having sent out a winner (City Island in the 2019 Ballymore Novices' Hurdle) and three seconds from ten runners in the past five years. He has the strong backing of Sean and Bernardine Mulryan, who owned City Island and now have a leading Gold Cup hope in Fastorslow and promising novice hurdler Built By Ballymore, who is a handicap possible.

BARRY CONNELL, a long-time owner and amateur rider, struck with his first festival runner as a trainer last year when Marine Nationale landed the Grade 1 Supreme Novices' Hurdle (his other runner, Good Land, was fourth in what is now the Baring Bingham Novices' Hurdle). Marine Nationale will return with a leading chance in the Arkle, although not in such good form as last year after his disappointing

defeat in the Irish equivalent at the Dublin Racing Festival.

FERGAL O'BRIEN (*above*) has the joint-highest number of runners-up (four) without a festival winner among current trainers but he has the stable strength to get on the scoreboard soon. The Cotswolds trainer sits fifth in the British trainers' table

milers and juvenile hurdlers, and he has a good prospect in the second category in Salver, who could go for the Triumph or try to exploit a decent mark in the juvenile handicap hurdle.

EMMET MULLINS has proved himself a notable threat when targeting the festival, with a winner, a runner-up, a third and two fourths from just 13 runners. The winner was heavily punted favourite The Shunter in the 2021 Plate Handicap Chase and market moves are worth noting, especially in the handicaps given Mullins' skill at placing horses. This year strong possibles include Corbetts Cross (in strong contention when running out in last year's Albert Bartlett) in the National Hunt Chase, Captain Conby in the Grand Annual, Almuhit in the Pertemps Final, So Scottish in the Plate, Noble Yeats in the Stayers' Hurdle and last year's runner-up Its On The Line in the Hunters' Chase.

ALAN KING, once a major force at the festival but now more focused on the Flat, has had only one winner at the meeting since 2016. That was in the 2022 Arkle Chase with Edwardstone, who is set to be his main contender again in the Champion Chase or Ryanair Chase. Edwardstone was fifth in the Champion Chase last year when he was one of just two festival runners for King and he will

and is well on course for a fourth consecutive century, operating at a strike-rate above 20 per cent. His most exciting prospect is course-and-distance winner Dysart Enos in the Mares' Novices' Hurdle and he has a good Grade 1 shot with Long Walk scorer Crambo in the Stayers' Hurdle, both on Thursday.

GARY MOORE last had a festival winner when Sire De Grugy took the Queen Mother Champion Chase in 2014 but could be a threat this time after a strong winter. Welsh Grand National winner Nassalam could lead the team in the Ultima Handicap Chase or the Gold Cup. Two of Moore's strengths are two-

return as a live threat after coming back to form with his Game Spirit win at Newbury. A bigger outsider is Favour And Fortune, rated the best of King's novice hurdlers and earmarked for the Supreme.

HARRY FRY, whose two festival winners are Unowhatimeanharry in the 2016 Albert Bartlett Novices' Hurdle and Love Envoi in the 2022 Mares' Novices' Hurdle, has decent prospects of more success. Love Envoi, runner-up in last year's Mares' Hurdle, is set to try again and the Dorset trainer has another Grade 1 hope with the highly rated Gidleigh Park in the Baring Bingham Novices' Hurdle. Boothill is a Champion Chase outsider and Altobelli and Might I are handicap possibles.

EDWARD O'GRADY, once a feared target trainer and still in the top 15 at the festival among current operators, has long been absent but could return with a decent chance this year in No Flies On Him. The JP McManus-owned five-year-old might go down the handicap route if not deemed good enough for a Grade 1.

OLIVER GREENALL AND JOSH GUERRIERO capped the first season of their training partnership with a festival breakthrough in the final race of last year's meeting when 6-1 shot Iroko (their only runner) took the Martin Pipe Handicap Hurdle.

Gidleigh Park: highly rated and unbeaten for Harry Fry (inset)

Iroko might well be back for one of the Grade 1 novice chases and an interesting handicapper is White Rhino for the Pertemps Final.

LUCINDA RUSSELL has been a notable player at the last two festivals with dual Ultima Handicap Chase winner Corach Rambler, who went on to win last year's Grand National and is now in the Cheltenham Gold Cup picture. With a runner-up also coming from just seven runners in the past five years, her ever-strengthening yard is one to take seriously. A couple of novice chasers to watch are Giovinco and the mare Apple Away, who might both end up in handicaps.

JOHN McCONNELL has been a trainer on the up in recent seasons and his rise continued with a festival breakthrough last year when Seddon took the Plate Handicap Chase at 20-1, taking his record to a winner and three thirds from just 14 runners in the past three years. The County Meath trainer might well have opened his account a couple of days earlier in the National Hunt Chase but for Mahler Mission's fall at the second-last when clear in front. Seddon is likely to go for a Plate repeat and Mahler Mission could contest the Ultima Handicap Chase en route to the Grand National.

JAMIE SNOWDEN broke his festival duck last year with You Wear It Well in the

Seddon (right): could bid for a Plate repeat for John McConnell

Mares' Novices' Hurdle and heads back there off a strong winter campaign headlined by Datsalrightgino's Coral Gold Cup success, albeit clouded by that stable star's sad demise on Cheltenham's Trials day. Ga Law, a 2m4½f handicap chase winner on Trials day, could fly the flag in the Plate or the Ultima and You Wear It Well is set to step up to the Mares' Hurdle.

JAMES OWEN looked a prime candidate to be a new name on the festival scoreboard after Burdett Road, a 1m2f handicap winner at Royal Ascot last summer, ran away with the Triumph Trial at Cheltenham in November, but then came a shattering ten-length defeat by Nicky Henderson's Sir Gino on Trials day. The Newmarket trainer, who has been operating above a 20 per cent strike-rate in his first full season, remains hopeful, especially if the ground is on the quicker side at the festival.

PHILIP HOBBS (now training jointly with long-time assistant **JOHNSON WHITE**) does not have the Grade 1 quality of Defi Du Seuil (the stable's last festival winner in 2019 in what is now the Turners Novices' Chase) or 2022 Stayers' Hurdle runner-up Thyme Hill. But their runners can be dangerous in handicap hurdles, with a second, third and fourth from 11 representatives at the past four festivals.

JONJO O'NEILL remains in the top five among current trainers with 27 festival winners, but his success rate has dropped considerably. He was on the scoreboard at 13 of the 14 festivals up to 2014 but has had seven blanks in the past nine years. His most recent winner was Sky Pirate in the Grand Annual Handicap Chase and a handicap tends to be his best route to success, although this year he has the promising Johnnywho for the Grade 1 Albert Bartlett Novices' Hurdle. The handicaps where he has done best are the Pertemps Final (four wins) and the Ultima Handicap Chase (three wins), both around 3m, and he has likely types in Springwell Bay (Pertemps) and Monbeg Genius (Ultima).

BEN PAULING has had three winners at the past seven festivals – a decent return from just 45 runners (six others finished in the first four). Shakem Up'Arry, course winner of the New Year's Day Handicap Chase, was third in last year's Plate Handicap Chase and looks a prime candidate again.

JOE TIZZARD had a best placing of fifth last year at his first festival, having taken the reins at Venn Farm from father Colin, but he might have better prospects of getting the stable back on the scoreboard for the first time since Native River's Gold Cup in 2018. He has exciting novice chaser JPR One and Elixir De Nutz, a lively

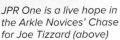

JPR One is a live hope in the Arkle Novices' Chase for Joe Tizzard (above)

outsider for the Champion Chase after his Grade 1 Clarence House success over Jonbon on Cheltenham's Trials day. With the stable ranking in the top ten for festival runners over the past five years, this remains one of Britain's strongest outfits.

DAVID PIPE needs one more winner to take the stable built by father Martin to a combined half-century but it is proving a long wait, with six blanks since Un Temps Pour Tout's second victory in the Ultima Handicap Chase in 2017. Pipe has had three runners-up in that time and a handicap looks his most likely route back to the winner's enclosure.

PAUL KEALY ON THE KEY PLAYERS

1.30 Sky Bet Supreme Novices' Hurdle
• 2m½f • Grade 1 • £135,000

ITV/RTV

Willie Mullins has gone a couple of years without success in this race, having won five in nine years before that, but he has a powerful trio at the top of the betting in Ballyburn, Mystical Power and Tullyhill. Much will depend on whether Ballyburn, deeply impressive in a Grade 1 at the Dublin Racing Festival last time, runs here or steps up in trip to the Baring Bingham. He'll be seen as a banker by many wherever he goes. Mystical Power and Tullyhill would be able deputies or second strings depending on how Mullins plays his hand. Gordon Elliott has Firefox, who became the only horse to beat Ballyburn when they met on their hurdling debuts in December, and Nicky Henderson looks to have the leading British contender in Jeriko Du Reponet, who like Mystical Power runs in the JP McManus colours.

Ballyburn
6 b g; Trainer Willie Mullins
Hurdles form 211, best RPR 158
Left-handed 11, best RPR 158
Right-handed 2, best RPR 132

Didn't take in the Champion Bumper at Cheltenham last season, but proved himself high class in that sphere with two wins, notably at the Punchestown festival in April. Was turned over at odds-on by Firefox on Fairyhouse maiden hurdle debut in December, but quickly banished that from the memory with a runaway 25-length success upped to 2m4f at Leopardstown later that month. Dropping back to 2m for the Grade 1 Tattersalls Ireland 50th Derby Sale Novice Hurdle at the Dublin Racing Festival, Ballyburn firmly established himself at the top of the Willie Mullins pecking order with a devastating performance of power and pace to beat Slade Steel by seven lengths with the rest strung out behind. The big question now is where he goes as Ballyburn is favourite for both the Supreme and the Baring Bingham. He clearly has the speed for 2m but Mullins also has the second favourite for the Supreme in Mystical Power, who looks more of an out-and-out two-miler. Ballyburn's pedigree, however, absolutely screams stamina. He has quite a few brothers and pretty much all of them were three-milers, including Noble Endeavor, who ran in the National Hunt Chase (fell) as well as the Grand National (also placed in the Martin Pipe and Ultima). Mullins is renowned for changing his mind at the last minute, so Ballyburn can't

be considered a betting proposition for either race yet. One thing is for certain, though. He'll deservedly be a hot favourite for whichever race he lines up in.

Going preference Seems to act on anything
Star rating ✪✪✪✪✪

Mystical Power
5 b g; Trainer Willie Mullins
Hurdles form (right-handed) 11, best RPR 144

By Galileo, Mystical Power is the first son of outstanding Champion Hurdle winner Annie Power, and he's well on the way to making his mark as a hurdler. A bumper winner on his debut at lowly Ballinrobe in May, Mystical Power got off the mark with a seven-length success in novice company at the Galway festival in July, and then confirmed himself a potentially top-class performer with a commanding success by the same margin in a four-runner Grade 2 Moscow Flyer Novice Hurdle at Punchestown in January. That race has more often than not been used by a horse who ended up as the Mullins first string for the Supreme, although last year he won it with Impaire Et Passe, who went to the Ballymore (as it was then) and won that instead. Mystical Power undoubtedly has bags of ability, but he's also far from the finished article as he's a little too keen and there's plenty of room for improvement in his jumping, although it's more a case of being a little untidy at times rather than making serious mistakes. Annie Power clearly stayed much further than 2m as she nearly won a Stayers' Hurdle two years before her Champion Hurdle success, but Mystical Power's keen-going tendencies surely make him more of a candidate for the 2m event this year. Much depends on whether Mullins wants to run his top two against each other, while Mystical Power's owner JP McManus also has other contenders for this. Anything is possible at the moment.

Going preference Has won on good and soft
Star rating ✪✪✪

Tullyhill
6 gr g; Trainer Willie Mullins
Hurdles form 211, best RPR n/a
Left-handed 1, best RPR 131
Right-handed 21, best RPR n/a

Had some warm form in bumpers, most notably when finishing second to A Dream To Share in Punchestown's version of the Champion Bumper. His hurdles career got off to an inauspicious start when he became one of the shortest-priced losers of the season at Punchestown in November, finishing a 24-length second at odds of 1-8 thanks to some shoddy jumping (went left a few times as well). A first run left-handed under rules went better as he made all and won by seven lengths from Lightkeeper at Naas, although that one was beaten just over three times that distance when second next time. He completed his preparation with a deeply impressive nine-length victory over the well-touted No Flies On Him in a Listed contest at Punchestown just before this book went to press, and in the process rocketed up the betting to give his trainer the first three in the market. They may not all run in this race, of course, but Tullyhill, who was neat and fast at his hurdles, has only the Supreme entry, so he's almost certainly going to be in the line-up.

Going preference Hurdles form on soft/heavy, won point on good
Star rating ✪✪✪✪

Jeriko Du Reponet
5 b g; Trainer Nicky Henderson
Hurdles form (left-handed) 111, best RPR 132

Called the "sort of horse you dream about" by Nicky Henderson in his pre-season Racing Post Stable Tour, Jeriko Du Reponet *(below)* won his point easily last March and has since made it 3-3 over hurdles. His first two outings came in maiden and novice company at Newbury and he won both very easily at odds-on, although he didn't beat much in slow times. He had more on his plate in the Grade 2 Rossington Main at Doncaster in January, coming through it well enough and finding plenty after the last despite hanging a little to win by a length and a quarter from Lump Sum. That form is nothing special in the context of a Supreme, though, with a best RPR of 132 being around 25lb shy of the figures you'd expect of just an average winner at the festival. It also gives him at least 26lb to find with Ballyburn and plenty with many of his other potential rivals despite his place in the betting. Jeriko Du Reponet certainly has the looks, but not necessarily the pedigree as his little-known sire Choeur Du Nord, a decent hurdler in France, has yet to produce a star, albeit it's still early days on that score.

Going preference Winning form on good and soft
Star rating ✪✪

Firefox
6 b g; Trainer Gordon Elliott
Hurdles form 414, best RPR 137
Left-handed 44, best RPR 135
Right-handed 1, best RPR 137

Is effectively a second-season novice as he finished fourth in a Navan maiden hurdle before running in the first of his four bumpers. Showed really good form in that sphere, running to an RPR of 135 on his final outing at Down Royal in November (A Dream To Share got 137 for winning at Cheltenham and went a bit higher at Punchestown), and he couldn't have got off to a better start back over hurdles at Fairyhouse in December. There it was very tight between him and Ballyburn (he was evens, his rival 10-11 in a field of 24), but it was he who found the better change of gear to win going away by two and a half lengths. Afterwards trainer Gordon Elliott was questioning whether he wanted to go further or not, and Firefox was subsequently tried in the 2m4f Grade 1 Lawlor's of Naas Novice Hurdle, but could finish only a laboured fourth to outsider of the field Readin Tommy Wrong. It's hard to know whether he didn't stay or ran flat for another reason, but it was a disappointing display given the promise he had shown, especially given that he jumped so well throughout the race. He's certainly bred for further, but he did show some gears when beating Ballyburn and it's surely too early to be writing him off given how impressive he was against a horse who's going to go off as a very warm favourite for whatever race he runs in.

Going preference No obvious preference
Star rating ✪✪✪

Slade Steel
6 b g; Trainer Henry de Bromhead
Hurdles form (left-handed) 112, best RPR 148

Decent enough bumper performer who made a fine start to hurdling career, first winning his maiden in good style from the useful King Of Kingsfield at Naas and then stepping up to 2m4f to edge out Lecky Watson by half a length in the Grade 2 Navan Novice Hurdle in December. A drop back down in trip at the Dublin Racing Festival resulted in a creditable seven-length second to Ballyburn, which was similar to the margin between them in a bumper the previous season. Right now he's a shorter price for the Baring Bingham than the Supreme, but he has twice finished behind Ballyburn and it's easy enough to see him being aimed at whatever race that one misses.

Going preference Wins have come on soft and heavy
Star rating ✪✪✪

Ile Atlantique
6 br g; Trainer Willie Mullins
Hurdles form 312, best RPR 146
Left-handed 32, best RPR 146
Right-handed 1, best RPR 133

Another who is essentially a second-season

novice over hurdles as he ran third at odds of 75-1 on his hurdles debut at Auteuil in April 2022 before joining Willie Mullins. Has since run to a good level in bumpers (just three-quarters of a length behind Firefox in the last of them) and run really well twice over hurdles. In the first he was a wide-margin winner of his maiden at Gowran in November, a performance impressive enough to make Paul Townend pick him ahead of three stablemates in the Grade 1 Lawlor's of Naas Novice Hurdle in January. That pick made him the default favourite and he was sent off at just 6-4, but went down by a neck to stablemate and outsider Readin Tommy Wrong. There's no doubt he stayed well enough there, although Mullins said afterwards that "Looking at that, Ile Atlantique could well be a Supreme horse." He clearly has a remarkable amount of juggling to do.

Going preference Acts on yielding and soft
Star rating ✪✪✪

King Of Kingsfield
6 b g; Trainer Gordon Elliott
Hurdles form 22213, best RPR 141
Left-handed 213, best RPR 141
Right-handed 22, best RPR 137

Has only a maiden hurdle win to show from five starts in this sphere, but has also shown a high level of form in finishing second to Farren Glory in the Royal Bond at Fairyhouse and third to Ballyburn at the Dublin Racing Festival. He was beaten 14 lengths in the latter, though, and that surely hints at limitation. As a novice who has already run five times, he'll have the option of handicaps, and while he hasn't tried further than 2m, his dam stayed well on the Flat, so the Martin Pipe, a race his trainer won in 2017 and 2018 for the same connections, could be on the cards.

Going preference No obvious preference
Star rating ✪✪

Jango Baie
6 b g; Trainer Nicky Henderson
Hurdles form 112, best RPR 140
Left-handed 1, best RPR 138
Right-handed 12, best RPR 140

It says something about the state of the

British challenge when the winner of the premier pre-Cheltenham 2m novice hurdle in Britain was still a 33-1 shot four weeks before the festival. Jango Baie may well have been fortunate to land the Grade 1 Formby Novices' Hurdle at Aintree following the fall of Farren Glory, but it was still a fair way out and he was a commanding winner in the end. That arguably gives him better form than the stable's number one Jeriko Du Reponet, but it's still some way removed from what will be required to beat Ballyburn and a few of the others. Lost his unbeaten record when a length-and-a-half second to the unbeaten Handstands upped to 2m3½f in the Sidney Banks at Huntingdon in February, but was conceding 5lb to the winner and clearly wasn't disgraced.

Going preference All form on soft
Star rating ✪✪

Asian Master
7 b g; Trainer Willie Mullins
Hurdles form 11, best RPR 139
Left-handed 1, best RPR 139
Right-handed 1, best RPR 123

Won the last of four points and then finished second in a bumper and fourth in a 3m hunter chase before joining Willie Mullins. That would give him a strange profile for a Supreme winner, but he has shown plenty of ability in maiden and novice company, winning both starts. In the second of those he bounded ten lengths clear of the 136-rated Better Days Ahead, although it has to be said he was getting 15lb if you include his jockey's claim. Useful but his trainer obviously has stronger candidates.

Going preference Has won on yielding and soft to heavy
Star rating ✪

Tellherthename
5 b g; Trainer Ben Pauling
Hurdles form 21P1, best RPR 132
Left-handed P
Right-handed 211, best RPR 132

Point winner who made subsequent Grade 1 winner Jango Baie pull out all the stops on their hurdling debuts at Ascot in November, going down fighting by a nose. A runaway

14-length winner at Huntingdon next time, he was sent off at a shorter price than Jango Baie for the Grade 1 Formby at Aintree (5-1 against 17-2), but apparently hated the ground and was beaten when pulled up, his jockey reporting he'd lost his action. Back on better ground just over two weeks later he was again a 14-length winner at Huntingdon, albeit in a weak race at odds of 1-4. Would have run in the Betfair Hurdle at Newbury in February if the ground hadn't gone against him, and is apparently considered very nicely treated on a mark of 135. That rating would put him close to the cutoff for the County Hurdle, though, and depending on the entries for

Ile Atlantique: one of many options for Willie Mullins

that, connections may decide they have to come here. He's at least as promising as the few shorter-priced British entries.

Going preference Doesn't want soft ground
Star rating ✪✪

Anotherway
5 b g; Trainer Willie Mullins
Hurdles form 01, best RPR 147
Left-handed 0, best RPR 114
Right-handed 1, best RPR 147

Would have a rating in the mid-80s on the Flat on his form in France, but wasn't exactly full of promise when only 11th of 28 on his debut for Willie Mullins at Leopardstown in December.

However, he won very easily from a horse with similar Flat ability on his second effort at the end of January at Punchestown, earning a hefty RPR of 147, a figure that puts him within spitting distance of all bar clear form horse Ballyburn. Has only the Supreme as an entry.

Going preference Won on good to soft on the Flat, heavy over hurdles
Star rating ✪

OTHERS TO CONSIDER
Even after the final forfeit stage before the five-day entries, Willie Mullins still had five others not listed, including the once-raced **Billericay Dickie**, who impressed at Punchestown at the

end of January, albeit in a desperate time. Other leading British hopes, if you can call them that considering their prices, would be **Favour And Fortune**, who was second to Jango Baie in the Formby, and **Lookaway**, who last ran down the field in the Betfair Hurdle. It's hard to see those being anything but bit-part players, though.

VERDICT

As usual it's going to be a case of Willie Mullins bingo and the final shape of this race isn't going to be known until he makes the final decision on whether **Ballyburn** goes here or in the Baring Bingham. I wouldn't be in a rush to oppose Ballyburn for either race, and it might boil down to which race Mullins thinks he has the best chance of winning without him. All the talk in February was that he's much more likely to come here than go back up in trip, but there will surely

be a lot of pondering to do yet. To my way of thinking, Mullins is much stronger in this race without Ballyburn than he would be in the Baring Bingham. He'd still have the first two in the betting here, but wouldn't have the favourite for the Baring Bingham if he ran Ballyburn in the Supreme, and if he wants to win both races, his best chance is to send Ballyburn over 2m5f. Mind you, as someone who backed Impaire Et Passe for the Supreme last year and Constitution Hill for the Baring Bingham the year before, I'm probably not best placed to be giving advice about running plans! Whatever the case, I'd be quite interested in **FIREFOX** coming back down in trip as it may simply have been a case of him not being ready for 2m4f last time. He certainly has the boot for 2m and his jumping is his chief asset.

SUPREME NOVICES' HURDLE RESULTS AND TRENDS

	FORM	WINNER	AGE & WGT	Adj RPR	SP	TRAINER	BEST RPR LAST 12 MONTHS (RUNS SINCE)
23	1111	Marine Nationale D	6 11-7	158-7	9-2	B Connell (IRE)	won Fairyhouse Gd1 nov hdl (2m) (0)
22	11	Constitution Hill D	5 11-7	159-1	9-4j	N Henderson	won Gd1 Tolworth Hurdle (2m) (0)
21	2-111	Appreciate It D	7 11-7	162T	8-11f	W Mullins (IRE)	won Leopardstown Gd1 nov hdl (2m) (1)
20	1-F11	Shishkin D	6 11-7	161-2	6-1	N Henderson	won Huntingdon Listed nov hdl (2m3½f) (0)
19	4P-11	Klassical Dream D	5 11-7	154-8	6-1	W Mullins (IRE)	won Leopardstown Gd1 nov hdl (2m) (0)
18	12231	Summerville Boy D	6 11-7	157-3	9-1	T George	won Gd1 Tolworth Hurdle (2m) (0)
17	11RR6	Labaik D	6 11-7	150-8	25-1	G Elliott (IRE)	won Navan Gd3 nov hdl (2m) (3)
16	61111	Altior CD	6 11-7	163T	4-1	N Henderson	won Kempton class 2 nov hdl (2m) (0)
15	2111	Douvan D	5 11-7	160-3	2-1f	W Mullins (IRE)	won Punchestown Gd2 nov hdl (2m) (0)
14	2-111	Vautour D	5 11-7	157T	7-2j	W Mullins (IRE)	won Gd1 Deloitte Hurdle (2m2f) (0)

WINS-RUNS: 4yo 0-2, 5yo 4-59, 6yo 5-66, 7yo 1-8, 8yo 0-4 **FAVOURITES:** -£1.40

TRAINERS IN THIS RACE (w-pl-r): Willie Mullins 4-6-30, Nicky Henderson 3-6-15, Gordon Elliott 1-2-8, Barry Connell 1-0-1, Alan King 0-0-4, Henry de Bromhead 0-2-8, Joseph O'Brien 0-0-3, Paul Nicholls 0-0-4, Nigel Twiston-Davies 0-0-3, Olly Murphy 0-2-4, Harry Fry 0-0-2, John McConnell 0-0-1, Fergal O'Brien 0-0-1, Ben Pauling 0-0-1, Neil King 0-0-1

FATE OF FAVOURITES: 1122044112 **POSITION OF WINNER IN MARKET:** 1120333113

Key trends

- Rated within 8lb of RPR top-rated, ten winners in last ten runnings
- Adjusted RPR of at least 154, 9/10
- Previously contested a Graded race, 9/10
- Won last time out, 9/10
- Ran within the last 66 days, 8/10
- Won at least 50 per cent of hurdle starts, 7/10

Other factors

- Only one winner had come via the Flat. Five of the other nine started their careers in bumpers, where they had earned an RPR of at least 110. Three started over hurdles in France, while another went hurdling straight from a point-to-point
- Only one winner had run in the Champion Bumper (Appreciate It second in 2020)

2.10 My Pension Expert Arkle Novices' Chase ITV/RTV
● 2m ● Grade 1 ● £175,000

Until the Dublin Racing Festival, this race looked to have a standout candidate in Barry Connell's Marine Nationale, last year's Supreme Novices' Hurdle winner who had raised the excitement level for his chasing career with an impressive debut success over Christmas. The Irish Arkle threw a spanner in the works, however, as Marine Nationale trailed in fifth while the Willie Mullins-trained Il Etait Temps just got the better of Gordon Elliott's Found A Fifty in a close finish. Horses can bounce back but the trends show it doesn't happen often in the Arkle and Marine Nationale's flat effort at Leopardstown has opened up this race. Il Etait Temps has put himself firmly in the reckoning but doesn't have much in hand from the Irish Arkle and has to prove he can perform at Cheltenham after a couple of unplaced runs at the festival. There will be interest in others from the Mullins squad, principally the relatively inexperienced but highly promising Hunters Yarn and Irish Arkle third Facile Vega, and Ireland's challenge could also feature Quilixios (Henry de Bromhead) and My Mate Mozzie (Gavin Cromwell). The leading British contender is last-time-out Grade 2 winner JPR One, whose trainer Joe Tizzard has a decent shot at a festival breakthrough in his second year after taking over the family stable from father Colin.

Marine Nationale

7 b g; Trainer Barry Connell
Chase form (left-handed) 15, best RPR 156
Cheltenham form (hurdles) 1, best RPR 158
At the festival 14 Mar 2023 Travelled strongly, towards rear of midfield, headway on outer 3 out, shaken up and went second before last, edged left and led when bumped run-in, ridden inside final 110yds, won going away, readily, won Supreme Novices' Hurdle by three and a quarter lengths from Facile Vega

A brief but very successful spell over hurdles culminated with Marine Nationale winning the Supreme Novices' Hurdle at Cheltenham under a very confident ride from Mikey O'Sullivan, and he was on everyone's radar as a potential Arkle horse as soon as his trainer confirmed he'd be going over fences. After a faultless display on his eagerly awaited chase debut over Christmas at Leopardstown, where he beat Firm Footings by eight and a half lengths on the bridle, he was already being quoted at odds-on for March and had his trainer openly talking about the following year's Champion Chase. Given he'd run to an RPR of 156, which is just 2lb shy of his peak hurdle form, in a beginners' chase without turning a hair, it was certainly easy to get excited. The bubble was spectacularly burst at the Dublin Racing Festival, though, as Marine Nationale jumped slowly and could manage only fifth of six in the Irish Arkle, finishing ten and a half lengths behind Il Etait Temps. His trainer was at a loss to explain the effort, which certainly was too bad to be true, but it does leave him questions to answer assuming, as is likely, he heads straight to Cheltenham.

Going preference Acts on good and soft
Star rating ✪✪✪

Il Etait Temps

6 gr g; Trainer Willie Mullins
Chase form 121, best RPR 156
Left-handed 1, best RPR 156
Right-handed 12, best RPR 152
Cheltenham form (hurdles) 55, best RPR 148
At the festival 18 Mar 2022 Took keen hold, in touch with leaders, bit short of room and not fluent 2 out, ridden up the centre before last, no extra run-in, finished fifth, beaten eight and three-quarter lengths by Vauban in Triumph Hurdle
14 Mar 2023 Didn't jump with fluency, took keen hold, raced wide, midfield, steady headway 3 out, ridden and outpaced on turn before last, soon edged left, kept on final 110yds, not reach leaders, finished fifth, beaten nine lengths by Marine Nationale in Supreme Novices' Hurdle

High-quality novice hurdler in his second season in that sphere last term, winning two of his five outings, most notably when causing a massive upset in the Tattersalls Ireland Novice Hurdle at the Dublin Racing Festival, a race in which hot favourite Facile Vega flopped. He had otherwise looked a level below that rival as he'd been four lengths behind him in the Future Stars at Leopardstown, the best part of six lengths away when they were second and fifth to Marine Nationale in the Supreme, and seven and a half lengths distant when second to him at Punchestown. Il Etait Temps made a fine start to his chase career, winning comfortably at Thurles in November, but then looked to have his limitations exposed by Gaelic Warrior, who beat him on the bridle at Limerick. However, back at the DRF he again found his best form to cause another upset (albeit when backed from 20-1 overnight to 6-1) to land the Irish Arkle by a neck from Found A Fifty, with the disappointing odds-on favourite Marine Nationale well beaten in fifth. That form gives him sound claims, but it was a proper staying performance over that 2m1f trip and he might find Cheltenham's sharper 2m just a tad too quick for him. He has already twice run better at the DRF than he did at Cheltenham, and that track might be more suitable, at least at the minimum trip (he is in the Turners).

Going preference Seems fine on most surfaces
Star rating ✪✪✪

Found A Fifty
7 b g; Trainer Gordon Elliott
Chase form 1212, best RPR 155
Left-handed 12, best RPR 155
Right-handed 12, best RPR 155

Decent enough performer over hurdles, although not quite at the level of some of his potential Arkle rivals. It has been a different story over fences, however, with two wins and two seconds from four starts, the last three coming in Grade 1 company. After a pleasing debut at Down Royal, Found A Fifty was seemingly outstayed by Irish National winner I Am Maximus in the Drinmore, but he made no mistake dropped to 2m1f at Leopardstown,

albeit in only a four-runner Racing Post Novice Chase, which he won by a length and a half from My Mate Mozzie despite jumping to his right throughout. He was straighter at the Dublin Racing Festival and arguably ran his best race, having just been pegged back by Il Etait Temps on the line in the Irish Arkle. There's nothing between them on that form and the slightly shorter trip is probably more in his favour, although that tendency to jump to his right will be tested.

Going preference Fine on yielding and soft
Star rating ✪✪✪

Hunters Yarn
7 b g; Trainer Willie Mullins
Chase form (right-handed) F1, best RPR 154
Cheltenham form 0, best RPR 140
At the festival 17 Mar 2023 Held up in rear, headway after 2 out, soon ridden, weakened approaching last, finished 12th, beaten 24 lengths by Faivoir in County Hurdle

Flopped when sent off at just 11-2 for last year's County Hurdle, but had otherwise been fairly progressive, and his trainer said last season that "he could be a very smart novice chaser". Things didn't quite go to plan on his chase debut at Fairyhouse in December as he fell at the last but he was cruising in a five-length lead at the time, and he made no mistake next time at the same track. Although giving the second-last a proper belt, he was soon back on the bridle to win eased right down by ten lengths and seven from Path D'Oroux and Firm Footings, the latter having been beaten half that distance by Marine Nationale earlier in the campaign. The form was given further substance when the runner-up finished second off a mark of 136 in a £100k handicap at the Dublin Racing Festival, and there can't be much doubt that Hunters Yarn's form claims are right up there with the best of these. He's a brother to Do Your Job, who was a Grade 2 novice chase winner over 2m4f for Michael Scudamore two seasons ago, but the Arkle is his only entry at Cheltenham, and that's surely where he's heading.

Going preference Best hurdles form on good, best chase form on soft
Star rating ✪✪✪

thought he was going to be, but there's also evidence to suggest there's no absolute standout contender for this Arkle, and his Cheltenham form – won the Bumper, second in the Supreme – is not to be sniffed at. It wouldn't be a major surprise to see him reverse form with the two ahead of him at Leopardstown or to win his second race at the festival.

Going preference Disappointing efforts came on yielding, and may need it considerably deeper
Star rating ✪✪✪

Facile Vega
7 b g; Trainer Willie Mullins
Chase form (left-handed) 143, best RPR 155
Cheltenham form (all) 12, best RPR 154
At the festival 16 Mar 2022 Towards rear of midfield, headway from over 6f out, close up 4f out, shaken up to challenge 2f out, led over 1f out, soon pushed along, went clear inside final furlong, readily, won Champion Bumper by three and three-quarter lengths from American Mike
14 Mar 2023 Midfield, smooth headway to lead before 2 out, pushed along when awkward on landing last, soon edged right and headed, kept on, no match for winner, finished second, beaten three and a quarter lengths by Marine Nationale in Supreme Novices' Hurdle

The 2022 Champion Bumper winner has long been considered a potential superstar by Willie Mullins, but it's fair to say he's had his share of ups and downs since that festival victory. It has hardly all been bad as he has won eight of his 12 starts, but he has blown out at short prices a couple of times, and did so on his second effort over fences when last of four to Found A Fifty in the Racing Post Novice Chase at Leopardstown following a really impressive first win at Navan. His previous flop had also come at Leopardstown, in the Dublin Racing Festival over hurdles the season before, but he performed better there in February, although he was still behind Il Etait Temps and Found A Fifty, who fought out the finish. There's mounting evidence to suggest he's not quite as good as connections

JPR One
7 bb g; Trainer Joe Tizzard
Chase form 1U31, best RPR 155
Left-handed 1U1, best RPR 155
Right-handed 3, best RPR 144
Cheltenham form (all) 25U, best RPR 147
At the festival 15 Mar 2022 Towards rear, hit 3rd, not fluent 4th, slightly hampered 3 out, soon pushed along and outpaced, weakened before 2 out, tailed off, finished fifth, beaten 57 lengths by Constitution Hill in Supreme Novices' Hurdle

The first, and only, British entry to get a full write-up, JPR One *(above)* may or may not be the sole representative of the home team on the day, but he certainly deserves his place. He may not have been anywhere near as good as his rivals over hurdles, but he looked a natural on his chase debut at Newton Abbot in October, and was in the process of winning with something to spare until unseating at the last in the Grade 2 Arkle Trial at Cheltenham in November. His one substandard effort came at right-handed Sandown when he was only third to Le Patron in the Henry VIII Novices' Chase, but he was back on track when pouncing late on Matata in the Lightning Novices' Chase at Lingfield. The RPR of 155 he earned there is just 1lb below the peak effort of Marine Nationale, who, assuming Gaelic Warrior doesn't run, is the form pick on Racing Post figures in what is a really tight race.

Going preference Doesn't seem to have any issues
Star rating ✪✪✪

Quilixios

7 b g; Trainer Henry de Bromhead
Chase form 161, best RPR 142
Left-handed 1, best RPR 142
Right-handed 16, best RPR 131
Cheltenham form (hurdles) 1, best RPR 149
At the festival 19 Mar 2021 Took keen hold, pressed leader, led going easily just before 2 out, ridden before last, edged right and went clear inside final 110yds, readily, won Triumph Hurdle by three and a quarter lengths from Adagio

Won the Triumph Hurdle in 2021, but had has his issues and managed only seven runs since. Three of them have been over fences this term, and he bagged his first win since the Triumph when scoring by a neck from Cool Survivor on his debut at Limerick in October. Tailed off when upped to 3m next time, he was back on track in plain novice company over 2m at Naas, jumping well and winning comfortably enough from Sa Fureur. However, an RPR of 142 for that effort puts him a long way behind those mentioned above him and some way behind plenty who didn't even get a mention, and he does seem priced up on his Triumph win and not chase form.

Going preference Acts on most, best on heavy
Star rating ✪✪

Blood Destiny

5 ch g; Trainer Willie Mullins
Chase form 12, best RPR 141
Left-handed 1, best RPR 141
Right-handed 2, best RPR 140
Cheltenham form (hurdles) 9, best RPR 120
At the festival 17 Mar 2023 Took keen hold, prominent, ridden after 2 out, soon weakened (jockey said gelding was never travelling from halfway), finished ninth, beaten 27 lengths in Triumph Hurdle by Lossiemouth

Tailed off when second favourite to stablemate Lossiemouth in last season's Triumph, Blood Destiny has run only three times since and been beaten at odds-on in two of them. Second at 8-11 in a Grade 2 four-year-old hurdle at Fairyhouse in April, he proved far too good for Heart Wood (subsequent runaway winner of a handicap chase at the Dublin Racing Festival) at Naas in December, but then went down at odds of 2-5 at Punchestown in

January. Has a lot to find on that form and likely this will be too hard.

Going preference Usually kept to soft ground
Star rating ✪✪

My Mate Mozzie

8 b g; Trainer Gavin Cromwell
Chase form 212, best RPR 150
Left-handed 12, best RPR 150
Right-handed 2, best RPR 130
Cheltenham form (all) 81, best RPR 146
At the festival 18 Mar 2022 Tracked leaders, disputing third home turn, soon ridden, no extra approaching last, finished eighth, beaten ten and a half lengths by State Man in County Hurdle

Strong traveller who cruised to victory at Cheltenham on his second chase outing and showed dramatically improved form when second to Found A Fifty in the Racing Post Novice Chase at Leopardstown, beaten just a length and a half. That puts him within hailing distance of these, and he did briefly trade at just above evens at Leopardstown despite going off at 12-1. That's his problem, though, as he does seem to save something for himself and he's lost when trading at odds-on six times in his life, including when getting beaten at 1.06 on his chase debut. Will likely back out of it when things get tough.

Going preference Seems best on better ground
Star rating ✪✪

OTHERS TO CONSIDER

The entry with the best chase form is **Gaelic Warrior**, but Cheltenham is the wrong way around for him, and he'd be a more likely runner in the Turners if connections want to have another go left-handed following his Leopardstown flop. **Matata** could prove a decent second string for the owners of Hunters Yarn as he went down by only half a length to JPR One at Lingfield, where he might have won with a more aggressive ride, and he has shown a good aptitude for Cheltenham. **Sharjah** is 11 now but he has been second in two Champion Hurdles, so does warrant at least a mention. He was also fourth under 12st in last year's County Hurdle, and there's a chance

ARKLE CHASE RESULTS AND TRENDS

	FORM WINNER	AGE & WGT	Adj RPR	SP	TRAINER	BEST RPR LAST 12 MONTHS (RUNS SINCE)
23	2-111 El Fabiolo D	6 11-7	174^T	11-10f	W Mullins (IRE)	won Leopardstown Gd1 nov ch (2m1f) (0)
22	B1111 Edwardstone D	8 11-4	174^T	5-2f	A King	won Sandown Gd1 nov ch (1m7½f) (2)
21	1-111 Shishkin C, D	7 11-4	180^T	4-9f	N Henderson	won Doncaster Gd2 nov ch (2m½f) (0)
20	11121 Put The Kettle On CD	6 10-11	165^-9	16-1	H de Bromhead (IRE)	won Cheltenham Gd2 nov ch (2m) (0)
19	6-231 Duc Des Genievres	6 11-4	165^-5	5-1	W Mullins (IRE)	won Gowran Park nov ch (2m4f) (0)
18	3-111 Footpad D	6 11-4	178^T	5-6f	W Mullins (IRE)	won Leopardstown Gd1 nov ch (2m1f) (0)
17	-1111 Altior C, D	7 11-4	185^T	1-4f	N Henderson	won Newbury Gd2 ch (2m½f) (0)
16	-1111 Douvan C, D	6 11-4	180^T	1-4f	W Mullins (IRE)	won Leopardstown Gd1 nov ch (2m1f) (1)
15	1-F11 Un De Sceaux D	7 11-4	181^T	4-6f	W Mullins (IRE)	won Leopardstown Gd1 nov ch (2m1f) (0)
14	1-261 Western Warhorse	6 11-4	148^-23	33-1	D Pipe	won Doncaster class 3 nov ch (2m3f) (0)

WINS-RUNS: 5yo 0-7, 6yo 6-23, 7yo 3-41, 8yo 1-11, 9yo 0-6, 10yo 0-1 **FAVOURITES:** £3.04

TRAINERS IN THIS RACE (w-pl-r): Willie Mullins 5-3-15, Henry de Bromhead 1-2-13, Gavin Cromwell 0-1-1, Gordon Elliott 0-0-5, Nigel Twiston-Davies 0-0-2, Venetia Williams 0-0-3, Gary Moore 0-0-1

FATE OF FAVOURITES: 2111106111 **POSITION OF WINNER IN MARKET:** 8111137111

he may go handicapping in something like the Grand Annual (Irish rating 147). The others either don't look good enough or are unlikely runners, and while there were rumours that **Inthepocket** could be supplemented, going to Cheltenham after just one chase outing in November (second to Facile Vega) would be a huge ask.

VERDICT

*If you accept that **Gaelic Warrior** is an unlikely runner, then on Racing Post Ratings there's no more than 2lb between the seven horses with the best form, and none of them has yet run to a level recorded by the worst winner of the Arkle over the last ten years. That doesn't mean it's a bad Arkle as something may stamp its authority on the division, but it does mean we have a more open race than is often the case, and one lacking a star, although that didn't look to be the case before **Marine Nationale** had his colours lowered at Leopardstown. His chances should not be written off after that, but he's still a shorter price than the four who finished ahead of him and he's therefore easy enough to discard as a potential bet. I wouldn't be remotely surprised to see Leopardstown form turned around on the day at Cheltenham, but given **Facile Vega** has finished first and second at two festivals and is the biggest-priced of the top four in the betting, I'd be more interested in him at*

Key trends

- Aged six or seven, 9/10
- RPR hurdles rating of at least 149, 9/10
- Finished in the first two on all completed chase starts, 9/10
- Rated within 9lb of RPR top-rated, 9/10 (seven were top rated)
- Adjusted RPR of at least 165, 9/10
- Three to five chase runs, 7/10
- SP no bigger than 5-1, 8/10 (exceptions 16-1 and 33-1)

Other factors

- Nine winners had previously won a 2m-2m1f Graded chase
- Six winners had previously run at the festival, showing mixed form in a variety of hurdle races

*10-1 than I would Marine Nationale, albeit only if the ground was soft at best. The one I've come down on, though, is **HUNTERS YARN**, who hasn't been properly tested yet but would be 2-2 over fences had he not fallen at the last on his debut, and trounced a subsequent big handicap winner in some style when last seen. His ownermate **Matata** is one I could see running a big race on the sharper 2m circuit of the Old course, although he'll be there to be shot at from the off.*

2.50 Ultima Handicap Chase

ITV/RTV

● *3m1f*   ● *Premier Handicap*   ● *£125,000*

This prized 3m1f handicap chase has an illustrious roll of honour and last year Corach Rambler became the latest winner to go on to Grand National glory, joining the likes of West Tip, Seagram and Rough Quest.

LAST YEAR'S WINNER Corach Rambler made it back-to-back wins for Lucinda Russell as 6-1 joint-favourite, edging out Fastorslow by a neck. The only others to achieve the feat were Sentina (1957 & 1958), Scot Lane (1982 & 1983) and Un Temps Pour Tout (2016 & 2017). With his second victory, Corach Rambler continued the long-established trend of second-season chasers doing well.

FORM The only winner in the past 18 runnings without any previous course form was the Irish-trained Dun Doire in 2006. With his first victory in 2016, Un Temps Pour Tout became the first horse since Dixton House in 1989 to land the prize having not won a race over fences before, although he did continue the recent trend towards inexperienced chasers. In the last ten years only The Druids Nephew (2015) and Vintage Clouds (2021) had run more than ten times over fences before landing the prize. Corach Rambler in 2022 became the seventh novice to land the race in the last 19 runnings.

WEIGHT AND RATINGS The low to mid 140s is a fruitful place to look (Corach Rambler last year became the sixth winner in the past decade rated 140-146). But it has been more possible for higher-rated runners to win in recent years. Un Temps Pour Tout (off 155 in 2017) carried 11st 12lb, the highest winning weight since Different Class with 11st 13lb in 1967, and Beware The Bear scored off 151 in 2019.

AGE Eight-year-olds have won the race ten times since the turn of the millennium, along with five seven year-olds. Together they account for almost two-thirds of winners (15-23) in that period.

TRAINERS Jonjo O'Neill and David Pipe are the two most successful current trainers with three wins each. The last three runnings have gone to the north, with Corach Rambler's double preceded by 28-1 shot Vintage Clouds for Sue Smith in 2021. While Irish-bred horses account for 14 of the last 16 winners, those trained across the Irish Sea have been successful only twice since 1966 with Youlneverwalkalone (2003) and Dun Doire (2006).

BETTING Corach Rambler (6-1 jf) last year became only the fourth winning favourite since 1977, but most winners have been well fancied with 18 of the last 24 returned at 10-1 or lower. The first five home last year were the top five in the betting. The other successful favourites since 1977 were Antonin (4-1 in 1994), Wichita Lineman (5-1 in 2009) and Coo Star Sivola (5-1 in 2018).

ONES TO WATCH This is one of the better opportunities for a trainer outside the big five to get on the scoreboard and among the leading fancies from Britain are **Chianti Classico** (Kim Bailey), **Monbeg Genius** (Jonjo O'Neill) and **Theatre Man** (Richard Bandey), while Irish possibles include **Stumptown** (Gavin Cromwell). Lurking dangerously, though, are **Meetingofthewaters** for Willie Mullins and Gordon Elliott's **The Goffer**, who was fourth last year.

Chianti Classico (right): Kim Bailey's novice is prominent in the betting

ULTIMA HANDICAP CHASE RESULTS AND TRENDS

	FORM	WINNER	AGE & WGT	OR	SP	TRAINER	BEST RPR LAST 12 MONTHS (RUNS SINCE)
23	U1-54	**Corach Rambler** CD	9 11-5	146-4	6-1j	L Russell	won Ultima Handicap Chase (3m1f) (2)
22	3114U	**Corach Rambler** C, D, BF	8 10-2	140-2	10-1	L Russell	won Chelt class 3 nov hcap ch (3m1½f) (2)
21	8-753	**Vintage Clouds** D	11 10-11	143-7	28-1	S Smith	5th Warwick class 2 hcap ch (3m) (1)
20	-3124	**The Conditional** CD, BF	8 10-6	139-3	15-2	D Bridgwater	2nd Newbury Gd3 hcap ch (3m2f) (1)
19	4P-41	**Beware The Bear** C	9 11-8	151T	10-1	N Henderson	won Cheltenham class 2 hcap ch (3m3½f) (0)
18	53421	**Coo Star Sivola** C, D	6 10-10	142-2	5-1f	N Williams	won Exeter class 3 nov hcap ch (3m) (0)
17	-1036	**Un Temps Pour Tout** CD	8 11-12	155-10	9-1	D Pipe	won Ultima Handicap Chase (3m1f) (5)
16	-1224	**Un Temps Pour Tout** D, BF	7 11-7	148-15	11-1	D Pipe	2nd Newbury Gd2 nov ch (2m7½f) (1)
15	-1275	**The Druids Nephew**	8 11-3	146T	8-1	N Mulholland	2nd Cheltenham Gd3 hcap ch (3m3½f) (1)
14	32U11	**Holywell** C, D	7 11-6	145-9	10-1	J O'Neill	won Doncaster class 4 nov ch (3m) (0)

WINS-RUNS: 5yo 0-1, 6yo 1-12, 7yo 2-48, 8yo 4-73, 9yo 2-48, 10yo 0-28, 11yo 1-10, 12yo 0-1 **FAVOURITES:** -£0.50

FATE OF FAVOURITES: 00021P3201 **POSITION OF WINNER IN MARKET:** 3253153051

OR 121-133 0-0-17, **134-148** 8-17-146, **149-164** 2-13-58

Key trends

- Ran no more than five times that season, 10/10
- Won over at least 3m, 9/10
- Officially rated 139-151, 9/10
- Aged seven to nine, 8/10
- Ran at a previous festival, 8/10
- No more than ten runs over fences, 8/10
- Top-three finish on either or both of last two starts, 7/10
- Carried no more than 11st 6lb, 7/10

Other factors

- Seven had recorded a top-four finish at a previous festival
- Seven winners had run well in a handicap at Cheltenham earlier in the season (three won, two placed and two fourth). The 2017 winner Un Temps Pour Tout had run well in a Grade 2 hurdle at the course
- This was once seemingly an impossible task for novices but five of the last ten winners have been first-season chasers

Constitution Hill was poised for greatness after a brilliant first season that culminated with his 22-length triumph in the Supreme Novices' Hurdle and he duly took his place in the hurdling pantheon with a second unbeaten campaign that peaked with his nine-length victory over State Man in last year's Champion Hurdle. Nicky Henderson's superstar has stretched his 100 per cent record to eight races, first wrapping up last season with victory over 2m4f in the Aintree Hurdle and then opening his latest campaign with another easy win in the Christmas Hurdle at Kempton. Both of those performances were below par on Racing Post Ratings but there is nothing to really test him in Britain and Willie Mullins' State Man remains his only serious opponent. Unfortunate to be born in the same year as Constitution Hill, State Man would have been a high-calibre divisional leader without him and has an outstanding record in his own right, having completed the same pre-Cheltenham winning sequence for the past two seasons in the Morgiana, Matheson and Irish Champion Hurdles. Whether anything will change at Cheltenham is the ultimate issue for him, however. Last year's Champion Hurdle win took Constitution Hill to an RPR of 177 (which puts him 7lb ahead of State Man) and within touching distance of Istabraq's top mark of 181. Many will be hoping he can go even higher this year.

Constitution Hill leads the string at Nicky Henderson's Seven Barrows stable in Lambourn in January

Constitution Hill comes home nine lengths clear of State Man in last year's Champion Hurdle

Constitution Hill

7 b g; Trainer Nicky Henderson
Hurdles form 11111111, best RPR 177
Left-handed 1111, best RPR 176
Right-handed 1111, best RPR 175
Cheltenham form 11, best RPR 177
At the festival 15 Mar 2022 Travelled strongly, tracked leaders, left in second 3 out, led going easily 2 out, nudged along and went clear on turn before last, shaken up and went further clear final 110yds, eased towards finish, impressive, won Supreme Novices' Hurdle by 22 lengths from Jonbon
14 Mar 2023 Travelled strongly, prominent, pressed leader from 3rd, led going easily 3 out, shaken up and went clear before last, impressive, won Champion Hurdle by nine lengths from State Man

The standout performer of his generation, Constitution Hill is now 8-8 over hurdles and has never once looked in trouble. His aggregate winning margin for those eight successes is just over 98 lengths, and he has looked unbeatable ever since he trounced stablemate Jonbon by 22 lengths in the 2022 Supreme Novices' Hurdle. Last season's unbeaten four-race campaign began with 12- and 17-length drubbings of stablemate and former Champion Hurdle winner Epatante in the Fighting Fifth at Newcastle and Christmas Hurdle at Kempton, after which he lined up for his first crack at the Champion Hurdle against the only horse thought capable of giving him a race, State Man. The 2022 County Hurdle winner had also completed an unbeaten preparation and was much too good for the reigning Champion Hurdle heroine Honeysuckle in the Irish version at the Dublin Racing Festival, but he couldn't lay a glove on Constitution Hill at Cheltenham, going down by nine lengths to the new champion, whose RPR of 177 puts him behind only the great Istabraq in the Racing

Post's historical list of top 2m hurdlers. Going further back, Timeform ranks Constitution Hill the joint sixth-best hurdler of all time, putting him behind only legends Comedy Of Errors, Persian War, Istabraq, Monksfield and the top-ranking Night Nurse. This was after just six starts, too, with his peak effort in the Champion Hurdle coming three days before his actual sixth birthday. There was much talk after his Cheltenham success about the prospect of going chasing with the ultimate aim of emulating Dawn Run by landing the Gold Cup, but although that gossip rumbled on through the summer, any real prospect of him doing so ended after a lacklustre (by his standards) display when he was upped to 2m4f in the Aintree Hurdle and saw off the veteran Sharjah by only three lengths. He was never in any danger and didn't really come under any pressure, but by the same token it wasn't the performance of a horse who was crying out for another six and a half furlongs over fences. Once it was finally confirmed Constitution Hill would be staying over hurdles, a similar campaign to the previous season was envisaged, but it hasn't turned out that way as the Fighting Fifth was abandoned due to the weather at Newcastle and trainer Nicky Henderson wasn't prepared to run him on heavy ground at Sandown when the race was rescheduled, reasoning it would be too close to the Christmas Hurdle 17 days later. His reappearance finally came at Kempton and once again he put in a faultless performance to maintain his unbeaten record. It was hard to put a big figure on a nine-and-a-half-length beating of the 149-rated Rubaud, and on RPRs it was actually a worse performance than his below-par Aintree run, but Constitution Hill was never asked to come out of second gear and his precision jumping and effortless galloping were

State Man: career-best RPR of 170 last time out in the Irish Champion Hurdle

still fully in evidence. Unfortunately a bad scope ruled him out of another run in the International Hurdle at Cheltenham on Trials day, so he goes into his defence on the back of just one run, but it's hard to deny he deserves to be a very warm favourite to land a second Champion Hurdle. Those looking for a performance to elevate him higher up the list of all-time great hurdlers will have to hope he beats an in-form State Man by an even bigger margin as there's nothing else around that can test him and he'll likely never run in a handicap.

Going preference Despite trainer's reluctance to run him again on heavy, he has no issues
Star rating ✪✪✪✪✪

State Man

7 ch g; Trainer Willie Mullins
Hurdles form 2F11111121111, best RPR 170
Left-handed 2F111211, best RPR 170
Right-handed 11111, best RPR 167
Cheltenham form 12, best RPR 166
At the festival 18 Mar 2022 Towards rear of midfield and on outer, smooth headway from 2 out, led approaching last, ridden final 110yds, ran on well, won County Handicap Hurdle by a length and a quarter from First Street
14 Mar 2023 Towards rear, headway on outer when good jump 5 out, soon in touch with leaders, went second after 2 out, pushed along before last, kept on but no match for winner, finished second, beaten nine lengths by Constitution Hill in Champion Hurdle

In most other eras State Man would be hailed as a proper champion himself as he has lost just once in 11 completed starts for Willie Mullins and has bagged eight Grade 1s. Unfortunately for him his defeat was a nine-length drubbing by Constitution Hill in the Champion Hurdle with the winner barely having been extended. State Man began that campaign with three Grade 1 wins, and he pushed two-time Champion Hurdle winner Honeysuckle towards the Mares' Hurdle when landing the first of his Irish Champion Hurdle successes. Having finished with another Grade 1 success at Punchestown in April, the seven-year-old has followed the same path as last year, first winning the Morgiana Hurdle at Punchestown in November and then putting last season's Ballymore winner Impaire Et Passe firmly in his place in the Matheson at Leopardstown. A repeat Irish Champion Hurdle victory was completed in effortless fashion, with State Man beating a resurgent Bob Olinger by five and a half lengths in February, and now he gets to have another crack at the only horse to beat him since he fell on his debut for Mullins in December 2021. If you want to clutch at straws you could argue he boasts better form than Constitution Hill this season as he achieved a higher RPR for all three of those efforts than the 163 posted by his rival at Kempton. A 170 for the Irish Champion is also a career best, so you can argue he has improved marginally. A good deal more is going to be needed for him to dethrone the champion, but at least there's at least one genuinely top-class horse to take on Constitution Hill.

Going preference No issues
Star rating ✪✪✪

Lossiemouth

5 gr m; Trainer Willie Mullins
Hurdles form 1112111, best RPR 155
Left-handed 11211, best RPR 155
Right-handed 11, best RPR 137
Cheltenham form 1, best RPR 143
At the festival 17 Mar 2023 In touch with leaders, carried right 3rd, headway and prominent 3 out, led after 2 out, hung left approaching last, ridden and kept on well run-in, won Triumph Hurdle by two and a quarter lengths from Gala Marceau

Lossiemouth was a commanding winner of the Triumph Hurdle last season and has won twice more since, but the fact she is third best in the ante-post betting tells you how weak the opposition is because, notwithstanding that her form is nowhere near the level of the big two, connections have no intention of running her anyway. At the time of writing she was 14-1 ante-post with those not offering a non-runner no bet concession but just 4-1 with some of those who were. It doesn't take a genius to work out she would be miles bigger than 4-1 if she turned up against both Constitution Hill and State Man (or even just the former) and those bookmakers have taken into account that the only prospect of her running is if the big guns don't go.

Going preference No definite preference
Star rating ✪

Irish Point

6 gr g; Trainer Gordon Elliott
Hurdles form 12241111, best RPR 159
Left-handed 24111, best RPR 159
Right-handed 121, best RPR 154

Had a bumper win to his name over Il Est Francais in France and was a serious novice hurdler last season despite not taking in Cheltenham. Beaten only a head by Marine Nationale in the Royal Bond in December of that season, he was fourth in another Grade 1 at 2m, but then bagged one of his own when stepped up to 2m4f at Aintree. A comfortable 2m1f win on his return at Down Royal – conceding 13lb to the 136-rated Magical Zoe (141 after she finished second of 21 in a handicap at the Dublin Racing Festival recently) – confirmed he was very useful at the shorter trip, but then he scooted up by 11 lengths upped to nearly 3m in the Christmas Hurdle at Leopardstown, prompting bookmakers to make him joint-favourite for the Stayers' Hurdle. The only problem is that the other joint-favourite, Teahupoo, is in the same stable and same ownership and there may be a desire to keep them apart. Still, if connections are going to consider taking on Constitution Hill you'd imagine they'd rather have a crack at him over 2m4f at Aintree (assuming he goes there again) than over 2m here. Arguably a little bit bigger in the betting than he should be with the firms offering non-runner, no bet (certainly shouldn't be ten points longer than Lossiemouth), but hard to see him winning even if he does line up, which still has to be considered doubtful.

Going preference No obvious preference
Star rating ✪

Not So Sleepy

12 ch g; Trainer Hughie Morrison
Hurdles form 415110PU1571553551, best RPR 160
Left-handed 0PU571535, best RPR 160
Right-handed 415111551, best RPR 160
Cheltenham form P555, best RPR 158
At the festival 10 Mar 2020 Raced keenly, headway to track leaders after 1st, weakened approaching 3 out, behind when pulled up before last in Champion Hurdle won by Epatante
16 Mar 2021 Took keen hold, tracked leaders, not fluent 3 out, soon lost position, not fluent and ridden 2 out, rallied approaching last, kept on but no impression run-in, finished fifth, beaten 13 lengths by Honeysuckle in Champion Hurdle
15 Mar 2022 Chased leader, not fluent but close up from 2nd, led before 3rd, headed and close up before 5 out, ridden and lost position when mistake 2 out, well held but kept on run-in, finished 6th, placed 5th, beaten nine lengths by Honeysuckle in Champion Hurdle
14 Mar 2023 Took keen hold, led, headed and prominent 1st, not fluent and lost position 5 out, mistake and pushed along in rear 4 out, ridden and well behind from 3 out, finished fifth, beaten 32 lengths by Constitution Hill in Champion Hurdle

Not So Sleepy is a little legend in his own right and time has certainly not dulled his enthusiasm or ability. Hughie Morrison's 12-year-old has held his form remarkably well over the years, and his two-length win on the Flat at Newbury in September ranked as the third-best run of his career in that sphere on RPRs. Back over hurdles last time, Not So Sleepy then matched his previous career-best hurdles RPR by winning a Grade 1 outright for the first time in his life in the Fighting Fifth (a race he dead-heated for two years earlier). There he took advantage of Constitution Hill's absence to slam a below-form Love Envoi by eight lengths. He has been well held in the last four Champion Hurdles, finishing fifth in each of the last three, and his best hope would be to better that this time. There are possibilities as it's hard to pinpoint more than three other definite runners at this stage, but there's always the chance that doing the donkey work for the big guns will soften him up and allow whatever is left to pass him in the straight.

Going preference Fine on all surfaces
Star rating ✪

Zarak The Brave

5 b g; Trainer Willie Mullins
Hurdles form 12231P1, best RPR 152
Left-handed 3P1, best RPR 152
Right-handed 1221, best RPR 152

Didn't line up for the Triumph Hurdle last season, but ran that race's winner Lossiemouth to a length and a half at Punchestown in April and then finished third in a Grade 1 in France. He confirmed himself

Not So Sleepy (right) heads to victory in the Grade 1 Fighting Fifth Hurdle at Sandown

a horse of serious ability when taking the Galway Hurdle off a mark of 145, and after being pulled up at odds of 1-8 in a Tipperary Grade 3 in October, he bounced back to beat Telmesomethinggirl by just over a length at Naas in January. That form is obviously nowhere near good enough for him to be a threat and his trainer seemed lukewarm on running him. He is, after all, just about rated low enough to be given a chance in another handicap.

Going preference No definite preference, unraced on heavy
Star rating ✪

Zanahiyr

7 ch g; Trainer Gordon Elliott
Hurdles form 1114212223dF7P5335124, best RPR 161
Left-handed 14223dF7P5332, best RPR 161
Right-handed 11212514, best RPR 154
Cheltenham form 43d3, best RPR 161
At the festival 19 Mar 2021 Took keen hold, tracked leaders, not fluent 3rd, going easily when bit short of room after 2 out, ridden and outpaced before last, rallied final 110yds, kept on, not pace to challenge, finished fourth, beaten four and three-quarter lengths by Quilixios in Triumph Hurdle
15 Mar 2022 Chased leaders, not fluent 1st, close up on outer from 5 out, ridden after 2 out, lost second approaching last, held but kept on run-in, no match for winner, finished 3rd, disqualified (banned substance in sample) from Champion Hurdle won by Honeysuckle
14 Mar 2023 Held up in rear, headway when mistake 3 out, soon ridden, awkward jump last, soon went third, kept on but no match for first two, finished third, beaten 13 lengths by Constitution Hill in Champion Hurdle

Has finished third in the last two Champion Hurdles, although he was disqualified from the first of them due to a banned substance. A 13-length third to Constitution Hill last year, he got almost ten lengths closer when third to him in the Aintree Hurdle, but was then beaten a long way by State Man at the Punchestown festival. After a straightforward win at Punchestown on his return and a fair second to Bob Olinger next time, he was below form on his next two starts, and jumped poorly when a distant second to Fact To File on his novice chase debut at Leopardstown, although he won on his second attempt in February, albeit again without jumping well. Most of his best form has come in the second half of the season, though, and he has run well every time he has gone to Cheltenham, so if you're looking for something to finish third to the big two he might be the one.

Going preference Handles any ground
Star rating ✪

OTHERS TO CONSIDER

That's just seven of the 18 who were still in the race at the end of February, but it's hard to see what else is going to run – not that the mentioned Lossiemouth or Irish Point are likely to anyway. Four of the next five in the betting are the mares **Echoes In Rain**, **Gala Marceau**, **Luccia** and **Love Envoi** and they'll all have the far more obvious option of the Mares' Hurdle. **Pied Piper** hasn't run since finishing last of four to State Man in the Morgiana, and he went handicapping last season, finishing second in the County, while the others are all rated so low you'd have to imagine handicaps are the plan.

VERDICT

*Seven runners went to post for last season's Champion Hurdle, but it's hard to envisage even that many lining up this time. On all known evidence **CONSTITUTION HILL** is as far clear of **State Man** as State Man is of the rest, and if you're that desperate for an each-way bet in the race at this stage you know you're effectively throwing away the win part of your bet. Even so, if you took the 66-1 each-way about **Zanahiyr** you'd get slightly more than 6-1 to your total stake for him finishing third. Looking at the likely shape of the field, it's unlikely he'd be anywhere that price without the big two on the day, although that's assuming Gordon Elliott lets him run there again rather than go down the handicap route. There's the small matter of £47,745 for third and £23,850 for fourth, though (plus smaller amounts down to eighth), and someone will surely be tempted to run for it rather than take their chance in a massive field of handicappers.*

CHAMPION HURDLE RESULTS AND TRENDS

	FORM	WINNER	AGE & WGT	Adj RPR	SP	TRAINER	BEST RPR LAST 12 MONTHS (RUNS SINCE)
23	11-11	**Constitution Hill** CD	6 11-10	180ᵀ	4-11f	N Henderson	won Gd1 Christmas Hurdle (2m) (0)
22	1-111	**Honeysuckle** CD	8 11-3	177ᵀ	8-11f	H de Bromhead (IRE)	won Punchestown Gd1 Hurdle (2m) (2)
21	11-11	**Honeysuckle** C, D	7 11-3	174ᵀ	11-10f	H de Bromhead (IRE)	won Gd1 Irish Champion Hurdle (2m) (0)
20	19-11	**Epatante** D	6 11-3	168ᵀ	2-1f	N Henderson	won Gd1 Christmas Hurdle (2m) (0)
19	4-111	**Espoir D'Allen** D	5 11-10	162⁻¹⁷	16-1	G Cromwell (IRE)	won Limerick Gd3 hdl (2m) (1)
18	1-111	**Buveur D'Air** CD	7 11-10	175ᵀ	4-6f	N Henderson	won Gd1 Aintree Hurdle (2m4f) (3)
17	1-111	**Buveur D'Air** D	6 11-10	163⁻⁷	5-1	N Henderson	won Gd1 Aintree nov hdl (2m½f) (1)
16	1F-11	**Annie Power** C, D	8 11-3	173ᵀ	5-2f	W Mullins (IRE)	won Gd1 Punchestown Mares Hurdle (2m2f) (1)
15	1-111	**Faugheen** C, D	7 11-10	173⁻⁴	4-5f	W Mullins (IRE)	won Gd1 Christmas Hurdle (2m) (0)
14	-1124	**Jezki** D	6 11-10	169⁻⁸	9-1	J Harrington (IRE)	2nd Gd1 Ryanair Hurdle (2m) (1)

WINS-RUNS: 5yo 1-22, 6yo 4-24, 7yo 3-25, 8yo 2-19, 9yo 0-7, 10yo 0-5, 11yo 0-2, 13yo 0-1 **FAVOURITES:** £5.16

TRAINERS IN THIS RACE (w-pl-r): Nicky Henderson 4-5-22, Willie Mullins 2-9-25, Henry de Bromhead 2-1-7, Gordon Elliott 0-1-6, Nigel Twiston-Davies 0-1-6, Hughie Morrison 0-0-4

FATE OF FAVOURITES: 4110161111 **POSITION OF WINNER IN MARKET:** 5112141111

Key trends

- Rated within 8lb of RPR top-rated, 9/10
- Won a Grade 1 hurdle, 9/10
- Won last time out, 9/10
- No more than 12 hurdle runs, 9/10
- Aged between six and eight, 9/10
- Adjusted RPR of at least 168, 8/10

Other factors

- Katchit (2008) became the first five-year-old to win since See You Then in 1985 but in 2019 Espoir D'Allen became the second in just over a decade (28 from that age group had failed in the interim)
- Three winners had not run since the turn of the year (two trained by Nicky Henderson)

4.10 Close Brothers Mares' Hurdle ITV/RTV
• 2m4f   • Grade 1   • £120,000

Willie Mullins once had a vice-like grip on this race with six-time winner Quevega and her successors, but it has been loosened in recent years with just one victory for his Closutton stable in the past seven runnings. Normal service looks set to be resumed this time, however, if hot favourite Lossiemouth lines up here as expected. Last year's impressive Triumph Hurdle winner returned to action after nine months off with a decisive victory by almost ten lengths over Love Envoi in the 2m1f International Hurdle on Cheltenham's Trials day and the only serious question still to answer is how she will handle a step up in trip.

Mullins has other leading contenders in Gala Marceau (runner-up to Lossiemouth in the Triumph) and the older Ashroe Diamond and Echoes In Rain (albeit the latter has been fifth and fourth in her two previous attempts).

Britain's main hopes are two mares who have run well in this race before. Marie's Rock won for Nicky Henderson in 2022 (but was a disappointing seventh as joint-favourite last year) and Harry Fry's Love Envoi was runner-up to Honeysuckle 12 months ago, having won the Mares' Novices' Hurdle at the festival the year before.

MARES' HURDLE RESULTS AND TRENDS

	FORM WINNER	AGE & WGT	Adj RPR	SP	TRAINER	BEST RPR LAST 12 MONTHS (RUNS SINCE)
23	1-132 **Honeysuckle** CD	9 11-5	169^T	9-4j	H de Bromhead (IRE)	won Gd1 Champion Hurdle (2m½f) (3)
22	371P1 **Marie's Rock**	7 11-5	151^{-10}	18-1	N Henderson	won Kempton class 3 hcap hdl (2m5f) (2)
21	2-331 **Black Tears** D	7 11-5	156^{-9}	11-1	D Foster (IRE)	won Punchestown Gd3 hdl (2m4f) (0)
20	1-111 **Honeysuckle** D	6 11-5	169^{-2}	9-4	H de Bromhead (IRE)	won Gd1 Hatton's Grace Hurdle (2m4f) (1)
19	112-3 **Roksana** D	7 11-5	153^{-8}	10-1	D Skelton	2nd Aintree Gd2 nov hdl (3m½f) (1)
18	/1-11 **Benie Des Dieux** D	7 11-5	156^{-13}	9-2	W Mullins (IRE)	Seasonal debutante (0)
17	12212 **Apple's Jade** D, BF	5 11-5	171^T	7-2	G Elliott (IRE)	won Aintree Gd1 juv hdl (2m1f) (5)
16	1-111 **Vroum Vroum Mag** D	7 11-5	160^T	4-6f	W Mullins (IRE)	won Ascot Gd2 hdl (2m7½f) (0)
15	7521 **Glens Melody** D	7 11-5	162^{-11}	6-1	W Mullins (IRE)	won Warwick Listed hdl (2m5f) (0)
14	1/11- **Quevega** CD	10 11-5	171^T	8-11f	W Mullins (IRE)	won Gd1 Punchestown World Hurdle (3m)(0)

WINS-RUNS: 5yo 1-9, 6yo 1-31, 7yo 6-42, 8yo 0-31, 9yo 1-14, 10yo 1-2, 11yo 0-1 **FAVOURITES:** -£4.98

TRAINERS IN THIS RACE (w-pl-r): Willie Mullins 4-8-27, Henry de Bromhead 2-0-5, Gordon Elliott 1-3-5, Dan Skelton 1-1-6, Nicky Henderson 1-1-9, Harry Fry 0-2-7, Jessica Harrington 0-1-5, Paul Nolan 0-1-1

FATE OF FAVOURITES: 1F133F2241 **POSITION OF WINNER IN MARKET:** 1213242381

Key trends

- At least eight career starts, 9/10
- Top-four finish in a Grade 1 or 2 hurdle, 9/10
- Adjusted RPR of at least 156, 8/10
- Rated within 10lb of RPR top-rated, 8/10
- Won last time out, 7/10

Other factors

- A runner priced 16-1 or bigger has finished in the first three in eight of the last ten runnings
- Willie Mullins has trained four of the last ten winners
- Quevega used to come here fresh when defending her crown but eight of the last nine winners had between two and five outings that season

4.50 Boodles Juvenile Handicap Hurdle RTV
● *2m½f* ● *Premier Handicap* ● *£80,000*

First run in 2005, this is a fiercely competitive and often wide-open handicap hurdle for four-year-olds only.

LAST YEAR'S WINNER Jazzy Matty scored at 18-1, becoming the third winner in the past six runnings for Gordon Elliott and the sixth in a row for Ireland (fifth was the best Britain could manage last year). He was the seventh French-bred to win in 19 runnings (a French-bred has finished first or second in all but one of the last ten).

FORM Thirteen of the 19 winners had won on one of their last two starts.

WEIGHT AND RATINGS Jazzy Matty last year became the second winner in three years off a low mark of 125 (following Jeff Kidder in 2021). Only three winners have been rated higher than 134, although they have come recently.

TRAINERS The big stables are always worth noting. Both Elliott and Paul Nicholls have had three winners, as well as several placed horses, and Nicky Henderson and David Pipe are also on the roll of honour. Joseph O'Brien is a significant player given the strength of his juvenile hurdling team.

BETTING Eight of the last 12 winners were at least 18-1, although the trend has been shifted recently by 7-2 favourite Band Of Outlaws in 2019, Diego Du Charmil (13-2 in 2016), Aramax (15-2 in 2020) and Brazil (10-1 in 2022).

ONES TO WATCH Irish trainers dominate the ante-post betting with **Lark In The Mornin** for Joseph O'Brien, Willie Mullins' **Batman Girac** and **Ethical Diamond**, and the Gordon Elliott-trained **Wodhooh**, **Ndaawi** and **Mighty Bandit**. The last home winner was in 2017 but there are decent hopes of another with Jane Williams' **Excelero** and the Olly Murphy-trained **Roaring Legend**.

BOODLES JUVENILE HANDICAP HURDLE RESULTS AND TRENDS

	FORM WINNER	AGE & WGT	OR	SP	TRAINER	BEST RPR LAST 12 MONTHS (RUNS SINCE)
23	52154 **Jazzy Matty** D, BF	4 10-6	125²	18-1	G Elliott (IRE)	won Fairyhouse mdn hdl (2m) (2)
22	6541 **Brazil** D	4 11-9	137⁶	10-1	P Roche (IRE)	won Naas nov hdl (2m) (0)
21	2217 **Jeff Kidder** D	4 10-8	125⁴	80-1	N Meade (IRE)	7th Leopardstown Gd 2 nov hdl (2m) (0)
20	31F31 **Aramax** D	4 11-8	138⁶	15-2	G Elliott (IRE)	won Naas nov hdl (2m) (0)
19	311 **Band Of Outlaws** D	4 11-8	139⁵	7-2f	J O'Brien (IRE)	won Naas nov hdl (2m) (0)
18	127 **Veneer Of Charm** D	4 11-0	129¹⁴	33-1	G Elliott (IRE)	2nd Fairyhouse hdl (2m) (1)
17	2P614 **Flying Tiger** D	4 11-5	134²	33-1	N Williams	won Newbury class 4 hdl (2m½f) (1)
16	322 **Diego Du Charmil** BF	4 11-1	133¹⁷	13-2	P Nicholls	2nd Enghien hdl (2m½f) (0)
15	3-421 **Qualando**	4 11-0	131⁹	25-1	P Nicholls	4th Auteuil Listed hdl (2m1½f) (2)
14	1216 **Hawk High** D	4 11-1	130¹²	33-1	T Easterby	won Warwick class 4 hdl (2m) (1)

FAVOURITES: -£5.50 **FATE OF FAVOURITES:** 000231P220 **POSITION OF WINNER IN MARKET:** 0020013047

Key trends

- Top-three finish in at least one of last two starts, 9/10
- Had lost maiden tag over hurdles, 9/10
- Won within last three starts, 9/10
- Officially rated 125 to 137, 8/10
- Three or four previous hurdle runs, 7/10

Other factors

- Two of the four winners who had run on the Flat had earned an RPR of at least 87; the other six were unraced on the Flat
- Three winners were French-bred
- Six winners were beaten on their first two starts over hurdles

5.30 National Hunt Novices' Chase RTV
• 3m6f • Grade 2 • Amateur riders • £125,000

LAST YEAR'S WINNER Gaillard Du Mesnil justified favouritism at 10-11 for Willie Mullins, although the result might have been different if clear leader Mahler Mission hadn't fallen two out.

WEIGHT AND RATINGS The recent rise in quality is reflected in the ratings. Last year Gaillard Du Mesnil was clear top on the official figures on 155 and runner-up Chemical Energy was next on 147.

AGE Eleven of the last 19 winners were seven-year-olds. The most recent older winners were both ten (Rathvinden in 2018 and Ravenhill in 2020).

TRAINERS The big yards have dominated in recent years with Mullins and Gordon Elliott winning eight times between them in 13 runnings since 2011.

BETTING Ten of the last 13 winners were in single-figure odds, although Gaillard Du Mesnil was the first successful favourite since 2013.

ONES TO WATCH Willie Mullins will have a major impact on the market here once he decides on running plans. **Embassy Gardens** will have strong claims if this is his chosen target. Another leading Irish novice who is shortest in the betting here is **Corbetts Cross** (Emmet Mullins).

NATIONAL HUNT CHASE RESULTS AND TRENDS

	FORMWINNER	AGE & WGT	Adj RPR	SP	TRAINER	BEST RPR LAST 12 MONTHS (RUNS SINCE)
23	3-213 **Gaillard Du Mesnil**	7 11-7	167[T]	10-11f	W Mullins (IRE)	3rd Gd1 Brown Advisory nov ch (3m½f) (4)
22	4-311 **Stattler**	7 11-6	166[T]	2-1	W Mullins (IRE)	won Naas Gd3 nov ch (3m1f)(0)
21	-1111 **Galvin** C	7 11-6	167[T]	7-2	I Ferguson (IRE)	won Cheltenham class 2 nov ch (3m½f) (0)
20	2152F **Ravenhill**	10 11-6	156-8	12-1	G Elliott (IRE)	2nd Listowel hcap ch (3m) (1)
19	12324 **Le Breuil**	7 11-6	155-9	14-1	B Pauling	3rd Newbury Gd2 nov ch (2m7½f) (2)
18	112BU **Rathvinden**	10 11-6	167[T]	9-2	W Mullins (IRE)	2nd Fairyhouse Gd1 nov ch (2m4f) (2)
17	22133 **Tiger Roll** C	7 11-6	159-6	16-1	G Elliott (IRE)	won Limerick hcap ch (3m) (2)
16	-3P62 **Minella Rocco**	6 11-6	159-7	8-1	J O'Neill	2nd Ascot Gd2 nov ch (3m) (0)
15	20-75 **Cause Of Causes**	7 11-6	159-2	8-1	G Elliott (IRE)	2nd Kim Muir hcap ch (3m1½f) (3)
14	61U21 **Midnight Prayer**	9 11-6	154-12	8-1	A King	won Warwick class 3 nov ch (3m2f) (0)

WINS-RUNS: 5yo 0-1, 6yo 1-17, 7yo 6-66, 8yo 0-42, 9yo 1-12, 10yo 2-7, 12yo 0-2 **FAVOURITES:** -£8.09

TRAINERS IN THIS RACE (w-pl-r): Gordon Elliott 3-2-12, Willie Mullins 3-3-15, Ben Pauling 1-0-4, Anthony Honeyball 0-1-1, Paul Nicholls 0-1-4, Gavin Cromwell 0-0-1, John McConnell 0-0-1, Nicky Henderson 0-1-5, Kim Bailey 0-0-1, Mark Bradstock 0-0-1, Neil Mulholland 0-0-3, Nigel Twiston-Davies 0-0-6, Paul Nolan 0-1-1

FATE OF FAVOURITES: 0045UFU321 **POSITION OF WINNER IN MARKET:** 4359254321

Key trends
- Adjusted RPR of at least 154, 10/10
- Top-two finish in a chase at 3m-plus, 9/10
- Hurdles RPR of at least 134, 9/10
- Rated within 9lb of RPR top-rated, 9/10
- Ran at least four times over fences, 9/10
- Top-three finish on last completed start, 8/10
- Aged six to eight, 7/10
- Had won over at least 3m (hurdles or chases), 7/10

Other factors
- The last two winners to have had less than four chase runs were both trained by Willie Mullins (Back In Focus in 2013 and Stattler in 2022)

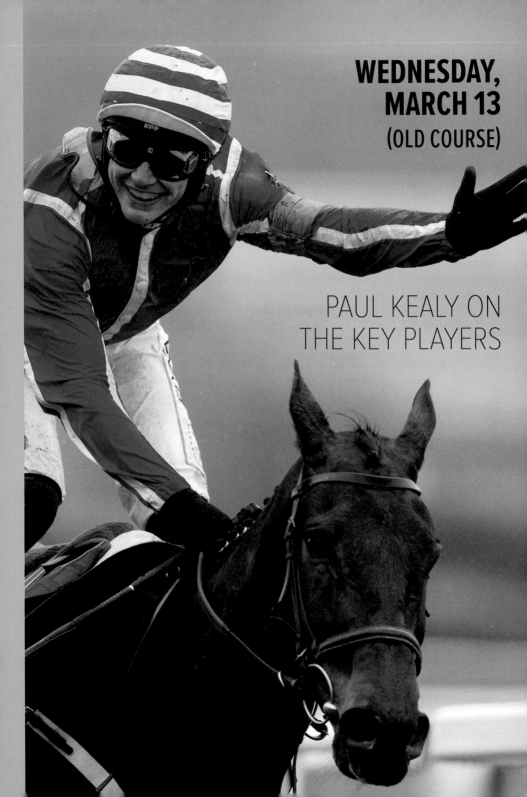

**WEDNESDAY,
MARCH 13**
(OLD COURSE)

PAUL KEALY ON
THE KEY PLAYERS

1.30 Baring Bingham Novices' Hurdle ITV/RTV
● 2m5f ● Grade 1 ● £135,000

Like the Supreme, the shape of this contest rests on where Willie Mullins decides to run Ballyburn, the ante-post favourite for both races. It's not an easy choice given that the Mullins number one showed an impressive turn of foot over 2m at the Dublin Racing Festival but had won over 2m4f before that. That combination of speed and stamina will make him a formidable opponent wherever he runs. The Irish contender with the best credentials after Ballyburn is Henry de Bromhead's Slade Steel, runner-up to him at the DRF but also previously a 2m4f winner. Mullins has good back-up in Readin Tommy Wrong and Ile Atlantique, a close first and second in a Grade 1 at Naas, along with possibly Mystical Power and the less well-tested Billericay Dickie. The best British hopes are Gidleigh Park (Harry Fry), Handstands (Ben Pauling) and Captain Teague (Paul Nicholls).

Ballyburn
6 b g; Trainer Willie Mullins
Hurdles form 211, best RPR 158
Left-handed 11, best RPR 158
Right-handed 2, best RPR 132

It's hardly unusual for Willie Mullins to have the favourite for the Supreme and Baring Bingham, and it's not even that unusual for it to be the same horse given the non-runner no bet concessions, but it is unusual to have almost no idea what race the horse will end up in. That was the case in mid-February regarding Ballyburn, who has been given a full write-up in the Supreme section after jumping to the top of the novice hurdling tree with his emphatic success over 2m at the Dublin Racing Festival. He has, however, also won at 2m4f and his pedigree says he's going to be a three-miler in time, so Mullins is going to have some serious thinking to do. Three Gold Cup winners have been second and another third in the Supreme this century, so there's no reason why Ballyburn can't go there, but at the time of writing Mullins seems to have a stronger hand in the Supreme without Ballyburn than he would in the Baring Bingham without him.

Going preference Doesn't seem to have any issues
Star rating ✪✪✪✪✪

Slade Steel
6 b g; Trainer Henry de Bromhead
Hurdles form (left-handed) 112, best RPR 148

As with many of these he also has the option of another novice hurdle at the festival, in his case the Supreme, but he's a much shorter price for this and according to the market will be favourite if Ballyburn stays at 2m. He was comprehensively put in his place by that one at Leopardstown, but was comfortably ahead of all the others, and is obviously a classy performer in his own right. He also has form over 2m4f, having edged Lecky Watson by half a length in the Grade 2 Navan Novice Hurdle, although considering the runner-up was a well-held third to Readin Tommy Wrong and Ile Atlantique in the Lawlor's of Naas Novice Hurdle that form is going to have to be improved upon. And, of course, there's always a chance Henry de Bromhead chooses to go wherever Ballyburn doesn't as he's twice been well beaten by him (first time in a Punchestown bumper).

Going preference Acts on yielding and heavy
Star rating ✪✪✪

Mystical Power
5 b g; Trainer Willie Mullins
Hurdles form (right-handed) 11, best RPR 144

Has been given a full write-up in the Supreme section as he's very keen and undoubtedly has his share of pace. He's a son of Annie Power, though, so should stay if asked. Unlikely he and Ballyburn will be asked to race against each other.

Going preference Has won on good and soft
Star rating ✪✪

Readin Tommy Wrong

6 b g; Trainer Willie Mullins
Hurdles form 11, best RPR 149
Left-handed 1, best RPR 149
Right-handed 1, best RPR 116

Showed useful form in winning two bumpers last spring, but his hurdling debut was a little underwhelming as he just scrambled home by a short head at odds of 8-15 from stablemate Lisnagar Fortune at Cork. That form turned out to be better than it looked at the time (runner-up won next time, third won next two), but it didn't stop Readin Tommy Wrong *(below)* from being chalked up as the 33-1 rank outsider overnight for the Grade 1 Lawlor's of Naas Novice Hurdle in January. However, despite his market position he was quite well backed on the day (sent off at 16-1) and he managed to edge out favourite and stablemate Ile Atlantique on the run-in. That was despite being two lengths down on the runner-up at the second-last and flattening the last, so he can clearly battle and stay well. Is also in the Albert Bartlett, but trainer said he looked like a Baring Bingham horse after that run. We all know how things can change, though.

Going preference Seems to act on anything, best form on soft
Star rating ✪✪✪

Ile Atlantique

6 br g; Trainer Willie Mullins
Hurdles form 312, best RPR 146
Left-handed 32, best RPR 146
Right-handed 1, best RPR 133

Won the first of three bumpers and showed decent form in the other two, most notably when second to Firefox at Fairyhouse in April. Outclassed modest opposition to get off the mark on hurdles debut at Gowran in November (19-length winner) and was then made 6-4 favourite for the Grade 1 Lawlor's of Naas Novice Hurdle in January. There he skipped two lengths clear approaching the second-last but was caught close home and edged out by Readin Tommy Wrong, losing by a neck. It's hard to say he did much wrong there, but he traded at 1.11 in running and got beaten and that's not the first time he has gone very low in the run as he hit Betfair's ceiling 1.01 when going down by a head to Stellar Story in his second bumper, also at Naas, and it was pretty much a carbon copy with the winner being fully under pressure a long way out while he was skipping two lengths clear and cruising. He does, therefore, have question marks when push comes to shove.

Going preference Doesn't seem to have any issues
Star rating ✪✪

Billericay Dickie

5 ch g; Trainer Willie Mullins
Hurdles form (right-handed) 1, best RPR 126

Had couple of runs in the French provinces in 2022, but was off for 548 before making his debut for Willie Mullins with an 11-length victory in just a six-runner maiden hurdle at Punchestown at the end of January. His jumping improved as the race went on but the time was pedestrian and it's impossible to rate the form too highly. Trainer was talking about looking at another novice hurdle with him before considering Cheltenham.

Going preference Hurdles win on heavy, Flat win on good
Star rating ✪

Gidleigh Park

6 b g; Trainer Harry Fry
Hurdles form 111, best RPR 136
Left-handed 11, best RPR 136
Right-handed 1, best RPR 115
Cheltenham form 1, best RPR 136

Won sole bumper in stylish fashion last March and did the same in first two hurdles outings, both in basic novice company at Exeter and Newbury. There wasn't a massive amount of substance to either, but he was still made odds-on to land the Grade 2 trial at Cheltenham at the end of January, and he just about maintained his unbeaten record. Trainer reckoned he was unsuited by the slow gallop and the resulting finish, but his form is a long way behind the best of the Irish and doesn't even make him the pick of the British. It's easy to argue that the string of 1s next to his name means the market likes him better than the level of his form deserves.

Going preference Fine on good to soft and soft
Star rating ✪✪

Handstands

5 br g; Trainer Ben Pauling
Hurdles form 111, best RPR 137
Left-handed 1, best RPR 128
Right-handed 11, best RPR 137

Point winner who is well regarded by Ben Pauling and has so far done everything asked of him. Looked potentially decent when winning two run-of-the-mill novice hurdles at Hereford and Newcastle in December and January, and then stepped up on that form when beating Formby Novices' Hurdle winner Jango Baie by a length and a half in the Sidney Banks at Huntingdon. The winner was conceding a 5lb Grade 1 penalty, so came out best at the weights. Promising but will be facing a different level if he comes here and has plenty to find.

Going preference Has won on good and soft
Star rating ✪✪

Captain Teague

6 ch g; Trainer Paul Nicholls
Hurdles form (left-handed) 121, best RPR 143
Cheltenham form 32, best RPR 143
At the festival 15 Mar 2023 Prominent, pushed along and made challenge over 2f out, disputed lead when hung right and hampered rivals inside final furlong, soon ridden and hung left, stayed on inside final 110yds, finished third, beaten two and a half lengths by A Dream To Share in Champion Bumper

Finished third to A Dream To Share and Fact To File in the Champion Bumper last season

and hasn't done much wrong over hurdles without suggesting he's ready to go two better. Started well enough with a nine-and-a-half-length success in the Grade 2 Persian War at Chepstow despite not being entirely fluent with his jumping and that not being the hottest race for the grade. At Cheltenham's Paddy Power meeting in November his jumping was better, but he found the concession of 5lb to Minella Missile (heading straight for Aintree) too much, going down by a length and a half. He then became Paul Nicholls' fourth consecutive winner of the Grade 1 Challow Hurdle, battling to a length-and-a-half success from Lookaway in a slow-motion finish in desperate conditions. The Challow has hardly been a great festival guide with the last winner to go on to novice hurdle glory there being Albert Bartlett winner Wichita Lineman in 2007, and Captain Teague also has that entry, with the state of the ground likely to determine where he goes. In his favour is the fact that he has festival form in a big field (incredibly few of last season's Champion Bumper runners are going to run in novice hurdles at the festival) and undoubtedly still has plenty of potential and is arguably the best of the British despite what the market suggests.

Going preference Acts on good to soft and slower
Star rating ✪✪✪

OTHERS TO CONSIDER

It's a bigger nightmare than ever trying to predict the final field as plenty of these are handy enough at 2m to drop back to that trip should Ballyburn turn up here. Other Willie Mullins contenders could include DRF second **Predators Gold**, while **Jingko Blue** could step out of handicap company for Nicky Henderson.

VERDICT

*This race revolves entirely around **BALLYBURN**, and while this is where I think he might end up, the market suggests otherwise. Only Willie Mullins knows for sure and he probably hasn't made his mind up yet. Ballyburn would be the selection if he shows up, but without him it would be much more open. **Readin Tommy Wrong** showed a good attitude when winning at Naas and has to be seriously considered.*

BARING BINGHAM NOVICES' HURDLE RESULTS AND TRENDS

	FORM	WINNER	AGE & WGT	Adj RPR	SP	TRAINER	BEST RPR LAST 12 MONTHS (RUNS SINCE)
23	1-11	**Impaire Et Passe** (below)	5 11-7	158-4	5-2	W Mullins (IRE)	won Punchestown Gd2 nov hdl (2m) (0)
22	1-311	**Sir Gerhard** C	7 11-7	159T	8-11f	W Mullins (IRE)	won Leopardstown Gd1 nov hdl (2m) (0)
21	1-211	**Bob Olinger**	6 11-7	159-5	6-4f	H de Bromhead (IRE)	won Naas Gd1 nov hdl (2m4f) (0)
20	1-111	**Envoi Allen** C	6 11-7	161T	4-7f	G Elliott (IRE)	won Fairyhouse Gd1 nov hdl (2m) (1)
19	-11d11	**City Island**	6 11-7	152-5	8-1	M Brassil (IRE)	won Naas nov hdl (2m3f) (0)
18	1-111	**Samcro**	6 11-7	161T	8-11f	G Elliott (IRE)	won Navan Gd3 nov hdl (2m4f) (1)
17	5-211	**Willoughby Court** D	6 11-7	154-5	14-1	B Pauling	won Warwick Gd2 nov hdl (2m5f) (0)
16	1-111	**Yorkhill**	6 11-7	159-8	3-1	W Mullins (IRE)	won Sandown Gd1 nov hdl (2m) (0)
15	-1142	**Windsor Park**	6 11-7	154-3	9-2	D Weld (IRE)	2nd Leopardstown Gd1 nov hdl (2m2f) (0)
14	1111	**Faugheen**	6 11-7	156T	6-4f	W Mullins (IRE)	won Limerick Gd3 nov hdl (3m) (0)

WINS-RUNS: 5yo 1-38, 6yo 8-66, 7yo 1-15 **FAVOURITES:** £0.03

TRAINERS IN THIS RACE (w-pl-r): Willie Mullins 4-8-27, Gordon Elliott 2-2-9, Ben Pauling 1-1-5, Henry de Bromhead 1-0-5, Martin Brassil 1-0-2, Nigel Twiston-Davies 0-0-2, Alan King 0-2-3, Dan Skelton 0-1-5, Paul Nicholls 0-0-3, Fergal O'Brien 0-0-6, Nicky Henderson 0-1-10, Pat Fahy 0-0-1, Harry Fry 0-1-1, David Pipe 0-0-1

FATE OF FAVOURITES: 13221P1116 **POSITION OF WINNER IN MARKET:** 1325141112

Key trends

- Started career in Irish points or bumpers, ten winners in last ten runnings
- Two or three hurdle runs, 10/10
- Rated within 5lb of RPR top-rated, 9/10
- Adjusted RPR of at least 154, 9/10
- Won at least 50 per cent of hurdle runs, 9/10
- Finished first or second in all hurdle runs, 9/10
- Won a Graded hurdle, 9/10
- Scored over at least 2m4f, 8/10
- Aged six, 8/10

Other factors

- Five of the last ten favourites have obliged and in that period only Willoughby Court's SP (14-1 in 2017) was bigger than 8-1

2.10 Brown Advisory Novices' Chase ITV/RTV
● 3m½f ● Grade 1 ● £175,000

Willie Mullins will be doing one of his juggling acts here and much depends on whether Dublin Racing Festival winner Fact To File runs here or in the Turners on Thursday. He will be the one to beat in either race after his impressive display at Leopardstown. Other options for Mullins include Embassy Gardens, Nick Rockett and Minella Cocooner. This is one of the best Grade 1 races for Britain with seven winners in the past decade, coming from six different stables, and there are major home chances again with Stay Away Fay (Paul Nicholls) and Grey Dawning (Dan Skelton). Stay Away Fay won last year's Albert Bartlett Novices' Hurdle, with several of his beaten rivals set to line up again here, and has excellent chase form at the track too, having finished third in open company in the Cotswold Chase on Trials day. Grey Dawning went to Aintree instead of Cheltenham last spring but has good course form now, with a somewhat unfortunate second place sandwiched between his two chase wins. The latest victory in a Grade 2 at Warwick was his most impressive yet, adding to his progressive profile. The best Irish contender outside the Mullins stable looks to be the Henry de Bromhead-trained Monty's Star, who still has to prove himself at this level but looked good when upped to 3m in a beginners' chase at Punchestown last time. He has form that ties in with Stay Away Fay and Albert Bartlett third Sandor Clegane (Paul Nolan) is set to renew rivalry too.

Fact To File
7 b g; Trainer Willie Mullins
Chase form (left-handed) 211, best RPR 164
Cheltenham form (bumper) 2, best RPR 136
At the festival 15 Mar 2023 Towards rear of midfield, headway on outer from over 3f out, pushed along over 2f out, ridden over 1f out, disputed lead when short of room and unbalanced inside final furlong, kept on but held inside final 110yds, finished second, beaten a length and a quarter by A Dream To Share in Champion Bumper

Finished second A Dream To Share at Leopardstown and in the Champion Bumper last season, after which connections opted to skip hurdling altogether and go straight over fences this season. It was an unusual decision but not without precedent as Willie Mullins did the same with his 1997 Champion Bumper winner Florida Pearl, who won what is now the Brown Advisory the next season and ended up bagging eight Grade 1s over fences. Fact To File was surprisingly beaten on his chase debut at Navan in November by American Mike, another Champion Bumper runner-up who is seemingly back on the up this season, but he stepped up on that dramatically on his next two outings. In the first he won his beginners' chase at Leopardstown in December, slamming dual Champion Hurdle third Zanahiyr by 17 lengths while barely coming off the bridle, and next time at the Dublin Racing Festival he was set to beat Gaelic Warrior by at least as far until that one unseated at the last. That was a bit of a farce of a Grade 1 with only two runners from the same stable, but the time was still three seconds faster than the winner of the 25-runner handicap chase, who carried 23lb less over the same course and distance later on the card, and he didn't come out of second gear. He's clearly a top-class novice who jumps really well and he's very much the one to beat assuming he comes here rather than staying at the shorter trip in the Turners. Mullins said he had no preference after Leopardstown, but his options for this race thinned out when Grangeclare West picked up an injury, and the vibes in mid-February were that he was more likely to run here than on the Thursday. He may not have run at the trip before, but that is no barrier to success, as L'Homme Presse was having his first crack at 3m-plus when winning in 2022.

Going preference No obvious preference
Star rating ✪✪✪✪✪

Stay Away Fay
7 b g; Trainer Paul Nicholls
Chase form 113, best RPR 162
Left-handed 3, best RPR 162
Right-handed 11, best RPR 154
Cheltenham form (all) 13, best RPR 162
At the festival 17 Mar 2023 Disputed lead, led narrowly after 2 out, pushed along approaching last, 2 lengths ahead last, ridden run-in, stayed on, always doing enough, won Albert Bartlett Novices' Hurdle by a length from Affordale Fury

Stay Away Fay's Albert Bartlett win provided Paul Nicholls with his first novice hurdle success at the festival since Al Ferof took the Supreme in 2011, and he did it in gutsy fashion, disputing the lead throughout and seeing off challenger after challenger for a length success from outsider Affordale Fury. His attitude certainly cannot be questioned and it has been fully in evidence on all three of his chase outings this term. First he had to rally after being passed to beat The Changing Man at Exeter in November. While Giovinco didn't quite pass him at Sandown the following month, he did pull alongside at the last looking to be going much the best, only for Stay Away Fay to pull out more on the run-in and win by a length and a half. The form of those two efforts didn't really entitle him to start favourite in open company for the Cotswold Chase on Trials day at Cheltenham next time and defeat shouldn't be held against him as he improved dramatically to run a three-and-a-half-length third to Capodanno and The Real Whacker. He looked set for a fair tussle with the winner, but didn't find that one's extra gear, and was passed on the run-in by The Real Whacker, although he was closing that down again at the line and trying his heart out as usual. It was a cracking effort for his first run outside novice company in any sphere and it gives him a perfectly good form chance, with the main worry being whether going a furlong shorter on the sharper Old course will provide enough of a test for him. However, if they do

Stay Away Fay after winning last year's Albert Bartlett

go hard and it turns into the sort of attritional race that used to be the norm in this contest, you wouldn't want anything else on your side.

Going preference Doesn't seem to have a preference, but the softer the better in terms of making it a proper stamina test
Star rating ✪✪✪✪

Grey Dawning
7 gr g; Trainer Dan Skelton
Chase form 3121 best RPR 162
Left-handed 121, best RPR 162
Right-handed 3, best RPR 139

Grade 2 novice hurdle winner at Warwick from now classy novice chaser Ginny's Destiny last season, but swerved Cheltenham and wasn't able to show what he was capable of behind Apple Away in the Sefton at Aintree as he fell at the ninth. He has since confirmed himself as one of Britain's leading chase prospects, though, improving with every outing. Although only third to Stay Away Fay on his Exeter debut, he was far from disgraced and was considerably better next time when slamming last season's National Hunt Chase winner Gaillard Du Mesnil by nine and a half lengths, albeit in receipt of 11lb. Sefton winner Apple Away was beaten a total of 14 lengths in third. Next time at Cheltenham Grey Dawning went down by three-quarters of a length to Paul Nicholls' Turners hope Ginny's Destiny (who has won again since), but he was conceding 3lb and the general consensus was that he'd have won but for a bad mistake two out. He made no mistake when winning Warwick's Grade 2 Hampton Novices' Chase in January, again beating Apple Away by 14 lengths, and that gives him some of the best form in a race which the British have won seven times in the last ten years. He's also in the Turners, but staying appears to be his game.

Going preference Very comfortable on deep ground
Star rating ✪✪✪✪

Monty's Star
7 b g; Trainer Henry de Bromhead
Chase form (right-handed) 31 best RPR 153
Cheltenham form (hurdles) P
At the festival 17 Mar 2023 Towards rear, not fluent 7th, pushed along after 3 out, soon weakened and behind, pulled up before 2 out

in Albert Bartlett Novices' Hurdle won by Stay Away Fay

Has some history with Stay Away Fay as he finished second to him in a point-to-point at Lingstown in December 2021 before being pulled up behind him in the Albert Bartlett last year. He had looked promising enough in his two previous hurdles starts, winning the second of them in Grade 3 company, and he has done better again in two chase outings this term. In the first of them he proved no match for Corbetts Cross and Three Card Brag over 2m5½f at Fairyhouse, but when upped to 3m next time at Punchestown he comprehensively reversed the form with the runner-up, winning by five and a half lengths. He's a good jumper and connections are entitled to expect a better show than at Cheltenham last year, although he does need to improve.

Going preference Thought to need plenty of dig in the ground
Star rating ✪✪

Embassy Gardens
8 b g; Trainer Willie Mullins
Chase form 11 best RPR 154
Left-handed 1, best RPR 154
Right-handed 1, best RPR 144
Cheltenham form (hurdles) P
At the festival 17 Mar 2023 Raced freely, disputed lead on outer, not fluent 3 out, pushed along and weakened quickly after 2 out, pulled up before last in Albert Bartlett Novices' Hurdle won by Stay Away Fay

Another who found the Albert Bartlett too much of a test for him last season, having been sent off at only 8-1 following a runaway 35-length novice hurdle win at Thurles. His final start at Punchestown last term wasn't great either as he finished a distant sixth of nine to Gaelic Warrior, but he has been a different proposition over fences in two outings this term. He jumped really well en route to a 13-length beginners' chase victory at Punchestown in December, although it's fair to say he wasn't highly tried given the runner-up was rated only 128. Better was to come in a Naas Grade 3 at the end of January, though, as he again jumped really well on his way to a comfortable ten-length success from Sandor Clegane. He's favourite for the

National Hunt Chase, although at the time of writing nothing had been made official. We have to assume it largely depends on where Fact To File goes.

Going preference Acts on yielding and heavy
Star rating ✪✪

Nick Rockett
7 b g; Trainer Willie Mullins
Chase form 412, best RPR 150
Left-handed 2, best RPR 148
Right-handed 41, best RPR 150

Didn't make his hurdles debut until two days before last year's festival, winning at Naas, and then ran away with a Grade 2 at Fairyhouse a month later, scoring by 15 lengths at odds of 9-1. He was fourth to Corbetts Cross, Monty's Star and Three Card Brag on his chase debut at Fairyhouse in December, but then won his beginners' chase on New Year's Day at the same track, recording a classy RPR of 150. That was over 2m5½f, and he was beaten next time at 3m in the Grade 2 Ten Up at Navan, going down by a length and a quarter to American Mike. He was beaten by a better horse rather than a lack of stamina, though, and he's a shorter price for the National Hunt Chase than this.

Going preference No obvious issues
Star rating ✪✪

Minella Cocooner
8 b g; Trainer Willie Mullins
Chase form 2313, best RPR 149
Left-handed 313, best RPR 146
Right-handed 2, best RPR 149
Cheltenham form (hurdles) 2, best RPR 154
At the festival 18 Mar 2022 Raced wide, took keen hold, tracked leaders, went second 5th, led before 7th, not fluent and stumbled 8th, switched to near side on turn before last, soon joined but went clear with winner, ridden and headed last, kept on, no match for winner, finished second, beaten five lengths by The Nice Guy in Albert Bartlett Novices' Hurdle

One of the best staying novice hurdlers in the division two seasons ago, winning a Grade 1 over 2m6f at the Dublin Racing Festival and then finishing second to The Nice Guy in the Albert Bartlett and again in the Irish version at Punchestown. Unfortunately he managed only one run last season, showing more than enough promise despite a two-and-three-quarter-length second to stablemate Classic Getaway on his chase debut at Gowran. There was considerably less promise when he was a 43-length third to Fact To File on his return this season in December, but that was his first run for 397 days and he was fully entitled to need it. Better was to come in January when he got off the mark in comfortable fashion back up to 3m and he seemed to be going the right way again. However, he flopped when backed into favouritism for the Ten Up at Navan in February despite being discarded by Paul Townend, finishing only third behind American Mike and stablemate Nick Rockett. More is going to be needed whether he runs here or in the National Hunt Chase, but he has finished outside the first two only twice and he's young enough to have a decent future.

Going preference Acts on any, but hurdles form suggests he may find more on better ground over fences
Star rating ✪✪

Apple Away
7 b m; Trainer Lucinda Russell
Chase form 3123, best RPR 143
Left-handed 32, best RPR 133
Right-handed 13, best RPR 143

Sprang a 14-1 upset in the Grade 1 Sefton Novices' Hurdle last season in a race in which stablemate Ahoy Senor also caused a stir a few years ago. Her victory was not so unexpected by her trainer, though, as she has always held her in high regard. Chasing hasn't quite gone to plan yet, though, as she was beaten 14 lengths into third by Grey Dawning on her debut at Haydock and was the same distance behind him but on 3lb better terms when the pair were first and second in the Grade 2 Hampton Novices' Chase at Warwick in January. In between she had shown more promise when romping to a 31-length victory at Leicester and, while it was only a three-runner race, the runner-up won a handicap chase at Newbury off a mark of 131 next time out. She made her share of mistakes when a close third in the Reynoldstown at Ascot in February, but that was a weak affair and she's not at the level she needs to be for this.

Going preference Seems to act on anything
Star rating ✪✪

Sandor Clegane

7 b g; Trainer Paul Nolan
Chase form 422, best RPR 140
Left-handed 2, best RPR 140
Right-handed 42, best RPR 135
Cheltenham form (hurdles) 1, best RPR 150
At the festival 17 Mar 2023 Towards rear, steady headway from 3 out, pushed along after 2 out, ridden approaching last, 3 lengths down and disputing third last, kept on well, finished third, beaten one and a quarter lengths by Stay Away Fay in Albert Bartlett Novices' Hurdle

Finished third in a pair of Grade 1 staying novice hurdles last season, most notably the Albert Bartlett when not beaten far by Stay Away Fay and Affordale Fury. That Cheltenham form is respected, but you certainly can't fancy him on what he has done over fences, as he has yet to win in three starts and has been comfortably held, his best run arguably coming on his final start when Embassy Gardens beat him by an easy ten lengths.

Going preference No ground worries
Star rating ✪

Broadway Boy

6 b g; Trainer Nigel Twiston-Davies
Chase form (left-handed) 12113, best RPR 155
Cheltenham form (all) 1211, best RPR 155

Was improving in handicap hurdles last season, winning his last two off marks of 119 and 126 (the second one at Cheltenham). That improvement has continued apace over fences with three wins in five starts, beginning with a comfortable success at Worcester in September. He appeared to be outclassed by Flooring Porter next time at Cheltenham, although he was conceding the easy two-and-a-half-length winner 5lb, and he improved rapidly after that anyway, winning next two at the track. The first was a Listed novice chase at the Paddy Power meeting, where he won by 20 lengths from stablemate Weveallbeencaught, while next time in December he landed quite a gamble to beat a bunch of much more experienced rivals. That progress came to an end when he was beaten out of sight by Grey Dawning at

Warwick, but the run was too bad to be true (beaten 32 lengths into third). On his best form back at Cheltenham he'd certainly have a shout of reaching the frame, although there is also the option of the National Hunt Chase and it doesn't look like he'll lack for stamina.

Going preference Best chase form on soft, best hurdles form on good
Star rating ✪✪✪

Giovinco

7 b g; Trainer Lucinda Russell
Chase form U12P1, best RPR 148
Left-handed 11, best RPR 148
Right-handed U2P, best RPR 148

Won all three novice hurdles for Lucinda Russell in impressive style last term and was expected to make up into a decent novice chaser this season. He has done that, but it has certainly been a rocky road, starting with a bump when he unseated on his debut at Carlisle in October. He then made a mockery of a mark of 143 in a four-runner novice handicap at Aintree over 3m1f, although it was hardly a jumping test with nine of the ten fences taken out. Giovinco's best run came when he was second to Stay Away Fay in the Grade 2 Esher Novices' Chase at Sandown in December. There he looked like winning for much of the home straight, especially when he challenged at the last seemingly going best, but it was Stay Away Fay who found the most for pressure to pull away again by a length and a half. Giovinco then had another bad experience when jumping poorly and never travelling in the Kauto Star at Kempton, eventually being pulled before two out. He managed to put another win on the board as a warm-up, but it's hard to say we learned any more given he was 4-11 in a two-runner race and they plodded round just fast enough to get over the fences. He clearly has plenty of talent when on song, but probably not enough to be a factor in this.

Going preference Has won on good and heavy
Star rating ✪✪

OTHERS TO CONSIDER

It's very hard to see **Gaelic Warrior** being asked to go 3m left-handed after his Leopardstown

BROWN ADVISORY NOVICES' CHASE RESULTS AND TRENDS

	FORM WINNER	AGE & WGT	Adj RPR	SP	TRAINER	BEST RPR LAST 12 MONTHS (RUNS SINCE)
23	2-011 The Real Whacker CD	7 11-7	167-3	8-1	P Neville	won Cheltenham Gd 2 nov ch (2m4½f) (0)
22	-1111 L'Homme Presse C	7 11-4	173-4	9-4f	V Williams	won Sandown Gd1 nov ch (2m4f) (0)
21	1-111 Monkfish C, D	7 11-4	180T	1-4f	W Mullins (IRE)	won Leopardstown Gd1 nov ch (2m5½f) (0)
20	1-11F Champ D, BF	8 11-4	169-5	4-1	N Henderson	Fell Cheltenham Gd 2 nov ch (2m4½f) (0)
19	12-22 Topofthegame D	7 11-4	170T	4-1	P Nicholls	2nd Kempton Gd 1 nov ch (3m) (0)
18	13112 Presenting Percy C, D, BF	7 11-4	171-1	5-2f	P Kelly (IRE)	won Fairyhouse hcap ch (3m5f) (1)
17	-21F1 Might Bite C, D	8 11-4	175T	7-2f	N Henderson	Fell Kempton Gd 1 nov ch (3m) (1)
16	4F121 Blaklion C, D	7 11-4	172-1	8-1	N Twiston-Davies	won Wetherby Gd 2 nov ch (3m) (0)
15	1-211 Don Poli C, D	6 11-4	165-2	13-8f	W Mullins (IRE)	won Leopardstown Gd1 nov ch (3m) (0)
14	4-2P1 O'Faolains Boy D	7 11-4	160-9	12-1	R Curtis	won Gd2 Reynoldstown Nov Ch (3m) (0)

WINS-RUNS: 5yo 0-1, 6yo 1-20, 7yo 7-58, 8yo 2-19, 9yo 0-2 **FAVOURITES:** £5.13

TRAINERS IN THIS RACE (w-pl-r): Nicky Henderson 2-2-10, Willie Mullins 2-5-19, Paul Nicholls 1-1-8, Gordon Elliott 0-2-7, Dan Skelton 0-0-1, David Pipe 0-0-2, Henry de Bromhead 0-2-5, Lucinda Russell 0-1-1, Noel Meade 0-1-2, Nigel Twiston-Davies 1-0-3

FATE OF FAVOURITES: 2131133112 **POSITION OF WINNER IN MARKET:** 8131133114

flop. **Kilbeg King** could represent the Kauto Star form. He was beaten nearly 15 lengths into third, but just failed to get up in the Reynoldstown, although than run screamed extra reserves of stamina and the National Hunt Chase looks more his race. It's hard to get excited about any of the others still among the entries at the time of writing, although **Meetingofthewaters** wouldn't be out of place if Willie Mullins wanted to take him out of handcap comany.

VERDICT

Without **FACT TO FILE** this would have an open look to it, but the vibes in February were that he's more likely to try 3m for the first time and, with due respect to the British runners, he could be different class. This is one novice in which the Brits have a pretty good recent record, though, and they have two big shouts in **Stay Away Fay** and **Grey Dawning**, with the latter just about preferred. Of those at bigger prices, **Broadway Boy** clearly loves Cheltenham and could get in the money at a decent price.

Key trends

- Contested a Graded chase, 10/10 (six won)
- Top-two finish last time out, 9/10 (exception fell)
- Six to 12 hurdle and chase runs, 9/10
- Aged seven or eight, 9/10
- Adjusted RPR of at least 165, 9/10
- Rated within 5lb of RPR top-rated, 9/10
- Ran three to five times over fences, 8/10

Other factors

- Of the combined 40 chase starts of winners, only 2016 scorer Blaklion had finished outside the first three when completing (five had fallen)
- Seven winners had previously run at the festival – four in the Albert Bartlett (4P1), one in the Baring Bingham (2), one in the Martin Pipe (1), one in the Pertemps Final (1) and one in the Coral Cup (2)

2.50 Coral Cup Handicap Hurdle

ITV/RTV

● 2m5f ● *Premier Handicap* ● £100,000

This highly competitive handicap hurdle was introduced in 1993 and regularly attracts a maximum field (currently set at 26).

LAST YEAR'S WINNER Langer Dan (9-1) became only the fourth winner at single-figure odds since 2004. The next four home were 16-1, 20-1, 50-1 and 22-1.

FORM Eleven of the last 14 winners had won or finished second last time out. Commander Of Fleet and Langer Dan did not fit that general trend in the last two years, although both had run in a Grade 2 last time.

WEIGHT AND RATINGS Langer Dan carried 11st 4lb to victory off a mark of 141. He was the fifth winner in the past decade rated in the narrow 138-143 band.

AGE This race tends to suit younger, less exposed types, and the number of hurdles runs is a key factor. Only three of the last 16 winners have been into double figures.

TRAINERS Nicky Henderson is the most successful with four wins, most recently with Dame De Compagnie in 2020. Ireland has had five of the last eight winners.

BETTING Only three favourites (outright or joint) have won in 30 runnings.

ONES TO WATCH Langer Dan, back down to last year's winning mark after a series of heavy defeats this winter, is set to head back here again for Dan Skelton, who also has Lanzarote Handicap Hurdle winner **Jay Jay Reilly** as an option. **Doddiethegreat** (Nicky Henderson), fourth in the Betfair Hurdle, could step up to this trip and **Sa Majeste** is in the picture for Willie Mullins.

CORAL CUP RESULTS AND TRENDS

	FORM WINNER	AGE & WGT	OR	SP	TRAINER	BEST RPR LAST 12 MONTHS (RUNS SINCE)
23	1-378 **Langer Dan**	7 11-4	141^T	9-1	D Skelton	won Aintree Gd3 hcap hdl (2m4f) (3)
22	F1P83 **Commander Of Fleet** D	8 11-5	152^{-4}	50-1	G Elliott (IRE)	won Navan hcap hdl (3m½f) (3)
21	75441 **Heaven Help Us** C	7 10-2	138^{-4}	33-1	P Hennessy (IRE)	won Leopardstown hcap hdl (2m2f) (0)
20	21/51 **Dame De Compagnie** C, D	7 10-12	140^T	5-1f	N Henderson	won Cheltenham class 2 hcap hdl (2m4½f) (0)
19	144-P **William Henry** C, D	9 11-10	151^{-6}	28-1	N Henderson	4th Ayr class 2 hcap hdl (2m5½f) (1)
18	115-0 **Bleu Berry**	7 11-2	143^{-5}	20-1	W Mullins (IRE)	won Fairyhouse Gd2 nov hdl (2m) (2)
17	48124 **Supasundae**	7 11-4	148^{-2}	16-1	J Harrington (IRE)	won Punchestown hdl (2m4f) (2)
16	P-421 **Diamond King**	8 11-3	149^{-5}	12-1	G Elliott (IRE)	won Punchestown hdl (2m4f) (0)
15	1-31 **Aux Ptits Soins**	5 10-7	139^{-4}	9-1	P Nicholls	won Auteuil hdl (2m1½f) (0)
14	-3312 **Whisper** C, D, BF	6 11-6	153^{-4}	14-1	N Henderson	2nd Ffos Las class 2 hcap hdl (2m4f) (0)

WINS-RUNS: 5yo 1-39, 6yo 1-70, 7yo 5-68, 8yo 2-42, 9yo 1-19, 10yo 0-16, 11yo 0-1 **FAVOURITES:** -£4.00

FATE OF FAVOURITES: 53004710PP **POSITION OF WINNER IN MARKET:** 5266001005

Key trends

● No more than nine hurdle runs, 8/10

● Not run for at least 32 days, 8/10

● Won between 2m2f and 2m6f over hurdles, 8/10

● Carried at least 10st 12lb, 8/10

● Won a race earlier in the season, 7/10 (four won last time out)

● No more than four runs that season, 7/10

● Officially rated 138 to 149, 7/10

● Aged five to seven, 7/10

Other factors

● The two winners to have had more than nine hurdle runs came in the last two runnings – Commander Of Fleet (13) and Langer Dan (16)

3.30 Betway Queen Mother Champion Chase ITV/RTV

● *2m* ● *Grade 1* ● *£400,000*

This was the last of the big championship races to be cracked by Willie Mullins but his breakthrough winner Energumene went back to back last year and, even though that one has been sidelined by injury, El Fabiolo has a strong chance of completing a Mullins hat-trick. Last year's Arkle scorer has won all six chase outings and ominously went up nearly half a stone on Racing Post Ratings with a dominant display last time in the Dublin Chase at Leopardstown. His main rival is the Nicky Henderson-trained Jonbon, as he has been since their novice hurdling days. Over fences the British hope has been just a step or two behind El Fabiolo most of the way and he was beaten five and a half lengths into second in their Arkle clash, but there's no doubt he's a high-class two-mile chaser at his best, as he showed in his Tingle Creek victory in December. They're the big two by far on form, but there are other Grade 1 regulars set to line up, notably 2022 Arkle scorer Edwardstone, back on winning form for Alan King in the Game Spirit at Newbury last time, and Henry de Bromhead's Captain Guinness, runner-up in this race last year.

El Fabiolo

7 b g; Trainer Willie Mullins
Chase form 111111, best RPR 179
Left-handed 111, best RPR 179
Right-handed 111, best RPR 173
Cheltenham form 1, best RPR 172
At the festival 14 Mar 2023 Prominent, not fluent 1st, led just after 2 out, 3 lengths ahead when not fluent last, soon ridden, kept on strongly and went further clear final 110yds, ridden out, won Arkle Novices' Chase by five and a half lengths from Jonbon

Hasn't lost since he first stepped out of maiden hurdle company for Willie Mullins and was beaten a neck by Jonbon in the Grade 1 Top Novices' Hurdle at Aintree in April 2022. Went through an unbeaten four-run first campaign over fences last term, with the last three coming in Grade 1 company. First he thrashed Banbridge by ten lengths in the Irish Arkle, while next time he gained handsome revenge over Jonbon with a five-and-a-half-length success from his old rival in the Arkle at Cheltenham, and then an 11-length romp followed at Punchestown. He returned to action looking every bit as good as ever in open company in the Grade 2 Hilly Way at Cork. There he gave 10lb and a four-and-three-quarter-length beating top the race-fit and 150-rated Fil Dor. While he looked to be tiring

at the end, he was entitled to on his first run for eight months and never looked in any danger. El Fabiolo, in any case, took his form to a new level with a resounding eight-and-a-half-length success in the Dublin Chase at Leopardstown in early February from stablemate and in-form mare Dinoblue. If you wanted to find a way of crabbing him you could say he jumped right at times and wasn't particularly fluent at some of his fences, but that has been him throughout his short chase career and so far his minor mistakes haven't cost him any real momentum and nothing has yet got close to beating him. Cheltenham's fences are a good deal softer than Leopardstown's anyway, and it's not as if his main rival doesn't have the same frailties. Willie Mullins waited an age to train his first Champion Chase winner, but El Fabiolo is rightly odds-on to make it three in a row following the dual successes of the sadly injured Energumene, and he's hard to bet against.

Going preference No ground issues
Star rating ✪✪✪✪✪

Jonbon

8 b g; Trainer Nicky Henderson
Chase form 111211112, best RPR 171
Left-handed 112112, best RPR 169
Right-handed 111, best RPR 171
Cheltenham form (all) 2212, best RPR 169

At the festival 15 Mar 2022 Tracked leader, joined leader after 5th, disputing lead when left in lead 3 out, headed and pushed along 2 out, ridden and outpaced on turn before last, soon no chance with winner, finished second, beaten 22 lengths by Constitution Hill in Supreme Novices' Hurdle

14 Mar 2023 Jumped slightly left throughout, raced in second, pushed along after 3 out, drifted left when challenging 2 out, soon ridden, 3 lengths down last, hung left and no extra run-in, beaten five and a half lengths by El Fabiolo in Arkle Novices' Chase

Has been runner-up to exceptional horses at the last two Cheltenham Festivals, being soundly thumped by stablemate Constitution Hill in the Supreme (22 lengths) before getting closer but ultimately being well held by El Fabiolo in the Arkle. He won three Grade 1s last term, though, starting with the Henry VIII Novices' Chase at Sandown, and finishing his season by landing the Maghull Novices' Chase at Aintree before stepping into opening company and beating Captain Guinness by a comfortable three and three-quarter lengths in the Celebration Chase back at Sandown despite making a pretty bad mistake at the fourth fence. Like El Fabiolo, he looked at least as good as ever on his first two starts this season as he slammed Edwardstone by nine and a half lengths in the Shloer at Cheltenham before beating the same horse in the Tingle Creek at Sandown. The margin of success was only two and three-quarter lengths there, but the ground was very deep and it's not easy to look that impressive when it's like that at the Esher track. Jonbon's unbeaten run came to an end, though, in the rescheduled Clarence House Chase on Trials day at Cheltenham, where he went down by a neck to Elixir De Nutz, a ten-year-old rated a stone inferior. The wheels didn't come off completely as it was obvious he was the best horse in the race, but he hadn't jumped well for new jockey James Bowen before the horrendous mistake at the fourth-last that nearly brought him to the floor. That he was able to rally and get back in front approaching the second-last speaks volumes for his attitude but, having got there, he then made a mess of the last and gave Elixir De Nutz first run up the hill. He was battling back again close

home, which shows how tough he is, but he's not going to win a Champion Chase jumping like that. Like El Fabiolo, he can measure his fences perfectly well, but he's going to need to put it together at the right time.

Going preference Has won on good and heavy. Better ground might help his jumping

Star rating ✪✪✪✪

Edwardstone
10 b g; Trainer Alan King
Chase form UB1111121U252241, best RPR 171
Left-handed UB11122521, best RPR 170
Right-handed 111U24, best RPR 171
Cheltenham form (all) 6551252, best RPR 164
At the festival 10 Mar 2020 Slowly away, towards rear, headway 3 out, ridden in close 6th after 2 out, weakened before last, finished sixth, beaten 23 lengths by Shishkin in Supreme Novices' Hurdle

19 Mar 2021 Midfield, pushed along and headway before last, ridden and kept on well run-in, not pace to challenge, finished fifth, beaten three lengths by Belfast Banter in County Handicap Hurdle

15 Mar 2022 Jumped well, travelled strongly, in touch with leaders, swerved sharply right to avoid faller just after 4th, steady headway 4 out, went second going easily 3 out, led and bumped 2 out, ridden and went clear run-in, readily, won Arkle Chase by four and a quarter lengths from Gabynako

15 Mar 2023 Held up in rear, not fluent 6th, pushed along briefly and some headway after 4 out, mistake 3 out, soon pushed along and weakened, finished fifth, beaten 63 and three-quarter lengths by Energumene in Champion Chase

The Arkle winner in 2022, Edwardstone began his next campaign with a nine-length romp in the Tingle Creek, but that was the last race he won until he suddenly bounced back to form in the Game Spirit at Newbury in February. He was sent off at just 15-8 for last season's Champion Chase, but was tailed off in fifth, and while his opening two seconds to Jonbon at Cheltenham and Sandown this season were much better, they did pretty much suggest he was yesterday's horse. Things didn't improve when Alan King gave him a first try at 2m4f in a chase (had placed in a good handicap at the trip over hurdles) at Kempton, but he was too keen and ended up finishing a 25-length fourth to Banbridge. Then came that remarkable return to form at Newbury. It wasn't remarkable that he won as he was 11-10 in a weakish four-runner race, but it was remarkable the way he did it. Having been held up in his races for his entire life, Edwardstone was bounced out in front by Tom Cannon and ran his rivals ragged, devouring every fence on his way to a 40-length victory from Funambule Sivola, who had won the race for the previous two years. It's fair to say the runner-up has looked regressive all season, but Boothill was around ten lengths down and going nowhere when coming down two out and he had been in career-best form this season and carried a rating of 158. It's hard to believe connections have finally found the way to ride him on his 28th career start, but Edwardstone apparently loved being out in front. He's still going to have to better the bare form at the age of ten if he's to beat the big two, but if he can go hard and jump that well out in front again he may well be able to draw some mistakes out of them. It'll certainly be some disappointment if he goes back to being held up, that's for sure.

Going preference Acts on most surfaces, although connections have avoided genuine good ground
Star rating ✪✪✪

Captain Guinness
9 b g; Trainer Henry de Bromhead
Chase form P12F3U13316412221P3, best RPR 165
Left-handed P2F313161221P3, best RPR 165
Right-handed 1U342, best RPR 165
Cheltenham form (all) B32, best RPR 165
At the festival 10 Mar 2020 In touch, badly hampered 3 out, close up and travelling well enough when brought down next in Supreme Novices' Hurdle won by Shishkin
16 Mar 2021 Took keen hold, close up and pressed leader, led but pestered 3rd, headed 4 out, lost second 3 out, pushed along and switched left home turn, outpaced 2 out, ridden run-in, briefly lost third towards finish, finished third, beaten 13 lengths by Shishkin in Arkle novices' Chase
15 Mar 2023 Took keen hold, in touch with leaders on inner, going easily 3 out, carried left and hampered rival home turn, soon went second, 2 lengths down when not fluent 2 out,

soon no chance with winner, ridden and kept on run-in, finished second, beaten ten lengths by Energumene in Champion Chase

Third to Shishkin in the 2021 Arkle and second to Energumene in last season's Champion Chase (albeit beaten 13 lengths the first time and ten the second), he's plenty capable of solid 2m form at his best. A comfortable Grade 2 winner on his return to action at Navan in November, he is nevertheless just short of top class and his pulled-up effort in the Paddy's Rewards Club Chase over Christmas and distant third to El Fabiolo in the Dublin Chase in February took his record to 0-13 in Grade 1 company. Hard to see him getting that monkey off his back here.

Going preference Has won on all surfaces
Star rating ✪

Ferny Hollow
9 b g; Trainer Willie Mullins
Chase form 11, best RPR 168
Left-handed 1, best RPR 168
Right-handed 1, best RPR 152
Cheltenham form (bumper) 1, best RPR 141
At the festival 11 Mar 2020 Held up in rear, headway when not clear run over 3f out, led inside final furlong, driven out and ran on well towards finish, won Champion Bumper by two and a half lengths from Appreciate It

Hasn't been beaten since December 2019, but that's largely because he has managed only five runs since, and only three since his Champion Bumper success in March 2020. He had two subsequent festival winners behind him that day (Appreciate It and Good Time Jonny), and another one when beating Bob Olinger on his hurdles debut in November 2020. That was his sole hurdles outing, though, as he missed a full year before winning both his chases in December 2021, recording an RPR of 168 when taking the Racing Post Novice Chase at Leopardstown in the second of them. That's it, though, and if he does get to Cheltenham it will be 808 days since his last run. Even now he's probably still just as big a price to line up as he is to win it.

Going preference Has run only on soft or heavy
Star rating ✪

CHAMPION CHASE RESULTS AND TRENDS

	FORM WINNER	AGE & WGT	Adj RPR	SP	TRAINER	BEST RPR LAST 12 MONTHS (RUNS SINCE)
23	1-113 **Energumene** CD, BF	9 11-10	181^T	6-5f	W Mullins (IRE)	won Punchestown Gd1 ch (2m) **(2)**
22	1-112 **Energumene** D	8 11-10	183^{-2}	5-2	W Mullins (IRE)	2nd Gd1 Clarence House Ch (2m1f) **(0)**
21	11-13 **Put The Kettle On** CD	7 11-3	170^{-10}	17-2	H de Bromhead (IRE)	3rd Leopardstown Gd 1 ch (2m1f) **(0)**
20	22-25 **Politologue** D	9 11-10	175^{-9}	6-1	P Nicholls	2nd Gd 1 Champion Chase (2m) **(3)**
19	1-111 **Altior** CD	9 11-10	187^T	4-11f	N Henderson	won Gd 1 Champion Chase (2m) **(4)**
18	111-1 **Altior** CD	8 11-10	181^T	Evensf	N Henderson	won Gd 1 Celebration Chase (1m7½f) **(1)**
17	-6315 **Special Tiara** D	10 11-10	174^{-8}	11-1	H de Bromhead (IRE)	3rd Gd 1 Champion Chase (2m) **(4)**
16	P2-11 **Sprinter Sacre** CD	10 11-10	177^{-1}	5-1	N Henderson	won Kempton Gd2 ch (2m) **(0)**
15	5-311 **Dodging Bullets** CD	7 11-10	178^{-6}	9-2	P Nicholls	won Gd1 Clarence House Ch (2m1f) **(0)**
14	12111 **Sire De Grugy** D	8 11-10	178^T	11-4f	G Moore	won Gd1 Clarence House Ch (2m1f) **(0)**

WINS-RUNS: 6yo 0-2, 7yo 2-19, 8yo 3-27, 9yo 3-22, 10yo 2-8, 11yo 0-5, 12yo 0-2, 13yo 0-1 **FAVOURITES:** -£0.69

TRAINERS IN THIS RACE (w-pl-r): Nicky Henderson 3-0-7, Henry de Bromhead 2-3-14, Paul Nicholls 2-2-11, Willie Mullins 2-3-12, Gary Moore 1-0-6, Alan King 0-1-4, Venetia Williams 0-1-2, Dan Skelton 0-1-2, Harry Fry 0-0-1

FATE OF FAVOURITES: 1P201143P1 **POSITION OF WINNER IN MARKET:** 1324112221

OTHERS TO CONSIDER

It almost feels criminal not to give the Clarence House Chase winner **Elixir De Nutz** a full write-up of his own, but it's unlikely he'll get as fortunate again and he's surely going to be no more than a bit-part player. **Gentleman De Mee** is talented on his day but must have good ground to be seen to best effect, while the likes of **Appreciate It**, **Editeur Du Gite** and **Boothill** are all talented enough without suggesting they have what it takes to figure when it matters.

VERDICT

With a due nod to the return to form of **Edwardstone**, *this really ought to boil down to who jumps best out of* **EL FABIOLO** *and* **Jonbon**. *Both are high-class 2m chasers who can jump very well when they get it right, but both also have mistakes in them. That said, El Fabiolo has yet to make a ghastly error of the type that nearly brought Jonbon to his knees at Cheltenham in January, and even when he does make mistakes he still wins easily. The chances are he's simply the best horse, and the market looks about right.*

Key trends
- Won over at least 2m1f, 10/10
- No more than 10lb off RPR top-rated, 10/10 (four were top-rated)
- Adjusted RPR of at least 174, 9/10
- Grade 1 chase winner, 9/10
- Won Graded chase within last two starts, 9/10
- No older than nine, 8/10
- Between seven and 16 runs over fences, 7/10

Other factors
- Five winners had previously won at the festival
- In the past ten years 37 French-breds have run, yielding five wins, seven seconds and six thirds

4.10 Glenfarclas Cross Country Chase   ITV/RTV
● *3m5½f* ● *£75,000*

Ireland has won 16 of the 19 runnings of this unusual event, introduced when the festival expanded to four days in 2005.

LAST YEAR'S WINNER Gordon Elliott's Delta Work confirmed this as a race for specialists when he became the fourth multiple winner.

TRAINERS Elliott has been the dominant force with five wins since the race was changed to a conditions event in 2016, having previously been a handicap (in 2021, while Elliott was suspended, Tiger Roll won in Denise Foster's temporary care).

BETTING It has generally paid to back horses at the head of the market, with 14 of the 19 winners returned at 11-2 or shorter.

ONES TO WATCH Elliott is set to field a strong team again with hat-trick seeker **Delta Work** alongside **Galvin**, last year's runner-up, and recent Punchestown banks winner **Coko Beach**. This has become a big target for Grade 1 winners once they hit the veteran stage and the latest in that mould is 2021 Gold Cup winner **Minella Indo**, who shaped promisingly for Henry de Bromhead when fourth under 12st in a course-and-distance handicap in December.

CROSS COUNTRY RESULTS AND TRENDS

FORM	WINNER	AGE & WGT	OR	SP	TRAINER	BEST RPR LAST 12 MONTHS (RUNS SINCE)
23 3-136	**Delta Work** CD	10 11-7	173⁻²	11-10f	G Elliott (IRE)	won Cheltenham cross-country ch (3m6f) **(3)**
22 3-466	**Delta Work** C	9 11-4	175⁻¹	5-2f	G Elliott (IRE)	4th Down Royal Gd1 ch (3m) **(2)**
21 52-P6	**Tiger Roll** CD	11 11-4	178⁻³	9-2	D Foster (IRE)	2nd Cheltenham cross-country ch (3m6f) **(1)**
20 -1111	**Easysland** CD	6 11-4	166⁻¹⁸	3-1	D Cottin (FR)	won Cheltenham cross-country ch (3m6f) **(1)**
19 11-41	**Tiger Roll** CD	9 11-4	159ᵀ	5-4f	G Elliott (IRE)	won Grand National hcap ch (4m2½f) **(2)**
18 P-2P5	**Tiger Roll** C	8 11-4	150⁻⁸	7-1	G Elliott (IRE)	won Cheltenham Gd2 NH Chase (4m) **(4)**
17 -5P05	**Cause Of Causes** C	9 11-4	142⁻³	4-1	G Elliott (IRE)	won Kim Muir Hcap Chase (3m2f) **(5)**
16 18119	**Josies Orders** CD	8 11-4	148⁻⁷	15-8f	E Bolger (IRE)	won Cheltenham cross-country ch (3m6f) **(1)**
15 4172F	**Rivage D'Or**	10 10-10	134⁻⁴	16-1	T Martin (IRE)	2nd Kilbeggan hcp ch (3m1f) **(2)**
14 P-111	**Balthazar King** CD	10 11-12	150⁻⁵	4-1	P Hobbs	won Cheltenham cl 2 hcap ch (3m½f) **(1)**

WINS-RUNS: 6yo 1-7, 7yo 0-9, 8yo 2-19, 9yo 3-32, 10yo 3-34, 11yo 1-22, 12yo 0-23, 13yo 0-4, 14yo 0-3, 15yo 0-1

FAVOURITES: £0.73 **FATE OF FAVOURITES:** 3013312211 **POSITION OF WINNER IN MARKET:** 2712312211

Key trends

● Won over at least 3m, 10/10

● At least 14 chase runs, 9/10

● Trained in Ireland, 8/10

● Top-three finish within last two completed starts, 8/10

● Won or placed in a cross country race at Cheltenham or Punchestown, 6/10

Other factors

● The last eight winners were owned by Gigginstown House Stud (five) or JP McManus (three)

● Two winners since 2008 had landed the PP Hogan at Punchestown in February, while 2013 winner Big Shu was runner-up in that event

● Only nine British-trained runners have made the first four, although in 2014 the home team had first, second and fourth

● Ireland has had the first four on three occasions and in 2009 had the first nine

4.50 Johnny Henderson Grand Annual Hcap Chase · RTV
• 2m • Premier Handicap • £125,000

With the switch from Friday to Wednesday, this hotly contested 2m handicap chase had a significant change three years ago by moving from the New course to the Old. The Old course is sharper and tighter, favouring a quicker, strong-travelling type.

LAST YEAR'S WINNER Maskada scored at 22-1 for Henry de Bromhead, comfortably clear of 7-2 favourite Dinoblue.

FORM Nine of the last 14 British-trained winners had won at Cheltenham before. Ireland has won eight of the last 22 runnings, including four in the past ten years.

WEIGHT AND RATINGS The quality has improved year on year and ten of the last 13 winners were rated at least 140 (2019 winner Croco Bay was just below at 139).

AGE This has been a good race for novices with 14 winners since 1983. Just three winners have been older than nine this century.

TRAINERS Paul Nicholls has won four times since 2004, although he has also had five beaten favourites.

BETTING Chosen Mate in 2020 became only the second successful favourite since 2004 and 13 of the last 17 winners were sent off 10-1 or bigger.

ONES TO WATCH Madara was a rare British runner at the Dublin Racing Festival and landed a notable victory for Sophie Leech, setting up a tilt at a first Cheltenham Festival win for the Gloucestershire trainer. Gavin Cromwell has been raiding successfully in the opposite direction this season and could send the novice **My Mate Mozzie** here.

GRAND ANNUAL HANDICAP CHASE RESULTS AND TRENDS

	FORM WINNER	AGE & WGT	OR	SP	TRAINER	BEST RPR LAST 12 MONTHS (RUNS SINCE)
23	-4F10 **Maskada** D, BF	7 11-1	142⁻⁹	22-1	H de Bromhead (IRE)	won Limerick hcap ch (2m3½f) (1)
22	92023 **Global Citizen** D	10 10-6	136⁻⁶	28-1	B Pauling	Seasonal debutant (0)
21	25112 **Sky Pirate** C, D	8 11-6	152⁻³	14-1	J O'Neill	won Warwick class 2 hcap ch (2m) (1)
20	60341 **Chosen Mate** D	7 11-4	147⁻⁸	7-2f	G Elliott (IRE)	won Gowran Park nov ch (2m) (0)
19	835/2 **Croco Bay** D	12 10-12	139⁻⁵	66-1	B Case	2nd Worcester class 3 hcap ch (2m½f) (0)
18	P-238 **Le Prezien** C, D	7 11-8	150⁻²	15-2	P Nicholls	3rd BetVictor Gold Cup hcap ch (2m4½f) (1)
17	63-3P **Rock The World** C, D	9 11-5	147⁻²	10-1	J Harrington (IRE)	2nd Punchestown hcap ch (2m) (2)
16	63-3P **Solar Impulse** D	6 11-0	140⁻⁸	28-1	P Nicholls	3rd Haydock class 2 ch (2m½f) (1)
15	5-604 **Next Sensation** D	8 11-2	143⁻⁵	16-1	M Scudamore	4th Newbury class 2 hcap ch (2m½f) (0)
14	-3439 **Savello** D	8 11-5	147⁻²	16-1	A Martin (IRE)	3rd Leopardstown hcap ch (2m1f) (1)

WINS-RUNS: 5yo 0-4, 6yo 1-17, 7yo 3-43, 8yo 3-61, 9yo 1-36, 10yo 1-26, 11yo 0-11, 12yo 1-4, 13yo 0-2 **FAVOURITES:** -£5.50

FATE OF FAVOURITES: 2430F01F22 **POSITION OF WINNER IN MARKET:** 9706201700

Key trends
- Distance winner, 10/10
- Carried no more than 11st 6lb, 9/10
- Top-three finish on at least one of last two starts, 9/10
- Aged nine or under, 8/10
- No more than 11 runs over fences, 8/10
- Officially rated 140 to 150, 7/10
- Yet to win that season, 7/10
- Had run at a previous festival, 6/10
- No more than four runs since August, 6/10

Other factors
- Three winners had won at the course – three of the exceptions had been placed in this race previously
- The record of the previous year's winner is 00909003

5.30 **Weatherbys Champion Bumper** RTV
• 2m½f • Grade 1 • £80,000

A Dream To Share was something of a fairytale success for John Kiely and the Gleeson family in last year's race, even if ultimately he was owned by JP McManus, but it won't be a surprise if the big two Irish stables re-establish their stranglehold this time. Before A Dream To Share, Willie Mullins (four) and Gordon Elliott (two) had won the previous six runnings between them and they have a host of leading candidates again. Elliott has a couple of the main fancies in Jalon D'Oudairies and Romeo Coolio, plus the longer-priced The Yellow Clay, but the Mullins squad is even deeper. Highest in the ante-post market for the 12-time winning trainer are Jasmin De Vaux and Maughreen, while further down the list are You Oughta Know, Cantico, Fleur Au Fusil and Argento Boy. Britain hasn't won since 2016 but there are decent chances this year with Teeshan (Paul Nicholls) and Let It Rain (Dan Skelton). The always well-stocked Irish ranks also feature Goldinthemountains (Martin Brassil) and Mywayofthinkin (Gavin Cromwell).

Jalon D'Oudairies
5 b g; Trainer Gordon Elliott
Bumper form 11, best RPR 128
Left-handed 1, best RPR 128
Right-handed 1, best RPR 117

Point winner just before last year's festival, and heads there this time as one of the market leaders after two comfortable successes, the latter from the useful if fragile Redemption Day at Leopardstown in December. Owners Gigginstown have not always been fans of this race, but Jalon D'Oudairies will be "bang there" according to trainer Gordon Elliott, who won it in 2017 and 2019, in his pre-festival Stable Tour.

Jasmin De Vaux
5 b g; Trainer Willie Mullins
Bumper form (left-handed) 1, best RPR 128

"Booked his ticket" according to Willie Mullins after romping to a 15-length success at Naas at the end of January on his bumper debut, some nine months after easily beating Largy Poet (now a 127-rated hurdler with Paul Nicholls) in his point. Recorded one of the best Topspeed figures of the contenders at Naas and is just about the shortest-priced runner for a yard which has won 12 of the 31 runnings.

Teeshan
5 b g; Trainer Paul Nicholls

Bumper form (right-handed) 1, best RPR 115

Wide-margin (41 lengths) point winner in October who has since joined Paul Nicholls and made a big impression on his bumper debut in a ten-runner race at Exeter in February. Bloodstock agent Tom Malone was singing his praises for this well before that outing and he represents the connections of last season's 40-1 third Captain Teague. He won't be that price.

Romeo Coolio
5 b g; Trainer Gordon Elliott
Bumper form (right-handed) 1, best RPR 113

Won his point on same day as stablemate Jalon D'Oudairies in March and won on his bumper debut well enough in January. It was only a five-runner affair, though, and the time was poor. Didn't warrant a mention in Elliott's pre-festival Stable Tour, so doesn't look first string.

Maughreen
5 b m; Trainer Willie Mullins
Bumper form (right-handed) 1, best RPR 121

Out of a half-sister to Champion Hurdle winner Faugheen and has inherited her fair share of talent judged on her January 12-length success at Punchestown, where she quickened up well. That was only a mares' race, but they have a good record in this .

You Oughta Know
6 b g; Trainer Willie Mullins
Bumper form 112, best RPR 132
Left-handed 2, best RPR 132
Right-handed 11, best RPR 125

Bumper winner in May and again in August and, while he lost that unbeaten record at the Dublin Racing Festival, his second to Jeroboam Machin (in the race that has provided the last two winners) gives him some of the best form. He was well held by an impressive winner (sadly injured during race and misses this) but stayed on powerfully and a strong gallop in a big field looks like it'll suit.

Cantico
5 b g; Trainer Willie Mullins
Bumper form (left-handed) 31, best RPR 127

Won point two days after Galopin Des Champs' Gold Cup victory and is now with the same owner. Bumper debut didn't quite go to plan as he was beaten five and a half lengths by Goldinthemountains when 5-4 favourite at Leopardstown over Christmas, but cruised home at Navan in February, recording an RPR of 127, and surely makes the team after that.

The Yellow Clay
5 b g; Trainer Gordon Elliott
Bumper form 114, best RPR 128
Left-handed 14, best RPR 128
Right-handed 1, best RPR 112

Won first two bumpers for Gordon Elliott without setting the world alight but improved dramatically when a 40-1 fourth to Jeroboam Machin at Leopardstown in February. Another who failed to get a mention in his pre-festival Stable Tour, though.

Goldinthemountains
5 ch g; Trainer Martin Brassil
Bumper form 41, best RPR 122
Left-handed 1, best RPR 122
Right-handed 4, best RPR 102

Flat-bred gelding, being by Irish and British Champion Stakes winner Almanzor out of a 1m2f Listed winner. Only fourth of 16 on bumper debut at Punchestown but improved markedly on that when beating Mywayofthinkin and Cantico at Leopardstown over Christmas. Didn't appear to be going as well as the runner-up two furlongs out but found plenty, which is a good sign. Given his pedigree, he may want a dry festival.

Mywayofthinkin
5 b g; Trainer Gavin Cromwell
Bumper form (left-handed) 2, best RPR 119

Second favourite to Cantico on bumper debut and beat that one, but found Goldinthemountains two lengths too good. That was his first run, though, and this half-brother to five decent jumps winners will have sound claims of reversing the form given a stronger test and softer ground.

Let It Rain
5 b m; Trainer Dan Skelton
Bumper form 11, best RPR 115
Left-handed 1, best RPR 108
Right-handed 1, best RPR 115

Dual bumper winner for Dan Skelton and was really strong at the end both times. Won Listed Ascot bumper in December in commanding fashion and, while the form doesn't look as strong as some of the Irish, she's got a good attitude and will stay very well. Reportedly wants soft ground to run.

Fleur Au Fusil
6 b m; Trainer Willie Mullins
Bumper form (left-handed) 11, best RPR 119

Won on bumper debut at Naas in November and followed up in Grade 2 mares' event at Leopardstown in early February. Form looks solid enough, but efforts to get her to settle properly have so far failed and she has carted her way to the front a long way out both times. Obviously has serious ability, but hard to believe that'll be the way to win a Champion Bumper.

Argento Boy
5 gr g; Trainer Willie Mullins
Bumper form (right-handed) 1, best RPR 115

Half-brother to a couple of decent winners, including Briar Hill, who won the Champion Bumper in 2013 as a relatively unconsidered 25-1 shot despite being ridden by Ruby Walsh. Briar Hill was a seven-length winner of his bumper debut in the January of his winning year, recording an RPR of just 115, and Argento Boy has done exactly the same.

CHAMPION BUMPER RESULTS AND TRENDS

	FORM	WINNER	AGE & WGT	Adj RPR	SP	TRAINER	BEST RPR LAST 12 MONTHS (RUNS SINCE)
23	111	A Dream To Share D	5 11-7	147^T	7-2	J Kiely (IRE)	won Leopardstown Gd2 bumper (2m) (0)
22	11	Facile Vega D	5 11-5	145^T	15-8f	W Mullins (IRE)	won Leopardstown Gd2 bumper (2m) (0)
21	11	Sir Gerhard D	6 11-5	140^{-11}	85-40	W Mullins (IRE)	won Navan Listed bumper (2m) (0)
20	221	Ferny Hollow D	5 11-5	138^{-9}	11-1	W Mullins (IRE)	won Fairyhouse bumper (2m) (0)
19	1-111	Envoi Allen D	5 11-5	144^T	2-1f	G Elliott (IRE)	won Leopardstown Gd2 bumper (2m) (0)
18	11	Relegate D	5 10-12	126^{-25}	25-1	W Mullins (IRE)	won Leopardstown Gd2 bumper (2m) (0)
17	811	Fayonagh D	6 10-12	140^T	7-1	G Elliott (IRE)	won Fairyhouse Listed bumper (2m) (0)
16	1121	Ballyandy CD	5 11-5	146^T	5-1	N Twiston-Davies	won Newbury Listed bumper (2m½f) (0)
15	-11	Moon Racer CD	6 11-5	140^{-7}	9-2f	D Pipe	won Cheltenham bumper (2m½f) (0)
14	3/2-1	Silver Concorde D	6 11-5	132^{-15}	16-1	D Weld (IRE)	won Leopardstown bumper (2m) (0)

WINS-RUNS: 4yo 0-22, 5yo 6-134, 6yo 4-49 **FAVOURITES:** £1.38

TRAINERS IN THIS RACE (w-pl-r): Willie Mullins 4-10-49, Gordon Elliott 2-2-13, Dan Skelton 0-1-3, Jonjo O'Neill 0-0-3, Stuart Crawford 0-0-2, Paul Nicholls 0-1-4, Nicky Henderson 0-1-3

FATE OF FAVOURITES: 2170412212 **POSITION OF WINNER IN MARKET:** 6123015212

OTHERS TO CONSIDER

With no entries for the Champion Bumper at the time of writing, there is plenty of guesswork involved, and one of the horses who was attracting money with some firms, **On Cloud Wine**, hadn't even run. He's a Sea The Stars gelding trained by Willie Mullins and in the ownership of Susannah Ricci. Mullins no doubt has plenty of others to consider as well, including dual winner **Baby Kate**, who is out of Grade 1-winning mare Augusta Kate (seventh in Ballyandy's Champion Bumper), and **Petit Secret**.

VERDICT

*The bumper at the Dublin Racing Festival has provided the winner for the last two years, but with impressive scorer Jeroboam Machin on the sidelines, this looks wide open. Runner-up **You Oughta Know** arguably still sets the standard but is obviously beatable. Bumpers wouldn't be my speciality, but I liked the way **MYWAYOFTHINKIN** went through his race at Leopardstown and it may have been a lack of experience and steady pace that did for him against the Flat-bred winner **Goldinthemountains**. Given a stronger gallop and a bit more dig in the ground he could turn into a very useful performer. **Jalon D'Oudairies** is second on a long shortlist with Gordon Elliott seemingly quite bullish.*

Key trends
- Won last time out, 10/10
- Aged five or six, 10/10
- Won a bumper worth at least £4,000 or €4,000 to the winner, 9/10
- Adjusted RPR of at least 138, 8/10
- Off the track for at least 32 days, 8/10 (four not seen since Christmas or earlier)
- Won a bumper with at least 12 runners, 8/10

Other factors
- Ireland has won eight of the last ten and 24 of the 31 runnings.
- Willie Mullins has had the most winners with 12 (four in the last ten years) but is often mob-handed. On four of the occasions he won, he saddled just one runner; on the other eight, the winner was not his most fancied in the market on all but one occasion (Facile Vega in 2022)
- Gordon Elliott has trained two of the last seven winners

THURSDAY, MARCH 14
(NEW COURSE)

PAUL KEALY
ON THE KEY
PLAYERS

1.30 Turners Novices' Chase ITV/RTV
• 2m4f • Grade 1 • £175,000

As with most of the novice races this will be shaped by Willie Mullins' decision making and his big choice here is whether to run Fact To File, who came straight from bumpers to chases this season and has been racing at this sort of trip. He has produced high-class form in his wins at Leopardstown over Christmas and at the Dublin Racing Festival, albeit the second time he had only one rival and finished alone. The main one who looks to have been set up for a tilt at this race is leading British hope Ginny's Destiny, whose trainer Paul Nicholls won this with Stage Star last year. Nicholls has run him exclusively at Cheltenham this season, including a last-time-out win on Trials day in the same race used as a stepping stone with Stage Star. There is plenty of class among the other possibles but no clear idea yet which ones will run here.

Fact To File
7 b g; Trainer Willie Mullins
Chase form (left-handed) 211, best RPR 164
Cheltenham form (bumper) 2, best RPR 136
At the festival 15 Mar 2023 Towards rear of midfield, headway on outer from over 3f out, pushed along over 2f out, ridden over 1f out, disputed lead when short of room and unbalanced inside final furlong, kept on but held inside final 110yds, finished second, beaten a length and a quarter by A Dream To Share in Champion Bumper

Another Willie Mullins-trained horse to find himself as a short-priced favourite for two races at the festival, and the shape of each race will look very different depending on where he goes. He has been given a full write-up in the Brown Advisory section because by mid-February the word was that he's far more likely to end up there. As always, though, nothing with Mullins is set in stone. If he does come here he's arguably the form choice and will be hard to beat.

Going preference No confirmed preference. Very useful on soft
Star rating ✪✪✪✪

Ginny's Destiny
8 b g; Trainer Paul Nicholls
Chase form (left-handed) 7111, best RPR 161
Cheltenham form 7111, best RPR 161

Decent enough novice hurdler without looking a superstar, with his best run arguably a five-length second to now fellow top British novice chaser Grey Dawning in the Grade 2 Leamington at Warwick last January. He has been a revelation over fences, though, bouncing back from a mediocre effort on his debut at Cheltenham in October to win his next three starts there and rocket 22lb up the handicap. The winning run started at the Paddy Power meeting in November when he jumped well, made all and bounded ten lengths clear of Es Perfecto. Hit with an 8lb rise for that, he went into novice company instead and again made virtually all to beat old rival Grey Dawning by three-quarters of a length. He was receiving 3lb from the runner-up there and there were many who thought Grey Dawning would have won but for a bad mistake two out, but jumping is the name of the game and that's Ginny's Destiny's chief asset. Upped a further 6lb for that, he was back in handicap company next time on Trials day at Cheltenham in January and, just like his stablemate and subsequent Turners winner Stage Star a year earlier, defied top weight of 12st as he powered to another comfortable win. Third-placed Es Perfecto was beaten only six and a quarter lengths this time, but he was a massive 15lb better off, so hasn't come close to matching the winner's rate of improvement. Given his obvious love for Cheltenham and his excellent jumping ability, Ginny's Destiny has to be considered a major player.

Going preference Seems to act on any ground
Star rating ✪✪

Facile Vega

7 b g; Trainer Willie Mullins
Chase form (left-handed) 143, best RPR 155
Cheltenham form (all) 12, best RPR 154
At the festival 16 Mar 2022 Towards rear of midfield, headway from over 6f out, close up 4f out, shaken up to challenge 2f out, led over 1f out, soon pushed along, went clear inside final furlong, readily, won Champion Bumper by three and three-quarter lengths from American Mike
14 Mar 2023 Midfield, smooth headway to lead before 2 out, pushed along when awkward on landing last, soon edged right and headed, kept on, no match for winner, finished second, beaten three and a quarter lengths by Marine Nationale in Supreme Novices' Hurdle

Considered more likely to run in the Arkle, so gets a full write-up in Tuesday's section as he has yet to be asked to try more than 2m1f in 12 starts. That said, his dam was a six-time festival winner at 2m4f and also won the 3m World Series Hurdle at Punchestown four times, so a step up in trip is sure to come at some point in his career. If it does come here and the ground is soft he'd have to be taken seriously given his two previous festival runs have yielded a Champion Bumper win and a Supreme second.

Going preference Disappointing efforts came on yielding and may need it considerably deeper
Star rating ✪✪✪

Gaelic Warrior

6 b g; Trainer Willie Mullins
Chase form 11U, best RPR 160
Left-handed U, best RPR 140
Right-handed 11, best RPR 160
Cheltenham form (hurdles) 22, best RPR 153
At the festival 15 Mar 2022 Jumped right throughout, led, pushed along home turn, 2 lengths ahead last, soon ridden and faced strong challenge, headed inside final 110yds, kept on well, finished second, beaten a short head by Brazil in Boodles Juvenile Handicap Hurdle
15 Mar 2023 Took keen hold, midfield, headway and prominent after 2 out, pushed along and went second 4 lengths down last, soon edged right, kept on final 110yds, no match for winner, finished second, beaten six and a half lengths by Impaire Et Passe in Ballymore Novices' Hurdle

Hugely talented six-year-old who has already paid two visits to the festival and finished second both times. In both seasons they were his only defeats for Willie Mullins and both came on left-handed tracks and there's no doubt he has a preference for going right-handed, even if there's not much difference between his best form on RPRs either way over hurdles. There was plenty of pre-season talk about a Stayers' Hurdle challenge, but Mullins eventually decided on a chase campaign and that looked a great call after his first two starts as he looked an absolute natural. He opened his account by winning in little more than a canter by 15 lengths from the useful Inothewayurthinkin over 2m3f at Punchestown and, while there was more fuss made about the row his rider Patrick Mullins had with Danny Mullins for attempting to go up his inside in the Grade 1 Faugheen Novice Chase at Limerick next time, Gaelic Warrior never looked like doing anything but winning easily, which he did by five and a half lengths from Il Etait Temps. That prompted a couple of firms to make him odds-on for the Turners, but the wheels rather fell off next time. While Il Etait Temps went on to land the Irish Arkle at the Dublin Racing Festival, Gaelic Warrior took his record left-handed for Mullins to 1-4 when unseating in the 2m5½f Ladbrokes Novice Chase. He had jumped straight enough early on against sole rival Fact To File, but went sharply to his right at the fence in front of the stands on the first circuit and was already well beaten when doing so again and shooting Paul Townend out of the saddle next time around (final fence). That's surely not his form, but whether he'll ever be able to show his best in a chase going left-handed has to be open to doubt because when you have that tendency over hurdles it's going to be even harder over fences.

Going preference Track much more of an issue than ground
Star rating ✪✪

Il Etait Temps

6 gr g; Trainer Willie Mullins
Chase form 121, best RPR 156
Left-handed 1, best RPR 156
Right-handed 12, best RPR 152
Cheltenham form (hurdles) 55, best RPR 148

At the festival 18 Mar 2022 Took keen hold, in touch with leaders, bit short of room and not fluent 2 out, ridden up the centre before last, no extra run-in, finished fifth, beaten eighth and three-quarter lengths by Vauban in Triumph Hurdle
14 Mar 2023 Didn't jump with fluency, took keen hold, raced wide, midfield, steady headway 3 out, ridden and outpaced on turn before last, soon edged left, kept on final 110yds, not reach leaders, finished fifth, beaten nine lengths by Marine Nationale in Supreme Novices' Hurdle

Has been given a full write-up in the Arkle section as that's the most likely destination. He has so far reserved his best for the Dublin Racing Festival, recording upset wins there for the last two seasons, including in the Irish Arkle last time. He only just got up there over 2m1f in testing ground, though, and appeared to find the 2m½f of the Supreme on the sharp side last season, so the 2m on Tuesday's chase track may provide the same problem. He'll get this trip if connections decide that's the way to go.

Going preference Seems fine on most surfaces
Star rating ✪✪✪

Iroko
6 b g; Trainer Oliver Greenall & Josh Guerriero
Chase form (left-handed) 1, best RPR 150
Cheltenham form (hurdles) 1, best RPR 144
At the festival 17 Mar 2023 Prominent, pushed along and outpaced after 2 out, rallied and went third just before last, 3 lengths down last, ridden and kept on well run-in, led towards finish, won Martin Pipe Conditional Jockeys' Handicap Hurdle by a length and a half from No Ordinary Joe

Excellent second season over hurdles last term, winning his first two handicaps at Wetherby before rocking up at Cheltenham and landing a gamble in the Martin Pipe. Fair effort at 3m when third to Apple Away on his final start at Aintree last season, and looked all set to make into an even better chaser following an impressive win on his return at Warwick in November. There he travelled strongly, jumped well and needed only to be shaken up briefly to beat Golden Son by three and a quarter lengths. It's fair to say the runner-up has done nothing for the form, but the 20-length third is now rated

142 and Iroko has bags of promise. However, an injury to the sole of his foot after that success has kept him off the track since, and a decision has to be made. His joint-trainers seem keen to go, but the final decision will be left to JP McManus. He has favourite Fact To File to call on and, while he's no stranger to running horses against each other, it won't be a surprise if they wait for Aintree with a horse so inexperienced. Plenty of untapped talent if he goes.

Going preference Has won on good and soft
Star rating ✪✪✪

American Mike
7 b g; Trainer Gordon Elliott
Chase form 141, best RPR 151
Left-handed 11, best RPR 151
Right-handed 4, best RPR 125
Cheltenham form (all) 27, best RPR 139
At the festival 16 Mar 2022 Travelled strongly, midfield, headway over 6f out, soon close up, going easily when led 3f out, shaken up when faced challenge 2f out, pushed along and headed over 1f out, switched left 1f out, kept on but no match for winner, finished second, beaten three and three-quarter lengths by Facile Vega in Champion Bumper
15 Mar 2023 Took keen hold, raced wide, didn't jump with fluency, prominent, pushed along after 2 out, weakened on turn before last, finished seventh, beaten 21 lengths behind Impaire Et Passe in Ballymore Novices' Hurdle

Runner-up in the Champion Bumper in 2022 but didn't progress as expected over hurdles, his seventh to Impaire Et Passe in the Ballymore being his best effort on RPRs. However, he wouldn't be the first horse to go missing for a season and then bounce back and, despite one blip, he's certainly on an upward curve again. He caused a minor upset when beating Fact To File by three and a quarter lengths on their chase debuts at Navan in November, but then came the blip when he was a 25-length fourth to Gaelic Warrior in the Grade 1 Faugheen at Limerick over Christmas. However, there was much to like about his victory in the Grade 2 Ten Up Novice Chase back at Navan in February. There he beat two well-backed Willie Mullins-trained rivals in Nick Rockett and Minella Cocooner and, while the winning distance was only a length and a quarter over the former, he looked like winning by a good deal further two out. He was definitely idling, though, as he pulled out more after the last to go away again. That was at 3m on heavy ground, though, and you wonder whether connections are now ruing the lack of entry in the Brown Advisory.

Going preference All best form on deep ground
Star rating ✪✪

Colonel Harry
7 ch g; Trainer Jamie Snowden
Chase form 1213, best RPR 150
Left-handed 11, best RPR 150
Right-handed 23, best RPR 148

Steadily progressive over hurdles last season and it was the same again on his first three runs over fences. Off the mark on his first run over fences at Chepstow in November, he was backed into favouritism for the Grade 1 Henry VIII Novices' Chase at Sandown but couldn't quite handle Le Patron, going down by a length and a quarter. However, he was better again upped to 2m3½f at Wetherby in January, winning going away by a length and three-quarters from the promising Trelawne. The wheels came off when he was a distant third to Nickle Back in the Grade 1 Scilly Isles back at Sandown, but that was his first run on good ground, so there's a possible excuse. Fair bit to find on balance, though.

Going preference Handles soft and heavy well
Star rating ✪✪

Djelo
6 b g; Trainer Venetia Williams
Chase form 111F2, best RPR 151
Left-handed 11F, best RPR 146
Right-handed 12, best RPR 151

Fair handicapper over hurdles in first season for Venetia Williams, although he won only first time out and lost his form in the second half of the campaign. Won first three outings over fences this term, improving his official rating from 128 to 149, his best success coming at Ascot in a Grade 2 by six lengths from Kandoo Kid. It wasn't his fault that he fell at the first next time as the leader jumped across him, and he was back going the right way when

a seven-length second to Nickle Back in the Scilly Isles at Sandown. The winner had stolen a massive lead and Djelo was the only horse who could make any serious ground on him, but that form is some way off what's required here. After five runs, he could go back handicapping too.

Going preference No obvious preference
Star rating ✪✪

Le Patron
6 b g; Trainer Gary Moore
Chase form 1114, best RPR 151
Left-handed 1, best RPR 133
Right-handed 114, best RPR 151

Huge early-season improver for Gary Moore, winning his first three chases, including the Grade 1 Henry VIII at Sandown, and taking his rating from 113 to 150. Was pretty weak in the market and never got into it back at Sandown in the Scilly Isles in February, though, and has questions to answer after that.

Going preference Has won on good and heavy
Star rating ✪✪

OTHERS TO CONSIDER
There were a few shorter-priced horses missed from this deliberately as it was a case of trying to give a mention to some more likely runners. **Grey Dawning** should be going for the Brown Advisory after his strong-staying performance at Warwick, but it would not be a great surprise if Dan Skelton decided to avoid Fact To File because he'll be a shorter price than he is for this without him in the field. **Found A Fifty** was a neck runner-up in the Irish Arkle and, having been outstayed by I Am Maximus over this sort of trip earlier in the season, should be staying at 2m. **Il Est Francais** isn't travelling according to his connections.

VERDICT
Around ten runners were quoted at 10-1 or shorter by most firms offering non-runner no bet, but in reality the only certain runner is **GINNY'S DESTINY**. *He brings some strong handicap form to the party and is following the same route as last year's winner Stage Star for the same stable. Willie Mullins said he had no preference for* **Fact To File**, *but the Brown Advisory has become increasingly*

TURNERS NOVICES' CHASE RESULTS AND TRENDS

	FORM WINNER	AGE & WGT	Adj RPR	SP	TRAINER	BEST RPR LAST 12 MONTHS (RUNS SINCE)
23	-1211 **Stage Star** CD	7 11-7	166-5	15-2	P Nicholls	won Cheltenham nov hcap chs (2m4½f) **(0)**
22	11-11 **Bob Olinger** C, D	7 11-4	175-3	6-5	H de Bromhead (IRE)	won Punchestown Gd3 nov ch (2m4f) **(0)**
21	3-131 **Chantry House** C, D	7 11-4	168-7	9-1	N Henderson	won Ascot class 3 nov ch (2m3f) **(2)**
20	5-1F2 **Samcro** C, D, BF	8 11-4	171-5	4-1	G Elliott (IRE)	Fell Fairyhouse Gd1 nov ch (2m4f) **(1)**
19	-5121 **Defi Du Seuil** C, D	6 11-4	166-2	3-1f	P Hobbs	won Sandown Gd1 nov ch (2m4f) **(0)**
18	11211 **Shattered Love**	7 10-11	168-3	4-1	G Elliott (IRE)	won Leopardstown Gd1 nov ch (3m) **(0)**
17	1-411 **Yorkhill** C, D	7 11-4	163-7	6-4f	W Mullins (IRE)	won Fairyhouse nov ch (2m) **(1)**
16	7-11F **Black Hercules** D, BF	7 11-4	169-2	4-1c	W Mullins (IRE)	won Warwick Listed nov ch (3m) **(1)**
15	-1121 **Vautour** C, D	6 11-4	165-10	6-4f	W Mullins (IRE)	won Leopardstown Gd2 nov ch (2m3f) **(0)**
14	11321 **Taquin Du Seuil** C, D	7 11-4	167-6	7-1	J O'Neill	won Haydock Gd2 nov ch (2m5f) **(0)**

WINS-RUNS: 5yo 0-6, 6yo 2-29, 7yo 7-32, 8yo 1-13, 9yo 0-6, 12yo 0-1 **FAVOURITES:** £0.67

TRAINERS IN THIS RACE (w-pl-r): Willie Mullins 3-4-23, Gordon Elliott 2-1-4, Henry de Bromhead 1-0-4, Nicky Henderson 1-4-9, Paul Nicholls 1-0-9, Dan Skelton 0-0-3, David Pipe 0-0-1, Gary Moore 0-1-1, Gavin Cromwell 0-0-1, Venetia Williams 0-0-1, Nigel Twiston-Davies 0-2-4

FATE OF FAVOURITES: 4111213FF3 **POSITION OF WINNER IN MARKET:** 4111213223

Key trends

- Ran over hurdles at a previous festival, ten winners in ten runnings
- Adjusted RPR of at least 165, 9/10
- Distance winner, 9/10 (exception had won over further)
- Graded winner over hurdles, 9/10
- Rated within 7lb of RPR top-rated, 9/10
- Won a Graded chase, 6/10

Other factors

- Eight winners won last time out – of the two exceptions, one finished second by a short head and the other fell when looking likely to win

*likely according to the rumour mill. **Iroko** would be most interesting of the others if given the go-ahead, which will surely be more likely if Fact To File is sent elsewhere, but if I owned **Gaelic Warrior** I'd be waiting for Punchestown and forgetting all about running left-handed over fences.*

Ginny's Destiny: following the same route as last year's winner Stage Star

2.10 Pertemps Network Final Handicap Hurdle — ITV/RTV
● *3m* ● *Premier Handicap* ● *£100,000*

The eligibility rules for this 3m handicap hurdle, first run at the festival in 1974, were tightened again last year. Now horses must finish in the first four in any of the scheduled qualifiers to be eligible for the final.

LAST YEAR'S WINNER Good Time Jonny scored at 9-1 for the shrewd Tony Martin, giving the trainer a seventh festival win (all in handicaps) and becoming the seventh Irish-trained winner of this race in eight years.

WEIGHT AND RATINGS All bar one of the first six last year was rated in the golden range from 138 to 142. Half the winners in the past decade have been in that bracket.

TRAINER The top trainer to note is Gordon Elliott, who won three straight runnings (with two 1-2s in that run) from 2018 to 2020 and had the runner-up again last year.

BETTING Favourites have a poor record, although nine of the past ten winners were in the top six in the market.

ONES TO WATCH Icare Allen hasn't run since finishing third for Willie Mullins in an Aintree qualifier in November and is prominent in the ante-post betting. **Gaoth Chuil** (Ted Walsh) and **Jody Ted** (Eoin Griffin) have won Irish qualifiers. **White Rhino** is a 3m winner on the New course this season for Oliver Greenall and Josh Guerriero.

PERTEMPS FINAL RESULTS AND TRENDS

	FORM	WINNER	AGE & WGT	OR	SP	TRAINER	BEST RPR LAST 12 MONTHS (RUNS SINCE)
23	P4030	**Good Time Jonny** D	8 11-4	142-2	9-1	T Martin (IRE)	3rd Leopardstown hcap hdl (3m) (1)
22	P-733	**Third Wind** D	8 10-11	141-6	25-1	H Morrison	3rd Warwick class 2 hcap hdl (3m1f) (1)
21	1324F	**Mrs Milner**	6 10-9	134-7	12-1	P Nolan (IRE)	won Galway hcap hdl (2m½f) (4)
20	8-494	**Sire Du Berlais** CD	8 11-12	152-3	10-1	G Elliott (IRE)	4th Navan hcap hdl (3m½f) (2)
19	48-86	**Sire Du Berlais**	7 11-9	145-6	4-1f	G Elliott (IRE)	4th Martin Pipe cond hcap hdl (2m4½f) (3)
18	33243	**Delta Work**	5 10-10	139^T	6-1	G Elliott (IRE)	4th Leopardstown hcap hdl (3m) (1)
17	11541	**Presenting Percy**	6 11-11	146-4	11-1	P Kelly (IRE)	won Fairyhouse hcap hdl (2m4f) (0)
16	31433	**Mall Dini**	6 10-11	139-7	14-1	P Kelly (IRE)	won Thurles mdn hdl (2m6½f) (3)
15	21-41	**Call The Cops** (5x) D	6 10-12	138-5	9-1	N Henderson	won Doncaster class 2 hcap hdl (3m½f) (0)
14	120-1	**Fingal Bay** C, D	8 11-12	148^T	9-2f	P Hobbs	won Exeter class 2 hcap hdl (2m7½f) (0)

WINS-RUNS: 5yo 1-6, 6yo 4-56, 7yo 1-67, 8yo 4-43, 9yo 0-34, 10yo 0-12, 11yo 0-9, 12yo 0-3, 13yo 0-2 **FAVOURITES:** +£0.50

FATE OF FAVOURITES: 1000212220 **POSITION OF WINNER IN MARKET:** 1365215693

Key trends
● Aged six to eight, 9/10
● Top-four finish last completed start, 8/10
● Winning form at 2m4f to 2m6f, 8/10
● Officially rated 138-148, 8/10
● Six to ten runs over hurdles, 7/10

Other factors
● Five winners had yet to win over 3m and five winners had run at the festival before

● In 2018, Delta Work became the first successful five-year-old since Pragada in 1988, while Buena Vista in 2011 was the first aged older than nine to oblige since 1981
● Five winners were set to carry at least 11st 9lb
● Lightly raced types are generally favoured, but three of the last four winners had 14 starts over hurdles

2.50 Ryanair Chase ITV/RTV
● 2m4½f ● Grade 1 ● £375,000

Allaho, the dominant winner in 2021 and 2022, is absent for a second consecutive year and that leaves the contest wide open again. Envoi Allen stepped up last year for Allaho's owners with his third festival success and is a leading contender again for Henry de Bromhead, albeit with the age stat to defy now at the age of ten. The leading Irish contender according to the ante-post betting is Joseph O'Brien's Banbridge, who ended his novice campaign with a Grade 1 win at Aintree and improved again on his only start this season with victory over Pic D'Orhy at Kempton. He missed Cheltenham last year, though, and almost certainly needs good in the going description if he's to line up. Paul Nicholls' Stage Star, last year's Turners Novices' Chase winner, has strong Cheltenham form but questions to answer after being pulled up there last time. A host of other possibles make this one of the most fascinating Grade 1 contests.

Banbridge
8 ch g; Trainer Joseph O'Brien
Chase form 113211, best RPR 169
Left-handed 121, best RPR 159
Right-handed 131, best RPR 169
Cheltenham form (all) 11, best RPR 158
At the festival 18 Mar 2022 Took keen hold, raced wide early, prominent, went second 7th, joined leader 3 out, led after 2 out, joined but clear with one other before last, soon ridden, kept on strongly final 110yds, won Martin Pipe Conditional Jockeys' Handicap Hurdle by a length and a half from Cobblers Dream

Terrifically consistent performer when conditions are in his favour, his form figures under all jumps codes on yielding or quicker ground being 1411011211. Had a really good first season over fences last term, winning his first two and taking his Cheltenham record to 2-2 when taking the Grade 2 Arkle Trial by six lengths from Tommy's Oscar that November. He was stuck in the mud when a distant third to the ill-fated Mighty Potter at Fairyhouse after that and then couldn't live with El Fabiolo's speed at Leopardstown. Little else has managed to do that, either, though, and Banbridge bagged his first Grade 1 success when beating fellow raider Saint Roi by a length and a half in the Manifesto Novices' Chase at Aintree in April. That wasn't the highest-quality Grade 1 ever run in Britain, but Banbridge at least showed he has come on again when beating the previous year's winner Pic D'Orhy in the Silviniaco Conti Chase on his belated return to action in January. He travelled to Britain, where he has won four of his five starts, for the better ground, and that's the issue for anyone thinking of an ante-post bet as he was taken out of the Turners due to soft ground last season.

Going preference The better the ground the better his chance
Star rating ✪✪✪✪

Envoi Allen
10 b g; Trainer Henry de Bromhead
Chase form 111FP16133171432, best RPR 167
Left-handed F131, best RPR 167
Right-handed 111P16317432, best RPR 167
Cheltenham form (all) 11F31, best RPR 167
At the festival 13 Mar 2019 Held up, headway 5f out, led over 3f out, ridden over 1f out, strongly pressed inside final furlong, ran on gamely and found extra near finish, won Champion Bumper by three-quarters of a length from Blue Sari
11 Mar 2020 Raced keenly, in touch, chased leaders 2 out, about 6 lengths off the pace home bend, closed quickly to lead just before last, edged left run-in, ran on to draw clear final 100yds, won Ballymore Novices' Hurdle by four and a quarter lengths from Easywork
18 Mar 2021 Prominent, fell 4th in Marsh Novices' Chase won by Chantry House
16 Mar 2022 Disputed lead at good pace, tracked leader from 2nd, disputed lead 3 out, pushed along when mistake 2 out, soon ridden and lost second, weakened gradually from last, finished third, beaten 13 lengths by Energumene in Champion Chase
16 Mar 2023 Took keen hold, jumped right on occasions, prominent, not fluent 4 out, pecked

on landing 3 out, disputed lead going easily before 2 out, pushed along and led clearly approaching last, ridden and edged left but kept on well run-in, won Ryanair Chase by two and three-quarter lengths from Shishkin

Was once considered the second coming in Ireland after Gordon Elliott guided him to an 11-race unbeaten start to his career, a run which included the Champion Bumper and Ballymore. His bid for a festival treble under new trainer Henry de Bromhead didn't last long, though, as he fell at the fourth when 4-9 favourite for what is now the Turners, and he has been a bit in and out ever since. However, while he hasn't turned out to be the superstar many had hoped, he has had a pretty illustrious career, and after finishing third to Energumene over a too-short 2m in the Champion Chase two years ago, he reverted to this trip last season to land his third festival success, winning by two and three-quarter lengths from Shishkin. He hasn't won since, but was far from disgraced when beaten only a neck by Gerri Colombe in the Champion Chase at Down Royal in November, although that was his first defeat at that meeting in five visits. He's going to arrive fresh as he bypassed the Savills at Leopardstown over Christmas due to the soft ground and missed another engagement due to a cough in January. In terms of form he's still right up there, but it's not easy to win a Grade 1 at Cheltenham when you hit double figures, and the last ten-year-old to do so in this race was Albertas Run in 2011.

Going preference Acts on any ground
Star rating ✪✪✪

Stage Star
8 b g; Trainer Paul Nicholls
Chase form (all left-handed) 1211151P, best RPR 171
Cheltenham form (all) P111P, best RPR 171
At the festival 16 Mar 2022 Raced freely, tracked leaders, dropped to midfield after 4th, pushed along when mistake 3 out, soon lost ground quickly, pulled up just after 2 out in Ballymore Novices' Hurdle won by Sir Gerhard 16 Mar 2023 Led, not fluent 4 out, pushed along and headed after 3 out, good jump and led again 2 out, soon ridden, kept on strongly and went clear run-in, won Turners Novices' Chase by three and a quarter lengths from Notlongtillmay

Won the Grade 1 Challow Hurdle in December

2021 and, while he disappointed in the Ballymore at Cheltenham, he improved in typical style for a Paul Nicholls-trained horse as soon as he went over fences. There were a couple of blips last season as he was beaten at odds of 2-7 on his second chase outing and was last of five on his final start at Aintree, but in between he proved himself a serious performer. At Cheltenham on Trials day he defied 12st to win by three and a quarter lengths from this season's ill-fated Coral Gold Cup winner Datalrightgino, while at the festival he made pretty much all the running and put in some big leaps when it mattered to score by three and a quarter lengths over another sadly ill-fated rival in Notlongtillmay. Then came the last of five to Banbridge at Aintree, but he was back with a massive career-best first time out in the Paddy Power Gold Cup, winning by four lengths from Notlongtillmay on slightly worse terms than in the Turners. That told only half the story as he was looking likely to win by at least twice that distance until making an uncharacteristically bad error and nearly falling at the last. He still won easily, though, and in recording an RPR of 171 he put himself right in the picture for this. Somewhat surprisingly, however, he was never travelling and didn't jump well when pulled up as a hot favourite in another big handicap at the track on New Year's Day, with his trainer saying he was stiff post-race. He has bounced back before, though, has won every time he has finished a race at Cheltenham, and will undoubtedly be fresh and ready come the day.

Going preference Best form on soft
Star rating ✪✪✪✪✪

Capodanno
8 ch g; Trainer Willie Mullins
Chase form 12U413P631, best RPR 164
Left-handed 1U4P31, best RPR 164
Right-handed 2136, best RPR 162
Cheltenham form 41, best RPR 164
At the festival 16 Mar 2022 Didn't jump with fluency, held up in rear, pushed along and outpaced after 3 out, rallied and went fourth before last, ridden and drifted left run-in, made no impression, finished fourth, beaten 12 and a quarter lengths by L'Homme Presse in Brown Advisory Novices' Chase

Was promising as a novice, and after running fourth to L'Homme Presse in the Brown Advisory, he won the 3m½f Champion Novice Chase at Punchestown. A Grand National preparation last season backfired, though, as he was pulled up at Aintree, and there wasn't a lot of promise in his return this season either, when he finished last of six at Thurles in November. However, he was back on track when third to Galopin Des Champs at odds of 80-1 in the Savills, albeit beaten 23 lengths, and he stepped up again when taking the Cotswold Chase in January from The Real Whacker and crack British novice Stay Away Fay. All his best form is at 3m-plus, though, so it's surprising that he didn't even get an entry in the Gold Cup even if he's not in the class of his stablemate and reigning champion Galopin Des Champs. The problem with coming back to this trip is not necessarily the distance, but the fact he's quite often slow through the air. He won't get away with that at the pace they're likely to go here.

Going preference Acts on any ground
Star rating ✪✪

Conflated
10 b g; Trainer Gordon Elliott
Chase form 321314U211F2313P53UU, best RPR 171
Left-handed 131U211F213PUU, best RPR 171
Right-handed 324353, best RPR 166
Cheltenham form F3, best RPR 171
At the festival 17 Mar 2022 Midfield, towards rear after 3rd, dropped to last before 9th, not fluent 10th, still plenty to do 5 out, pushed along and headway on outer from 3 out, ridden and 5 lengths down disputing second when fell 2 out in Ryanair Chase won by Allaho
17 Mar 2023 In touch with leaders, slightly hampered and left in fourth 17th, ridden and not clear run just before 2 out, hung left and outpaced but went third approaching last, weakened run-in, finished third, beaten 13 and a half lengths by Galopin Des Champs in Gold Cup

Talented performer whose finest hours came at Leopardstown in 2022 when he won both the Irish Gold Cup and Savills Chase, although he has run well at Cheltenham too as he was third in last season's Gold Cup, albeit beaten 13 and a half lengths. He hasn't been quite as good this season, failing to finish in the Savills in December and the Irish Gold Cup in February, although he was only about three lengths down on Galopin Des Champs and Fastorslow on the latter occasion, so wasn't that far off his best even if he looked about to finish third. The problem with him might well be the trip, as while he would have finished second to Allaho in the 2002 running of this but for falling two out, he looked rushed off his feet throughout and hasn't attempted anything so short since. He's also a ten-year-old, which is another negative for Grade 1s at the festival.

Going preference Has won on all types of going
Star rating ✪✪

Fil Dor
6 gr g; Trainer Gordon Elliott
Chase form 13522, best RPR 153
Left-handed 1352, best RPR 153
Right-handed 2, best RPR 153
Cheltenham form 20, best RPR 141
At the festival 18 Mar 2022 Disputed lead, briefly led on turn before last, ridden and kept on final 110yds, no match for winner, finished second, beaten two and a half lengths by Vauban in Triumph Hurdle
15 Mar 2023 Midfield, lost position 5th, ridden and dropped to rear before 3 out, soon beaten, finished 19th, beaten 47 lengths by Langer Dan in Coral Cup

Talented six-year-old who has tasted his share of success and finished second to Vauban in the 2022 Triumph Hurdle. Took well enough to fences on first two attempts last season, but went back over hurdles after being thumped by El Fabiolo in the Irish Arkle. Has been back chasing this term and arguably put up his best two performances, although he was beaten both times. On the first occasion he was second to in-form mare Dinoblue in a Grade 3 at Naas, while next time he ran El Fabiolo to just under five lengths, albeit the winner was making his reappearance and conceding 10lb. Still, it was a fair enough effort, although a peak RPR of 153 puts him more than a stone behind the best in this field. Add the fact his two efforts at around 2m4f have resulted in a 47-length 19th of 26 in last season's Coral Cup and a 54-length last of six at Fairyhouse and his price of around 10-1 is pretty hard to fathom. Not quite as hard to fathom as his price of €620,000 at the Andy and

Gemma Brown dispersal sale, however.

Going preference Acts on any, best form on soft

Star rating ✪

Appreciate It

10 b g; Trainer Willie Mullins
Chase form 113432253, best RPR 160
Left-handed 1345, best RPR 156
Right-handed 13223, best RPR 160
Cheltenham form (all) 2164, best RPR 163
At the festival 11 Mar 2020 In touch, led going well over 2f out, ridden over 1f out, headed inside final furlong, not pace of winner towards finish, finished second, beaten two and a half lengths by Ferny Hollow in Champion Bumper 16 Mar 2021 Jumped well, travelled strongly, chased clear leader, steady headway and pressed leader before 3rd, led going easily 2 out, shaken up and went clear before last, 6 lengths ahead when left clear 15 lengths ahead last, pushed out, impressive, won Supreme Novices' Hurdle by 24 lengths from Ballyadam 15 Mar 2022 Led, headed before 3rd, not fluent 3rd, led again before 5 out, pushed along and headed after 2 out, ridden and weakened before last, finished sixth, beaten nine and a quarter lengths by Honeysuckle in Champion Hurdle 16 Mar 2023 Held up in rear, not fluent 10th, headway when mistake 4 out, went third 2 out, soon hung badly left, ridden run-in, no extra and lost third final strides, finished fourth, beaten four and a half lengths by Stage Star in Turners Novices' Chase

A runaway winner of the 2021 Supreme Novices' Hurdle, he hasn't quite hit the same heights since, although it looked like he might when he won his first two outings over fences last season. It seems hard to believe now, but he was 11-8 favourite when a ten-length third to El Fabiolo in the Irish Arkle, and after that he finished fourth in the Turners and then third and second in Grade 1s at Fairyhouse and Punchestown. His best effort as a chaser came first time this season when he split Fastorslow and a below-par Galopin Des Champs in the John Durkan at Punchestown, but there have been backward steps since with a remote fifth in the Savills and a not so distant but still well beaten third of four at Thurles. Plenty to prove and isn't going to improve at the age of ten.

Going preference Has never run on good or better

Star rating ✪

Hitman

8 b g; Trainer Paul Nicholls
Chase form 12F13223221P236092, best RPR 164
Left-handed 1133221236092, best RPR 164
Right-handed 2F22P, best RPR 164
Cheltenham form 39, best RPR 163
At the festival 16 Mar 2023 Prominent, not fluent 5th, not fluent 11th, ridden 2 out, switched right and went second approaching last, lost second towards finish, finished third, beaten three lengths by Envoi Allen in Ryanair Chase

Talented albeit frustrating character who has managed just three minor chase wins in 18 starts over the last four seasons. Often runs well at a good level, though, and has managed three seconds and two thirds in Grade 1s and four seconds and a third in Grade 2s. Seemed to have lost the plot when tailed off in the Old Roan Chase on his return at Aintree, and while he ran a bit better after a wind operation on Trials day at Cheltenham, he was still a long way below form. That all changed in the Denman Chase at Newbury in February, though, when he came as close as he ever will to staying 3m and looked set for a tussle with Shishkin after the last. Ultimately he failed to quite get home, finishing just over a four-length second, with third-placed Protektorat, who he'd passed going easily just after three out, coming back at him at the line. Third in this race last year when just caught for second by Shishkin, he'll likely run well again and it won't be a surprise to see him place. It'll be quite an upset if he wins, though.

Going preference All ground seems to come alike

Star rating ✪

Fugitif

9 b g; Trainer Richard Hobson
Chase form 1P144821225413, best RPR 162
Left-handed 1P14821225413, best RPR 162
Right-handed 4, best RPR 112
Cheltenham form 222413, best RPR 162
At the festival 16 Mar 2023 Midfield, headway 3 out, went second after 2 out, made challenge last, soon ridden and edged left, kept on until no extra final 110yds, finished second, beaten two lengths by Seddon in Magners Plate Handicap Chase

Banbridge: four wins in five British starts but better ground a must

A proper Cheltenham specialist who has run plenty of good races in big handicaps at around this trip on both courses, including finishing second in the Plate last year. The only time he has finished out of the first three in six track starts came when he was fourth to Stage Star on his return in the Paddy Power Gold Cup, and he improved dramatically on that to win the December Gold Cup next time, coming from a mile back to collar Il Ridoto by a short head. That was off a mark of 151, so he still has a bit more to find, but he could arguably be marked up for that considering he was around 20 lengths behind the front two five out and that pair finished second and third. Fugitif was given a shot at Grade 1 glory next time when the Clarence House Chase was moved to Cheltenham, but he didn't have the raw speed to be competitive and finished a staying-on third to Elixir De Nutz and Jonbon, who would clearly have won easily if he hadn't nearly fallen four out. Nevertheless, it was another good run at Cheltenham over the wrong trip, and he's fully entitled to another crack at a Grade 1 over the correct distance. In a race that lacks an absolute standout performer and could attract a reasonably sized field, there are grounds for suggesting he represents a little bit of each-way value.

Going preference Best form on soft but seems happy enough on any ground
Star rating ✪✪✪

Ahoy Senor

9 b g; Trainer Lucinda Russell
Chase form U121215351F2PP43, best RPR 172
Left-handed 1121531F2PP4, best RPR 172
Right-handed U253, best RPR 155
Cheltenham form 21F4, best RPR 170
At the festival 16 Mar 2022 Took keen hold, led, not fluent and headed 7th, not fluent 14th, lost second after 4 out, mistake and lost position 3 out, soon pushed along, rallied and left in second 3 lengths down 2 out, ridden and hung left final 110yds, kept on, no match for winner, finished second, beaten three and a half lengths by L'Homme Presse in Brown Advisory Novices' Chase
17 Mar 2023 Jumped slightly right, led, fell 17th in Gold Cup won by Galopin Des Champs
Cracking horse over the last few years and was

still going well in last season's Gold Cup when falling at the 17th. After that he returned the best RPR of his life when second to Shishkin at Aintree, which does appear to be his favourite track. First two outings this season suggested his star was on the wane as he was pulled up in the Charlie Hall and the Coral Gold Cup, but there were signs of life when he finished fourth to Capodanno in the Cotswold Chase on Trials day, albeit he ran better when winning it the previous year. He wasn't helped by the fact his stirrup leather broke when he belted the third-last (usual four out), but for which he may have finished a deal closer. He's still in the Gold Cup, but he was nibbled at in the market for this and had an attempt at this sort of trip for the first time in a long while in the Betfair Chase at Ascot in February, finishing third to Pic D'Orhy and L'Homme Presse. On the face of it, he didn't exactly advertise his chances, but the winner was given an easy time in front, and he certainly showed enough pace for a drop in trip, but jumped terribly, which has, of course, been his Achilles heel for a while.

Going preference Handles all ground
Star rating ✪✪✪

OTHERS TO CONSIDER

At the final forfeit stage before the five-day declarations the likes of **Fastorslow**, **El Fabiolo** and **Edwardstone** were still among the entries, but the former is surely going to the Gold Cup and the latter pair to the Champion Chase. **Protektorat** has finished third and fifth in the last two Gold Cups and, while he was run out of things in the Denman Chase in February after making the running, it wasn't a lack of stamina that cost him, so he's probably Gold Cup-bound too. **Janidil** was second in this a couple of years ago and could have another crack, while **French Dynamite** has a Paddy Power Gold Cup second to his name but has seemingly lost the plot this season. **Pic D'Orhy** obviously has some strong form at the Ryanair trip but has not been given a full profile because he has long been thought better going right-handed.

VERDICT

This is a difficult race to bet in ante-post as

RYANAIR CHASE RESULTS AND TRENDS

	FORM WINNER	AGE & WGT	Adj RPR	SP	TRAINER	BEST RPR LAST 12 MONTHS (RUNS SINCE)
23	3-317 Envoi Allen C, D	9 11-10	171⁻¹²	13-2	H de Bromhead (IRE)	won Down Royal Gd1 Chase (3m) (1)
22	1-211 Allaho CD	8 11-10	182ᵀ	4-7f	W Mullins (IRE)	won Gd1 Ryanair Chase (2m4½f) (3)
21	3-641 Allaho D	7 11-10	171⁻⁵	3-1f	W Mullins (IRE)	won Thurles Gd2 chs (2m4f) (0)
20	1-212 Min D	9 11-10	182ᵀ	2-1	W Mullins (IRE)	won Gd1 Melling Chase (2m4f) (3)
19	-1211 Frodon CD	7 11-10	180ᵀ	9-2	P Nicholls	won Cheltenham Gd3 hcap chs (2m4½f) (1)
18	-1232 Balko Des Flos D	7 11-10	172⁻⁶	8-1	H de Bromhead (IRE)	2nd Gd1 Christmas Chase (3m) (0)
17	-1611 Un De Sceaux C, D	9 11-10	178ᵀ	7-4f	W Mullins (IRE)	won Cheltenham Gd1 chase (2m½f) (0)
16	11-12 Vautour CD	7 11-10	184ᵀ	Evensf	W Mullins (IRE)	2nd Gd1 King George VI Chase (3m) (0)
15	-418U Uxizandre C	7 11-10	170⁻⁵	16-1	A King	Won Cheltenham Listed chase (2m) (2)
14	21-25 Dynaste C, D, BF	8 11-10	179ᵀ	3-1f	D Pipe	2nd Gd1 Betfair Chase (3m1f) (1)

WINS-RUNS: 6yo 0-5, 7yo 5-24, 8yo 2-33, 9yo 3-25, 10yo 0-9, 11yo 0-2, 12yo 0-3 **FAVOURITES:** £4.32

TRAINERS IN THIS Willie Mullins 5-4-20, Henry de Bromhead 2-2-10, Alan King 1-0-5, Paul Nicholls 1-1-8, Gordon Elliott 0-1-6, Nicky Henderson 0-3-10, Joseph O'Brien 0-1-1, Mouse Morris 0-0-2, Noel Meade 0-2-2, Dan Skelton 0-0-2

FATE OF FAVOURITES: 1311203112 **POSITION OF WINNER IN MARKET:** 1811322113

there has to be a major doubt about the favourite depending on ground conditions. I made the mistake of backing **Banbridge** for the Turners last season when he was a no-show because of soft ground, and his record suggests he's one of the most ground-dependent horses at the meeting. Three of the last four Thursdays at the festival have featured soft ground and, while it won't always be that way, he can't be punted right now. He'll be the one to beat on good ground because he's so effective on it, clearly likes the track and we haven't seen the best of him. Looking in advance, though, I'd rather back something each-way at a big price and **FUGITIF** makes some appeal. He clearly has a bit to find with the main protagonists, but if there's a decent-sized field on the day and a strong pace he'll have his perfect conditions and could easily run through some better-fancied rivals after the last and hit the frame. Of the others, I would place lay **Capodanno** all day long over this trip, while it would be foolish to completely write off **Ahoy Senor** based on his Ascot Chase third as that was the wrong way round for him. His jumping keeps letting him down, though.

Key trends

- No more than four runs since October, 10/10
- Rated within 6lb of RPR top-rated, 9/10
- Top-two finish in at least one of last two starts, 9/10
- Adjusted RPR of at least 171, 9/10
- No more than 12 runs over fences, 8/10
- Course winner, 7/10

Other factors

- Six winners had recorded a top-four finish in a Grade 1 or 2 chase over 3m-plus
- The first five winners (2005-2009) had either won or been placed in the Paddy Power Gold Cup or December Gold Cup. However, 2019 winner Frodon is the only one in the last ten years to have run in those races

3.30 Paddy Power Stayers' Hurdle — ITV/RTV
● 3m ● Grade 1 ● £325,000

Gordon Elliott saddled beaten favourite Teahupoo in last year's race but still won with the veteran Sire Du Berlais and he holds another strong hand. Teahupoo is one of the aces again as he tries to improve on last year's close third off a quieter preparation, having been rested since his repeat win in the Hatton's Grace at Fairyhouse in early December. Soft ground looks crucial to his chance, though, and he still has to prove he's fully effective up the Cheltenham hill. Elliott also has the year-younger Irish Point, who has come out of his Grade 1-winning novice campaign to strike at the top level as a stayer in Leopardstown's Christmas Hurdle. That gives him strong claims but he's in the same ownership as Teahupoo and it's open to question whether both will run. The other main new challenger is Crambo, who won the Grade 1 Long Walk at Ascot and offers plenty of hope that trainer Fergal O'Brien can make his festival breakthrough this year. There are plenty of old faces too, including past winners Sire Du Berlais, Flooring Porter (Gavin Cromwell) and Paisley Park (Emma Lavelle) and several high-class performers who have switched from chasing back to hurdling for various reasons. The shortest-priced of them is Emmet Mullins' 2022 Grand National winner Noble Yeats, who set up a tilt at this prize with victory over Paisley Park in the Cleeve Hurdle on Cheltenham's Trials day. Festival winners Sir Gerhard and Monkfish have also been turned back to hurdling by Willie Mullins for last-time-out successes.

Teahupoo
7 b g; Trainer Gordon Elliott
Hurdles form 11121119611341, best RPR 168
Left-handed 1193, best RPR 163
Right-handed 1121161141, best RPR 168
Cheltenham form 93, best RPR 163
At the festival 15 Mar 2022 Midfield, bit short of room 1st, pushed along and dropped to last 3 out, weakened before 2 out, finished ninth, beaten 33 lengths by Honeysuckle in Champion Hurdle
16 Mar 2023 Held up in rear, steady headway from 3 out, not fluent 2 out, switched left then ridden and pressed leader approaching last, switched right final 110yds, kept on well, finished 3rd, placed 2nd, demoted to 3rd after appeal, beaten three-quarters of a length by Sire Du Berlais in Stayers' Hurdle

High-quality hurdler who has won nine of 14 starts and went some way to proving his stamina for 3m when running out a 15-length winner of the Galmoy at Gowran Park last February. That was a dreadful race for the grade, though, and Teahupoo was just held by Sire Du Berlais and Dashel Drasher in the Stayers' Hurdle, finishing a three-quarter-length third, although he didn't get the best of runs in the straight. He was gaining on the runner-up at the line (promoted to second, demoted on appeal), although not the winner, and he was a little bit further behind Sire Du Berlais when the pair were third and fourth in the Punchestown version, having been outpaced turning in but staying on again late. Teahupoo surprised Impaire Et Passe when beating last season's Ballymore winner in the 2m4½f Hatton's Grace at Fairyhouse on his return in December, and he has been deliberately kept fresh for this, which is understandable given he won on his debut and has form figures after a break of at least 52 days of 1111111. The ground, however, may be the biggest key, as he's one of two big-race favourites on the Thursday card who appear very ground-dependent. However, while it's case of the quicker the better for Ryanair favourite Banbridge, the opposite is true of Teahupoo, who is 111111131 on soft or worse with a best RPR of 166, but 21964 on good to soft or quicker with a best RPR of 157.

Going preference The more mud the better
Star rating ✪✪✪✪

Irish Point

6 gr g; Trainer Gordon Elliott
Hurdles form 12241111, best RPR 159
Left-handed 24111, best RPR 159
Right-handed 121, best RPR 154

Very useful novice last season who swerved Cheltenham but bagged his Grade 1 when stepped back up to 2m4f in the Mersey Novices' Hurdle at Aintree in April, winning by a comfortable three and a half lengths in a race that has produced plenty of winners. He proved he had the pace for 2m when giving 13lb and a near two-length beating to the talented mare Magical Zoe in a Grade 3 at Down Royal on his return, but then provided connections with a quandary when he cruised to an 11-length success in the Grade 1 2m7½f Christmas Hurdle at Leopardstown on heavy ground. That was a very steadily run race and his stamina will face a sterner test if he lines up. The quandary is because he's in the same ownership as favourite Teahupoo, and trainer Gordon Elliott said in his pre-Cheltenham Stable Tour he was at least half considering taking on Constitution Hill in the Champion Hurdle instead. It may all depend on how suitable the ground looks like being for Teahupoo. Irish Point surely has far too much to find to win Tuesday's big race, but he had a Grade 1 bumper success to his name over Il Est Francais in France and has been very classy since day one.

Going preference No obvious issues.
Star rating ✪✪✪✪

Irish Point: young up-and-comer in the staying division —

Crambo

7 b g; Trainer Fergal O'Brien
Hurdles form 1P117131, best RPR 159
Left-handed P1713, best RPR 141
Right-handed 111, best RPR 159

Won both bumpers and had a good first season over hurdles, winning three of his first four starts, including the big EBF Final on heavy ground at Sandown the weekend before the Cheltenham Festival. He found the step up to Grade 1 company too much for him at Aintree on his final start, finishing only seventh to Irish Point, but has made rapid further progress this season. That started when he won the 2m4f Aintree handicap hurdle taken by Paisley Park at the start of his Stayers' Hurdle-winning season, and while he couldn't emulate that one by winning the big 3m handicap hurdle at Haydock on his next outing, he probably should have done as he was given plenty to do and encountered trouble in the straight before powering home fastest of all to finish third. He did emulate Paisley Park by winning the Grade 1 Long Walk Hurdle at Ascot next time out, though, and the horse he beat was none other than Paisley Park, the veteran failing by just a short head to win that race for the third time. It's fair to say, however, that Paisley Park is not nearly as good as he was a few years ago, so Crambo is going to have to improve again, although that's perfectly plausible given his profile, and he has been kept fresh for this.

Going preference Best form on heavy last season, best form on good this season
Star rating ○○○

Noble Yeats

9 b g; Trainer Emmet Mullins
Hurdles form 121, best RPR 150
Left-handed 11, best RPR 150
Right-handed 2, best RPR 128
Cheltenham form (all) 9341, best RPR 170
At the festival 15 Mar 2022 Towards rear, steady headway into midfield 11th, raced wide and ridden 3 out, weakened before 2 out, finished ninth, beaten 19 and three-quarter lengths by Corach Rambler in Ultima Handicap Chase
17 Mar 2023 Prominent, lost position 9th, not fluent 10th, dropped to rear and pushed along 15th, behind when ridden 4 out, stayed on from 2 out, went fourth towards finish, finished fourth, beaten 15 lengths by Galopin Des Champs in Gold Cup

It's not unusual for a Grand National horse to enjoy a prep over hurdles, but it is for one to take in Grade 1 company as part of its build-up, but that has been the plan for Noble Yeats en route to a third crack at the Aintree prize he won in 2022 (fourth last year). He's remarkably light on hurdling experience as after winning a weak maiden on his debut in that sphere in March 2021 he was sent straight over fences. The second run over hurdles didn't come until December this season, when he was a beaten 10-11 shot over 2m4f at Limerick, recording an RPR of just 128. However, irrespective of his odds, that trip was always going to be way too short and Noble Yeats showed what he was capable of when edging out Paisley Park by a head in the Cleeve Hurdle on Trials day in January. He was receiving 6lb from the 12-year-old runner-up, though, and he's likely to need to step up on that by around a stone to be winning this. Having finished fourth in last year's Gold Cup, he has the requisite class, but even 3m is short for him these days and it's going to have to be a proper slog for him to get competitive.

Going preference Handles any ground
Star rating ○○

Sir Gerhard

9 b g; Trainer Willie Mullins
Hurdles form 11131, best RPR 158
Left-handed 111, best RPR 157
Right-handed 31, best RPR 158
Cheltenham form (all) 119, best RPR 154
At the festival 17 Mar 2021 Made all, pushed along and 4 lengths ahead home turn, reduced lead when ridden and hung right final furlong, kept on, always doing enough, won Champion Bumper by half a length from Kilcruit
16 Mar 2022 Held up in rear, headway into midfield after 4th, mistake 4 out, tracked leaders going easily 3 out, pushed along after 2 out, 4 lengths down and ridden when left in second last, held but kept on run-in, won Ballymore Novices' Hurdle by three and a half lengths from Three Stripe Life
15 Mar 2023 In rear, headway 5 out, went fourth before 2 out, shaken up and weakened quickly after 2 out, finished ninth, beaten 46 lengths by The Real Whacker in Brown Advisory Novices' Chase

Another who has reverted to hurdles from fences, but in his case because he's been a failure over the bigger obstacles, winning only on his chase debut last season in a three-runner race at odds of 1-6 despite nearly falling at the third. It was a big ask for him to go straight to the Brown Advisory after that, but given his Cheltenham record (Champion Bumper and Ballymore winner) he was sent off at just 3-1 before finishing a 46-length last of the nine finishers, having travelled strongly (without jumping that well) for a long way but weakened quickly from two out. He did finish second in a 2m4f Grade 1 at Fairyhouse in April, but then made mistakes and was pulled up over 3m at Punchestown 16 days later, and he fell on his return behind Dinoblue at Naas in November. That led to the return to hurdles and Sir Gerhard showed he retained all his ability with a straightforward success in a conditions event at Punchestown over 2m3f. How much ability he has is open to question, though, as neither of his Cheltenham wins came in vintage renewals and he has yet to record an RPR as high as 160 or, just as importantly, give any indication he wants to go 3m.

Going preference Highly effective on soft
Star rating ✪

Monkfish
10 ch g; Trainer Willie Mullins
Hurdles form 2111291, best RPR 160
Left-handed 1, best RPR 154
Right-handed 211291, best RPR 160
Cheltenham form (all) 11, best RPR 170
At the festival 13 Mar 2020 Prominent, led 3rd, headed 6th, remained handy, blundered 8th, led on bend between last 2, edged right when strongly pressed approaching last, headed run-in, rallied to regain lead near finish, won Albert Bartlett Novices' Hurdle by a neck from Latest Exhibition
17 Mar 2021 Led, not fluent 2nd, not fluent and headed but close up 8th, disputed lead 14th, led 3 out, three and a half lengths ahead and going easily when blundered last, ridden run-in, won Brown Advisory Novices' Chase by six and a half lengths from Fiddlerontheroof

Another dual festival winner on the comeback trail for Willie Mullins, Monkfish won the Albert Bartlett in 2020 and the Brown Advisory the following year, and was one of the favourites for the Gold Cup before suffering an injury and missing the best part of two years. Eased back into action over hurdles with a creditable second to Asterion Forlonge in a 2m4f Grade 2 at Fairyhouse last April and was then tailed-off last in the Champion Stayers Hurdle at Punchestown. That led to another nine months off the track, but Monkfish was back with a bang in the Galmoy at Gowran in late January with a five-and-a-half-length success from Summerville Boy. What he achieved is hard to tell as the runner-up was a 12-year-old rated only 141, but Mullins evidently retains faith in him as he was still talking about taking on stablemate Galopin Des Champs in the Gold Cup in his pre-Cheltenham Stable Tour. That would be a considerably stiffer task than this – and this is stiff enough.

Going preference Acts on any ground
Star rating ✪

Paisley Park
12 b g; Trainer Emma Lavelle
Hurdles form
122011111117213P3331352137222, best RPR 172
Left-handed 220111111723P331323722, best RPR 172
Right-handed 1113512, best RPR 164
Cheltenham form 01117313372, best RPR 172
At the festival 16 Mar 2018 Raced keenly in midfield, lost place after 6th, behind 8th, finished 13th, beaten 53 and three-quarter lengths by Kilbricken Storm in Albert Bartlett Novices' Hurdle
14 Mar 2019 Looked well, midfield, headway before 2 out, ridden before bend between last 2, closed for pressure to lead approaching last where mistake, pressed early run-in, stayed on well to draw away final 75yds, won Stayers' Hurdle by two and three-quarter lengths from Sam Spinner
12 Mar 2020 Midfield, headway approaching 7th, ridden after 3 out, hit 2 out, effort when hampered on bend between last 2, no impression under pressure approaching last, weakened final 100yds, finished seventh, beaten 14 and a half lengths by Lisnagar Oscar in Stayers' Hurdle
18 Mar 2021 Towards rear, pushed along before 4 out, raced wide and steady headway after 3 out, soon ridden and outpaced, rallied and close up when edged left before last, kept on final 110yds, went third towards finish, finished

third, beaten five lengths by Flooring Porter in Stayers' Hurdle

17 Mar 2022 Slowly into stride, held up in rear, not fluent 1st, pushed along after 3 out, outpaced and still plenty to do 2 out, soon ridden, rallied before last, went third inside final 110yds, stayed on, finished third, beaten two and three-quarter lengths by Flooring Porter in Stayers' Hurdle

16 Mar 2023 Always towards rear, pushed along briefly 4 out, ridden and outpaced after 3 out, minor headway approaching last, finished seventh, beaten 12 and a quarter lengths by Sire Du Berlais in Stayers' Hurdle

It's five years since Paisley Park went through a career-best season which culminated in his victory in this race, and while he has had his share of big days since – two more Long Walk Hurdles and two more Cleeve Hurdles – there is little doubt he's a shadow of his former self in terms of ability. The enthusiasm hasn't dulled one iota and he was less than a length away from compiling an unbeaten first half of the season, the only problem being he hasn't won once. He went down battling by a head conceding 6lb to Dashel Drasher in the Long Distance Hurdle at Newbury in December, while there was only a short head between him and Crambo in the Long Walk at Ascot, the pair pulling six lengths ahead of Dashel Drasher. Noble Yeats did him by a neck in the Cleeve at Cheltenham, but that one was also receiving 6lb, so in three runs Paisley Park has come out best at the weights twice and been inches from being so on the other occasion. Crambo and Noble Yeats are considerably shorter than he is in the betting for the obvious reason that he's 12 now, but he won't give up if within hailing distance at the last and it won't be that much of a surprise if he beats a few of his better fancied rivals on the day.

Going preference Acts on all ground
Star rating ✪✪

Sire Du Berlais

12 b g; Trainer Gordon Elliott
Hurdles form 3130248861849411322P40145 5P41137, best RPR 166
Left-handed 314861849411322P4015P4117, best RPR 166
Right-handed 3028453, best RPR 159
Cheltenham form 411201, best RPR 165

At the festival 16 Mar 2018 Mid-division, headway after 2 out, soon ridden, stayed on to go 4th final 120yds but not pace to get on terms, finished fourth, beaten seven and a half lengths by Blow By Blow in Martin Pipe Conditional Jockeys' Handicap Hurdle

14 Mar 2019 Midfield, jumped slowly 2nd, ridden when not much room and hampered on bend after 3 out, headway 2 out, chased leaders before last, stayed on gamely to lead final 75yds, driven out, won Pertemps Final by a neck from Tobefair

12 Mar 2020 Midfield, pushed along briefly after 8th and 9th, headway 2 out, challenging approaching last, led inside final 100yds, stayed on gamely, won Pertemps Final by half a length from The Storyteller

18 Mar 2021 Held up in midfield, not fluent 3rd, steady headway 3 out, pushed along and went third after 2 out, ridden and outpaced before last, rallied and went second final 110yds, soon edged right, kept on, no match for winner, finished second, beaten three and a quarter lengths by Flooring Porter in Stayers' Hurdle

17 Mar 2022 Towards rear of midfield, badly hampered by faller and dropped to rear 4th, steady headway when on outer from 7th, midfield when ridden after 2 out, made no impression, finished 11th, beaten 11 and three-quarter lengths by Third Wind in Pertemps Final

16 Mar 2023 Midfield, mistake 5 out, headway on inner just before 2 out, ridden after 2 out, pressed leaders approaching last, led final 110yds, kept on well, won Stayers' Hurdle by three-quarters of a length from Dashel Drasher

Hardy battler with one of the best Cheltenham Festival records in recent seasons, having compiled form figures on the track in March of 411201. Having won back to back Pertemps Finals in 2019 and 2020 and then finished second to Flooring Porter in the 2021 Stayers', he was made joint-favourite for another crack at the Pertemps but could manage only a midfield finish, his days of being a challenger seemingly over. He was having none of it, though, and whether by accident or design (he missed the Warwick Pertemps qualifier with a vet's certificate) he ended up back in the Stayers' at the age of 11 last year and powered up the centre of the track for a famous three-quarter-length victory from Dashel Drasher and favourite Teahupoo. To confirm that wasn't some sort of fluke, he then won the Liverpool Hurdle for the second year in a row before failing to complete a remarkable treble by just three-quarters of a length at Punchestown, where he finished third to Klassical Dream and Asterion Forlonge but was one place ahead of Teahupoo. Given a long break after that, Sire Du Berlais was a tailed-off seventh of eight on his return in the Boyne Hurdle at Navan in February. He has only one target, though, and he's sure to go out on his shield on the day that matters most.

Going preference Fine on most surfaces
Star rating ✪✪

Flooring Porter

9 b g; Trainer Gavin Cromwell
Hurdles form 780714162132111PF21244439, best RPR 168
Left-handed 162111F21244439, best RPR 168
Right-handed 780741132P, best RPR 147
Cheltenham form (all) 1141, best RPR 168
At the festival 18 Mar 2021 Jumped well, made all, going easily 2 out, shaken up and went clear approaching last, kept on strongly, unchallenged, won Stayers' Hurdle by three and a quarter lengths from Sire Du Berlais
17 Mar 2022 Jumped well, made all, soon 4 lengths ahead, reduced lead but going easily after 3 out, shaken up when jumped left last, pushed along and went clear final 110yds, unchallenged, won Stayers' Hurdle by two and three-quarter lengths from Thyme Hill
16 Mar 2023 Soon led, set good pace, clear before 5 out, reduced lead 3 out, mistake 2 out, ridden and headed approaching last, hung left run-in, no extra final 110yds, finished fourth, beaten three and a half lengths by Sire Du Berlais in Stayers' Hurdle

Sire Du Berlais: last year's win extended his superb record at Cheltenham

Back-to-back winner of this in 2021 and 2022 and lost his crown when only fourth to Sire Du Berlais last season. That was the first winless season of his career, and after failing to reverse form in the Liverpool Hurdle (third) and finishing tailed off in France, he was sent for a chase campaign this term. Things started well enough as he again showed how much he likes Cheltenham with a cosy win from the since much-improved Broadway Boy, but going right-handed at Punchestown proved disastrous as he started hanging violently left after the fifth fence in the Florida Pearl, and while he was back going his favoured way around in the Grade 1 Neville Hotels Novice Chase, he got stuck in the mud and finished only a 16-length third behind Grangeclare West and Corbetts Cross. Gavin Cromwell seems keenest on a crack at the National Hunt Chase, but Keith Donoghue, his new rider this season, would love to have a crack on him in this. Both Stayers' Hurdle wins came on ground officially described as soft and good to soft, but in reality it was a good deal quicker, and the better the ground the better his chance in either race. He's only nine, so still young enough to be a factor, and he loves the course.

Going preference Doesn't want it too deep
Star rating ✪✪

STAYERS' HURDLE RESULTS AND TRENDS

	FORM	WINNER	AGE & WGT	Adj RPR	SP	TRAINER	BEST RPR LAST 12 MONTHS (RUNS SINCE)
23	455P4	Sire Du Berlais CD	11 11-10	166-7	33-1	G Elliott (IRE)	Won Gd1 Liverpool Hurdle (3m½f) (5)
22	1-PF2	Flooring Porter CD	7 11-10	173-2	4-1	G Cromwell (IRE)	Won Gd1 Stayers' Hurdle (3m) (3)
21	13211	Flooring Porter D	6 11-10	169-5	12-1	G Cromwell (IRE)	Won Leopardstown Gd1 hdl (3m) (0)
20	239F3	Lisnagar Oscar D	7 11-10	155-21	50-1	R Curtis	3rd Gd2 Cleeve Hurdle (3m) (0)
19	-1111	Paisley Park CD	7 11-10	176T	11-8f	E Lavelle	won Gd2 Cleeve Hurdle (3m) (0)
18	4112-	Penhill CD, BF	7 11-10	159-10	12-1	W Mullins (IRE)	won Gd1 Albert Bartlett Nov Hurdle (3m) (1)
17	-312F	Nichols Canyon CD	7 11-10	170-2	10-1	W Mullins (IRE)	won Punchestown Gd1 hurdle (2m) (2)
16	-2111	Thistlecrack CD	8 11-10	176T	Evensf	C Tizzard	won Gd2 Cleeve Hurdle (3m) (0)
15	-1234	Cole Harden	6 11-10	162-7	14-1	W Greatrex	2nd Newbury Gd2 hdl (3m½f) (2)
14	1-111	More Of That C	6 11-10	165-14	15-2	J O'Neill	won Gd2 Relkeel Hurdle (2m4½f) (0)

WINS-RUNS: 5yo 0-2, 6yo 3-20, 7yo 5-39, 8yo 1-29, 9yo 0-17, 10yo 0-20, 11yo 1-6, 13yo 0-1 **FAVOURITES:** -£5.63

TRAINERS IN THIS RACE (w-pl-r): Willie Mullins 2-3-19, Gavin Cromwell 2-0-3, Emma Lavelle 1-2-5, Gordon Elliott 1-1-4, C Byrnes 0-0-1, Fergal O'Brien 0-0-2, Henry de Bromhead 0-0-1, Jeremy Scott 0-1-1, Nicky Henderson 0-1-8, Noel Meade 0-0-3, Joseph O'Brien 0-0-2, Jessica Harrington 0-1-5

FATE OF FAVOURITES: 2213517353 **POSITION OF WINNER IN MARKET:** 3614519729

OTHERS TO CONSIDER

Home By The Lee went off at just 9-1 last year and was far from disgraced in fifth. His opening Lismullen Hurdle third to Bob Olinger this season was a fair enough effort, but he never went a yard behind Irish Point at Leopardstown in December, hence his price now. He could easily bounce back. Last year's runner-up **Dashel Drasher** has improved his RPR with every run this season, but only because he started so poorly, and he does seem to be some way below last season's form.

VERDICT

*Teahupoo is going to be the one to beat if he gets proper soft ground as his record fresh is impeccable. There are no guarantees on that score, though, and the one I really want to be with is **IRISH POINT** if he's allowed to take on his ownermate. It may have been a soft and slowly run Christmas Hurdle he won at Leopardstown, but he has exuded class on both outings this term and is the youngest in the race. Just don't back him without the NRNB concession. **Noble Yeats**, **Sir Gerhard** and **Monkfish** are too short given the various question marks over them, and it wouldn't surprise me if the likes of **Paisley Park**, **Sire Du Berlais** and **Flooring Porter** (if he runs) beat all of those three. It just depends on*

Key trends

- Ran no more than four times since August, 9/10
- Aged six to eight, 9/10
- Top-three finish on last completed start, 8/10
- Ran between eight and 16 times over hurdles, 8/10
- Won a Graded hurdle over at least 3m, 8/10
- Previously ran at the festival, 7/10
- Adjusted RPR of at least 165, 7/10
- Finished in first three in all completed hurdle starts that season, 6/10

Other factors

- Five of the ten Irish winners since the mid-1980s prepped in the Boyne Hurdle at Navan
- The record of Cleeve Hurdle winners is 2131738

*whether the young guns, two of whom, **Crambo** and **Irish Point**, have yet to run at Cheltenham, come up to scratch. Flooring Porter might end up ahead of some of those in the market if Keith Donoghue gets his way and the ground is decent.*

4.10 TrustATrader Plate Handicap Chase — ITV/RTV
• 2m4½f • Premier Handicap • £120,000

Established in 1951 and traditionally known as the Mildmay of Flete, this is a highly competitive 2m4½f handicap chase that usually attracts a maximum field of 24.

LAST YEAR'S WINNER Seddon became a first festival winner for trainer John McConnell and conditional rider Ben Harvey with his 20-1 success. He was the fifth Irish-trained winner in eight years.

FORM Seddon was the fifth last-time-out winner to strike in the past eight runnings (one of the other winners had been second the time before).

WEIGHT AND RATINGS Eight of the last ten winners were in the 140-145 range and mostly carried less than 11st.

TRAINERS Some of the bigger stables struggle to get runners at the lower end of the handicap and Gordon Elliott (with The Storyteller in 2018) is the only one of the current big five trainers to have taken the prize in the past 16 years.

BETTING This race has been the biggest graveyard for favourites over the years. Last year the first four were all in double figures at least (fourth-placed Gevrey was 125-1).

ONES TO WATCH Leopardstown's 2m5½f handicap chase at the Dublin Racing Festival is worth checking, not just the winner **Heart Wood** (Henry de Bromhead) but also unplaced horses like **Inothewayurthinkin** (Gavin Cromwell). Course regulars **Ga Law** (Jamie Snowden) and **Il Ridoto** (Paul Nicholls) could be in the home defence.

PLATE RESULTS AND TRENDS

	FORM WINNER	AGE & WGT	OR	SP	TRAINER	BEST RPR LAST 12 MONTHS (RUNS SINCE)
23	F2311 **Seddon** C, D	10 10-9	143-2	20-1	J McConnell (IRE)	won Leopardstown hcap ch (2m5f) **(0)**
22	2F187 **Coole Cody** CD	11 11-2	145-2	22-1	E Williams	won Cheltenham Gd3 hcap ch (2m1½f) **(2)**
21	14131 **The Shunter** C, D	8 10-5	140ᵀ	9-4f	E Mullins (IRE)	3rd Leopardstown hcp ch (2m1½f) **(0)**
20	-1121 **Simply The Betts** CD	7 11-4	149ᵀ	10-3f	H Whittington	won Cheltenham class 2 hcap ch (2m4½f) **(0)**
19	3-111 **Siruh Du Lac** CD	6 10-8	141-6	9-2	N Williams	won Cheltenham Gd3 hcap ch (2m4½f) **(0)**
18	-2137 **The Storyteller** D	7 11-4	147-7	5-1f	G Elliott (IRE)	7th Leopardstown Gd1 nov ch (2m5f) **(0)**
17	14322 **Road To Respect**	6 10-13	145-16	14-1	N Meade (IRE)	3rd Leopardstown Gd1 nov ch (2m1f) **(2)**
16	-F2P1 **Empire Of Dirt** D	9 10-11	142-13	16-1	C Murphy (IRE)	2nd Punchestown hcp ch (2m6f) **(2)**
15	7/157 **Darna** D	9 10-11	140-6	33-1	K Bailey	won Sedgefield class 3 hcp ch (2m3½f) **(2)**
14	P18-P **Ballynagour** D	8 10-9	140-1	12-1	D Pipe	8th Cheltenham Gd3 hcap ch (2m5f) **(1)**

WINS-RUNS: 5yo 0-2, 6yo 2-18, 7yo 2-42, 8yo 2-52, 9yo 2-47, 10yo 1-40, 11yo 1-12, 12yo 0-5 **FAVOURITES:** +£3.58

FATE OF FAVOURITES: 22PP12112P **POSITION OF WINNER IN MARKET:** 6087121180

Key trends

- Won between 2m3f and 2m5f, 10/10
- No more than 11 runs over fences, 8/10
- Won a Class 3 or higher, 8/10
- Officially rated 140 to 145, 8/10
- Carried no more than 10st 13lb, 7/10

Other factors

- Only two of the last ten winners placed in one of the big 2m4f-2m5f handicaps at Cheltenham that season (Siruh Du Lac and Coole Cody)
- Irish trainers have won five of the last eight runnings (their last winner before them was Doubleuagain in 1982)
- Five winners scored last time out but four of the other five failed to place

4.50 Ryanair Mares' Novices' Hurdle

● 2m1f   ● Grade 2   ● £105,000

RTV

Ireland took the first six runnings after this race was introduced in 2016 but the home side has hit back with consecutive wins for Harry Fry with Love Envoi and Jamie Snowden with You Wear It Well.

Those two came from further down the betting at 15-2 and 16-1 but Britain has one of the leading fancies this time in unbeaten course winner Dysart Enos, whose trainer Fergal O'Brien is seeking a first festival success and could have a big day as he's also set to field Stayers' Hurdle contender Crambo.

Of course the top Irish yards have plenty of ammunition and Jade De Grugy (Willie Mullins) and Brighterdaysahead (Gordon Elliott) are well ahead of Dysart Enos on Racing Post Ratings. Those two are unbeaten and have won at Grade 3 level this season.

Other possibles include Fun Fun Fun (Mullins), Joyeuse (Nicky Henderson) and Queens Gamble (Harry Derham).

MARES' NOVICES' HURDLE RESULTS

	FORM WINNER	AGE & WGT	Adj RPR	SP	TRAINER	BEST RPR LAST 12 MONTHS (RUNS SINCE)
23	-1121 **You Wear It Well** D	6 11-7	143-6	16-1	J Snowden	won Sandown Gd2 nov hdl (2m4f) (0)
22	-1111 **Love Envoi** D	6 11-7	140-8	15-2	H Fry	won Sandown Gd2 nov hdl (2m4f) (0)
21	13113 **Telmesomethinggirl** D	6 11-2	149-4	5-1	H de Bromhead(IRE)	3rd Leopardstown hcap hdl (2m2f) (0)
20	2-433 **Concertista**	6 11-2	154T	9-2	W Mullins (IRE)	3rd Leopardstown hcap hdl (2m2f) (0)
19	1-13 **Eglantine Du Seuil** D	5 11-2	135-13	50-1	W Mullins (IRE)	3rd Listowel nov hdl (2m) (0)
18	F2-11 **Laurina** D	5 11-7	155T	4-7f	W Mullins (IRE)	won Fairyhouse Gd3 nov hdl (2m2f) (0)
17	21111 **Let's Dance** D	5 11-7	153T	11-8f	W Mullins (IRE)	won Leopardstown Gd2 nov hdl (2m4f) (0)
16	11 **Limini** D	5 11-7	148-4	8-11f	W Mullins (IRE)	won Fairyhouse Gd3 nov hdl (2m2f) (0)

WINS-RUNS: 4yo 0-8, 5yo 4-56, 6yo 4-57, 7yo 0-19, 8yo 0-5 **FAVOURITES:** -£2.33

TRAINERS IN THIS RACE (w-pl-r): Willie Mullins 5-3-31, Henry de Bromhead 1-2-12, Paul Nicholls 0-0-2, Gordon Elliott 0-3-10, Fergal O'Brien 0-1-2, Nicky Henderson 0-2-14, John McConnell 0-0-1, Jessica Harrington 0-0-3, Peter Fahey 0-0-1

FATE OF FAVOURITES: 11190004 **POSITION OF WINNER IN MARKET:** 11103248

Key trends

- Aged five or six, 8/8
- Top-three finish last time out, 8/8
- Top-three finish in a Listed or Graded hurdle, 8/8
- Adjusted RPR of at least 143, 6/8
- Rated within 6lb of RPR top-rated, 6/8
- Two to four hurdle starts, 6/8

Other factors

- Six winners had won over further than 2m1f
- One was still a maiden but she was beaten a short head in the race the previous year
- Willie Mullins has trained five of the eight winners (the first five)

5.30 Fulke Walwyn Kim Muir Handicap Chase   RTV
• 3m2f   • Amateur riders   • £75,000

LAST YEAR'S WINNER A fourth success in five years for Ireland as 10-1 shot Angels Dawn became a first festival winner for trainer Sam Curling and rider Patrick King. The first seven were Irish-trained.

FORM There is a trend of Kim Muir winners bouncing back from disappointing efforts (14 of the past 23 winners had been unplaced on their previous run).

WEIGHT AND RATINGS The higher-rated runners have started to do well and 11 of the last 15 winners carried 11st 4lb or more.

AGE Only four horses aged older than nine have won in the last 30 runnings and horses aged seven or eight have won ten of the last 13.

TRAINERS This tends to get shared around and Curling was the 11th different winning trainer in the past 12 runnings. Gordon Elliott has become the most powerful force with two winners, two seconds, two thirds and two fourths from 18 runners.

BETTING Only one favourite has won in the past decade but most winners in that time have come from the top six in the market.

ONES TO WATCH Ireland has to be the first port of call and a chief fancy is **Good Time Jonny**, who looks set to bid for a second consecutive festival win after taking last year's Pertemps Final Handicap Hurdle for trainer Tony Martin. **Perceval Legallois** (Gavin Cromwell) and **Cool Survivor** (Gordon Elliott) are likely types. **Angels Dawn** will have to defy a higher mark to make it back-to-back wins for Sam Curling.

KIM MUIR HANDICAP CHASE RESULTS AND TRENDS

	FORM WINNER	AGE & WGT	OR	SP	TRAINER	BEST RPR LAST 12 MONTHS (RUNS SINCE)
23	8421U **Angels Dawn** BF	8 11-0	131-9	10-1	S Curling (IRE)	Unseated Punchestown hcap ch (3m4f) **(0)**
22	12211 **Chambard** (5x)	10 10-12	134-10	40-1	V Williams	won Hunt class 3 nov hcap ch (2m7½f) **(0)**
21	0-312 **Mount Ida**	7 11-9	142-10	3-1f	D Foster (IRE)	2nd Thurles Gd2 nov ch (2m4f) **(0)**
20	52422 **Milan Native**	7 11-1	141-2	9-1	G Elliott (IRE)	2nd Thurles nov ch (2m2f) **(3)**
19	-5253 **Any Second Now**	7 11-11	143-4	6-1	T Walsh (IRE)	5th Leopardstown hcap ch (3m½f) **(1)**
18	-P632 **Missed Approach**	8 11-5	138-2	8-1	W Greatrex	8th Scottish Grand National (4m1f) **(4)**
17	45683 **Domesday Book**	7 11-4	137-6	40-1	S Edmunds	3rd Leicester class 3 hcap ch (2m4f) **(0)**
16	8-005 **Cause Of Causes** C	8 11-9	142-6	9-2	G Elliott (IRE)	5th Naas Gd2 ch (2m) **(0)**
15	30-6P **The Package** CD	12 11-4	137T	9-1	D Pipe	6th Cheltenham Gd3 hcap ch (3m3½f) **(1)**
14	13280 **Spring Heeled** (2ow)	7 11-8	140-5	12-1	J Culloty (IRE)	2nd Limerick hcap ch (3m) **(2)**

WINS-RUNS: 6yo 0-12, 7yo 5-45, 8yo 3-62, 9yo 0-53, 10yo 1-26, 11yo 0-16, 12yo 1-7, 13yo 0-2 **FAVOURITES:** -£6.00

FATE OF FAVOURITES: 00UU287122 **POSITION OF WINNER IN MARKET:** 6320326105

Key trends

- Officially rated 134 to 142, 8/10
- Aged seven to nine, 8/10
- No more than ten runs over fences, 8/10
- Rated within 6lb of RPR top-rated, 7/10 (last three winners the exceptions)
- Ran at a previous festival, 7/10
- Finished in first three in either or both of last two starts, 7/10
- Ran over at least 3m last time, 6/10

Other factors

- Irish trainers have won six of the last ten runnings – the last Irish-trained winner before them was Greasepaint in 1983
- Four winners had yet to win over three miles or beyond

FRIDAY, MARCH 15
(NEW COURSE)

PAUL KEALY
ON THE KEY
PLAYERS

1.30 JCB Triumph Hurdle
• 2m1f • Grade 1 • £135,000

ITV/RTV

The standout performance in this division came on Cheltenham's Trials day when the Nicky Henderson-trained Sir Gino overpowered previous Triumph favourite Burdett Road with a hugely impressive ten-length victory over course and distance. His trainer is the record-holder in this race and has excellent prospects of an eighth success with his latest highly promising recruit. The Spring Juvenile Hurdle, well established as the best proving ground in Ireland, did not produce anything that measured up to Sir Gino in quite a bunched finish. Several of the principals are likely to head here, although as with so many races the decision making of Willie Mullins will be crucial as he had the first four (Kargese, Storm Heart, Majborough and Bunting), albeit all with different high-profile owners. Burdett Road, a Royal Ascot winner last summer and twice an impressive winner over hurdles before coming up against Sir Gino, is not out of it for Newmarket trainer James Owen, although a turnaround with the favourite looks difficult. Salver (Gary Moore) and Liari (Paul Nicholls) are other British possibles.

Sir Gino
4 b g; Trainer Nicky Henderson
Hurdles form 111, best RPR 143
Left-handed 11, best RPR 143
Right-handed 1, best RPR 127
Cheltenham form 1, best RPR 143

Listed hurdle winner on debut at Auteuil in April and justified lofty reputation on first run for Nicky Henderson when scooting home by 14 lengths under a penalty in a juvenile contest at Kempton over Christmas. That race didn't look particularly good on paper at the time, but the runner-up won his next two and third scored next time as well. What they were like behind him became irrelevant anyway when Sir Gino stormed to the head of the Triumph Hurdle market with a deeply impressive ten-length success from previous favourite and Royal Ascot winner Burdett Road. He had clearly learned plenty from that Kempton run a month earlier as his jumping was considerably better, particularly at the last, although he didn't really need a good one considering how well he was going. Big horse who will surely jump a fence sooner rather than later, but right now is in pole position to give the race's most successful trainer an eighth Triumph and it's hard to argue with his odds-on quotes.

Going preference Has won on heavy and good to soft
Star rating ✪✪✪✪✪

Majborough
4 b g; Trainer Willie Mullins
Hurdles form (left-handed) 13, best RPR 138

Another big horse who is likely to prove a long-term chaser rather than a hurdler, and is evidently highly regarded by Willie Mullins, who in his recent pre-Cheltenham Stable Tour said: "Every time I see him, I think of the Gold Cup rather than the Triumph Hurdle." It's going to be the Triumph first, though, and in it he's going to have to reverse form with a couple of stablemates let alone deal with Sir Gino, as he was only third to Kargese and Storm Heart in the Grade 1 Spring Juvenile Hurdle at the Dublin Racing Festival and was beaten just under two lengths. His two rivals were race-fit, though, whereas he was having his first run since a debut success at Auteuil in early April, and both of them were ahead of him in the betting. There's no doubt he filled the eye on looks, however. Six of the last seven Irish-trained Triumph winners ran in the Spring, and four of them were beaten there, so his defeat is far from a negative, and it just depends how strong the form is. With five horses finishing within three lengths of each other and another who probably would have if he'd been put in the race earlier, that is the big question.

Going preference Has raced only on soft
Star rating ✪✪✪

Kargese

4 b f; Trainer Willie Mullins
Hurdles form (left-handed) 12121, best RPR 133

Won two of three spring outings in mares' company at Auteuil, including a Grade 3, before joining Willie Mullins in the ownership of Kenny Alexander and it has been Graded races all the way since. Second to Kala Conti in the Grade 2 South Dublin Juvenile Hurdle at Leopardstown over Christmas, she reversed that form in the Grade 1 Spring Juvenile Hurdle at the same track in February, beating three stablemates with Kala Conti back in fifth, albeit beaten only two and three-quarter lengths. She's certainly a battler as she made a mess of the last but still kept pulling out more, but she can be keen (wears a hood) so will have to deal well with the preliminaries, and there might be others better suited to the ground if we get a dry festival. While the Irish have dominated the Triumph in recent years, the Spring form has been overturned more often than not.

Going preference Untried on good, goes very well on soft
Star rating ✪✪✪

Burdett Road

4 b g; Trainer James Owen
Hurdles form 112, best RPR 130
Left-handed 12, best RPR 130
Right-handed 1, best RPR 118
Cheltenham form 12, best RPR 130

Decent Flat performer for Michael Bell and won the Golden Gates Handicap at Royal Ascot off a mark of 90 before running with some credit in Group company afterwards. Subsequently gelded and switched by his owners to James Owen for a hurdling campaign, he got off to the best possible start when cantering to a 12-length success at Huntingdon in November. The opposition was far from challenging, but he did show a reasonable aptitude for jumping, although a first-time hood didn't stop him from racing keenly. Just a couple of weeks later he leapt to the head of the Triumph market after showing a smart change of pace on the run-in to beat subsequent winner An Bradan Feasa in a Triumph Trial at the Paddy Power meeting. On that occasion he didn't jump at all well in an eventful race, but his Flat class was there for all to see. The acid test came in the Grade 2 trial over the Triumph course and distance in January, though, and it's one he failed, going down by ten lengths to new odds-on Triumph favourite Sir Gino. He actually jumped a lot better but still raced keenly for the best part of a circuit and, while he still looked to be going well enough approaching the last, he couldn't pick up. Rider Harry Cobden wasn't hard on him after the last, but that was equally true of James Bowen on the winner, and it's hard to see how he turns the form around if he doesn't learn to settle. Connections won't be throwing in the towel just yet, but while Sir Gino's performance had Triumph Hurdle winner written all over it, Burdett Road's screamed Aintree.

Going preference Handles soft, but good to firm winner at Royal Ascot and better ground will help
Star rating ✪✪

Storm Heart

4 b g; Trainer Willie Mullins
Hurdles form 12, best RPR 139
Left-handed 2, best RPR 139
Right-handed 1, best RPR 132

Would have been rated around 75 on the Flat in France after five runs in the provinces, and burst on to the Triumph scene with a 22-length Punchestown success for Willie Mullins at the end of December. The race was run at a crawl, but he took up the running only approaching the last and showed an impressive change of gear. That run was enough to make him a strong initial favourite for the Spring Juvenile Hurdle at Leopardstown, but he was pretty weak in the market on the day, although still went off jolly. He didn't do much wrong either, but there seemed to be no excuses with his second to Kargese, and the market now expects both the winner and the less experienced third to have his measure at Cheltenham.

Going preference Has run mostly on soft/heavy but Flat win was on good
Star rating ✪✪

Givemefive

4 b g; Trainer Harry Derham
Hurdles form 11, best RPR 124
Left-handed 1, best RPR 124
Right-handed 1, best RPR 103

Won one of ten starts on the Flat for Johnny Murtagh and was rated just 69. However, he has started well over hurdles with wins at Market Rasen and Warwick, the second by 18 lengths under a penalty. Form isn't strong, though, and initial target was the Fred Winter, although he needs another run for that.

Going preference Best Flat form away from soft ground
Star rating ✪✪

Liari

4 b g; Trainer Paul Nicholls
Hurdles form 111, best RPR 126
Left-handed 1, best RPR 118
Right-handed 11, best RPR 126

Rated around 7lb better than Storm Heart on the Flat in France and, while his hurdles form doesn't compare, he's unbeaten in three, including Listed races at Aintree and Musselburgh. Trainer called him a horse for the future, and was in no rush to commit him for this. He did give him an entry, though, which is more than he did with Aintree Grade 1 winner Monmiral three years ago.

Going preference Has won on anything from good to heavy
Star rating ✪✪

Wodhooh

4 b f; Trainer Gordon Elliott
Hurdles form 11111, best RPR 123
Left-handed 111, best RPR 119
Right-handed 11, best RPR 123

Best form in four Flat runs was on the all-weather in Britain (rated 71) and has been very well placed by Gordon Elliott to win five in a row over hurdles. Nothing special about any of her form, though, with a top RPR of just 123, and no surprise if she goes for something easier elsewhere.

Going preference Has won on good and soft
Star rating ✪

Anzadam

4 b g; Trainer Willie Mullins
Hurdles form 11, best RPR 105
Left-handed 1, best RPR 105
Right-handed 1, best RPR 105

Was 2-2 over hurdles in France in the autumn, but hasn't managed an outing since joining Willie Mullins. Hard to know what the form is worth (no rating given in France), but did beat an odds-on dual winner easily on the second occasion. Looks a way down the pecking order, with no mention in trainer's pre-Cheltenham Stable Tour.

Going preference Has run only on soft/heavy
Star rating ✪

Bunting

4 b g; Trainer Willie Mullins
Hurdles form 114, best RPR 138
Left-handed 14, best RPR 138
Right-handed 1, best RPR 119

The fourth of five potential runners for Mullins from the Spring Juvenile Hurdle. He finished fourth, which wasn't a bad achievement considering he jumped so poorly. Will need to improve in that department, but most of the jumping is done in the early part of the race on the New course, and the way he finished suggests he'll appreciate the extra furlong.

Going preference All runs on soft/heavy
Star rating ✪✪

Mighty Bandit

4 b g; Trainer Warren Greatrex
Hurdles form 19, best RPR 128
Left-handed 9, best RPR 117
Right-handed 1, best RPR 128

First two starts for Gordon Elliott, but sold at the Andy and Gemma Brown dispersal sale in February, and it was some gamble by new connections to shell out €420,000 for a horse who finished ninth of 12 last time out. He was favourite for that Grade 2, though, and reportedly finished with a nasal discharge. He'd been impressive in a near ten-length maiden hurdle debut for his previous powerful owners in November, and is very much an unknown quantity for Warren Greatrex now.

Going preference Win was on soft
Star rating ✪

TRIUMPH HURDLE RESULTS AND TRENDS

	FORM	WINNER	AGE & WGT	Adj RPR	SP	TRAINER	BEST RPR LAST 12 MONTHS (RUNS SINCE)
23	1-112	**Lossiemouth** D, BF	4 10-9	161ᵀ	11-8f	W Mullins (IRE)	won Leopardstown Gd2 hdl (2m) **(1)**
22	21	**Vauban** D	4 11-0	158ᵀ	6-4f	W Mullins (IRE)	won Gd1 Leopardstown nov hdl (2m) **(0)**
21	1-111	**Quilixios** D	4 11-0	158⁻⁴	2-1	H de Bromhead (IRE)	won Down Royal hdl (2m½f) **(1)**
20	1	**Burning Victory** D	4 10-7	139⁻²¹	12-1	W Mullins (IRE)	won Gd3 Fairyhouse nov hdl (2m) **(0)**
19	1	**Pentland Hills** D	4 11-0	139⁻²¹	20-1	N Henderson	won Plumpton class 4 nov hdl (2m) **(0)**
18	22	**Farclas**	4 11-0	155⁻³	9-1	G Elliott (IRE)	2nd Gd1 Leopardstown nov hdl (2m) **(0)**
17	11111	**Defi Du Seuil** CD	4 11-0	164ᵀ	5-2f	P Hobbs	won Gd1 Finale Hurdle (2m) **(1)**
16	14	**Ivanovich Gorbatov** D, BF	4 11-0	149⁻⁵	9-2f	A O'Brien (IRE)	won Leopardstown maiden hdl (2m) **(1)**
15	111	**Peace And Co** CD	4 11-0	159ᵀ	2-1f	N Henderson	2nd Doncaster Gd2 hdl (2m½f) **(1)**
14	12	**Tiger Roll** D	4 11-0	150⁻²	10-1	G Elliott (IRE)	2nd Gd1 Leopardstown nov hdl (2m) **(0)**

FAVOURITES: £6.88

TRAINERS IN THIS RACE (w-pl-r): Willie Mullins 3-8-31, Gordon Elliott 2-4-8, Nicky Henderson 2-3-11, Henry de Bromhead 1-1-3, Denis Hogan 0-0-1, Noel Meade 0-0-1, Gary Moore 0-0-5, Joseph O'Brien 0-1-5, Paul Nicholls 0-0-12, Thomas Mullins 0-0-1

FATE OF FAVOURITES: 41114PU411 **POSITION OF WINNER IN MARKET:** 6111575211

Key trends

- Last ran between 18 and 55 days ago, ten winners in the last ten runnings
- Won at least 50 per cent of hurdle races, 9/10 (exception still a maiden)
- Top-two finish last time out, 9/10 (six won)
- By a Group 1-winning sire, 8/10
- Adjusted RPR of at least 150, 7/10
- Ran no more than three times over hurdles, 7/10

Other factors

- Five of the last ten winners were undefeated over hurdles (two had just run once)
- Six winners had landed Graded events
- Three winners had raced on the Flat in Britain, Ireland or France and all had recorded an RPR of at least 77
- Since the introduction of the Fred Winter Handicap Hurdle in 2005, 16 of the 19 winners have had an SP of 10-1 or shorter

Nurburgring
4 b g; Trainer Joseph O'Brien
Hurdles form 1213, best RPR 130
Left-handed 123, best RPR 130
Right-handed 1, best RPR 129

Rated as high as 96 on the Flat and has made a fair fist of hurdling, winning two of his four starts. Confirmed himself a better horse than Kala Conti on last two runs in Graded company at Fairyhouse and Leopardstown, first beating her by half a length conceding 3lb and then running a three-quarter-length third on 7lb worse terms. More needed, though.

Going preference Appreciates soft ground
Star rating ✪

Peking Opera
4 b g; Trainer Gary Moore
Hurdles form (right-handed) 1, best RPR 102

Runs in the colours of Goshen and was better than him on the Flat, carrying a rating of 105 when a six-length third to Vauban in a Group 3 at Naas in August. Made a meal of beating a 125-rated older rival who was giving him 17lb at Sandown on February hurdles debut, though, and will have to find a huge amount on that.

Going preference Acts on good or soft
Star rating ✪

Salver
4 b g; Trainer Gary Moore
Hurdles form 1111, best RPR 125
Left-handed 111, best RPR 125
Right-handed 1, best RPR 114

Same price as stablemate Peking Opera, but has miles better hurdling form, having won all four outings in comfortable fashion. The first two came in modest races at Warwick and Exeter, but he then ran out an impressive 21-length winner from the 125-rated Balboa in the Grade 2 Finale Juvenile Hurdle at Chepstow. Can't say we learned any more with an odds-on win at Haydock in February, but he's promising and "more than just a juvenile" according to Gary Moore.

Going preference Said to want soft ground
Star rating ✪✪

Golden Move
4 b g; Trainer Paul Nicholls
Hurdles form Unraced

Best form on soft or worse on the Flat, in which sphere he was rated 81 for Richard Fahey. Yet to make debut over hurdles for new trainer Paul Nicholls, but he's not averse to throwing them straight into the Adonis at Kempton to see what he's got and then leaving them as novices for the next season if they're not quite up to it.

Going preference Seems to want cut
Star rating ✪

Kala Conti
4 b f; Trainer Gordon Elliott
Hurdles form 11215, best RPR 130
Left-handed 1115, best RPR 130
Right-handed 2, best RPR 126

Ten-length winner on French debut in May and started well for Gordon Elliott, winning at Navan, running second to Nurburgring in a Grade 3 at Fairyhouse and then beating Kargese at Leopardstown, albeit in receipt of 3lb. That form was turned around in the Spring, though, with Kala Conti only fifth, although beaten less than three lengths. More than enough runs to take in the Fred Winter, but finishing that close up in a Grade 1 probably didn't help.

Going preference Acts on soft and heavy
Star rating ✪

Salvator Mundi
4 b g; Trainer Willie Mullins
Hurdles form (left-handed) 2, best RPR 110

In the same ownership as favourite Sir Gino and a length-and-three-quarter second to him when they made their debuts at Auteuil in April. Figured among the five-day entries for the Spring, but not the final line-up, and if he goes without a run it will be 11 months since he saw a racecourse.

Going preference Sole run on heavy
Star rating ✪

Ethical Diamond
4 b g; Trainer Willie Mullins
Hurdles form (left-handed) 06, best RPR 135

Showed promise in first two Flat maidens last spring at around 1m2f, but evidently appreciated the step up to 1m4½f at Limerick on final start, recording an RPR of 96 when winning going away. That was enough to persuade Willie Mullins to shell out 320,000gns for him, but in two runs over hurdles he has clawed back just £1,304. He showed very little first time when well beaten at odds of 6-5, but was much better than a 50-1 sixth in the Spring Juvenile Hurdle, finishing with some purpose under a considerate ride. Beaten just over five lengths, he could well prove a good deal better than that and, while the Fred Winter has been the plan, Mullins admitted he was struggling to get another run into him, so he might come here.

Going preference Better ground will help
Star rating ✪✪

VERDICT
*I backed **Ethical Diamond** each-way straight after the Spring as I thought he was much better than the bare result, and half those ahead of him in the race are considered the biggest dangers to **SIR GINO**. That bet will be sunk, though, if Willie Mullins manages to get another run into him before the Fred Winter on the Tuesday. In any case, Nicky Henderson's four-year-old looked the real deal when thrashing previous favourite Burdett Road on Trials day at Cheltenham, and whatever beats him is likely to have to make a huge amount of improvement.*

2.10 County Handicap Hurdle · 2m1f · Premier Handicap · £100,000 — ITV/RTV

LAST YEAR'S WINNER Faivoir struck at 33-1 for Dan Skelton, who has now won four of the last eight runnings.

FORM The Betfair Hurdle and the Liffey Handicap Hurdle at the Dublin Racing Festival have been key pointers – ten of the past 23 winners had run in one of those.

WEIGHT AND RATINGS All bar four winners since 2006 were rated in the 130s with five of the last ten having run off 137-139. Ch'tibello in 2019 and State Man in 2022 are among just ten winners since 1970 to carry more than 11st.

TRAINERS Ireland has accounted for 11 of the last 16 winners, with six of them trained by Willie Mullins. Paul Nicholls has done best of the British trainers, winning four times since 2004, but Skelton has been the one to watch recently.

BETTING Mullins' State Man (11-4 in 2022) was only the fourth market leader to succeed since 2002 (one of the others was Saint Roi for Mullins in 2020).

ONES TO WATCH Iberico Lord is a clear contender for Nicky Henderson after his Betfair Hurdle victory at Newbury. Skelton had runner-up **L'Eau Du Sud**, as well as **Faivoir** in fifth. Willie Mullins has a host of novices and handicappers to juggle, including **Zenta**, **Mistergif** and **Absurde**.

COUNTY HURDLE RESULTS AND TRENDS

	FORM WINNER	AGE & WGT	OR	SP	TRAINER	BEST RPR LAST 12 MONTHS (RUNS SINCE)
23	05-4P **Faivoir** C, D	8 10-7	134^T	33-1	D Skelton	5th Aintree cond/am hcap hdl (2m½f) (2)
22	2-F1 **State Man** D	5 11-1	141^{-9}	11-4f	W Mullins (IRE)	won Limerick mdn hdl (2m) (0)
21	12562 **Belfast Banter** D	6 10-0	129^{-8}	33-1	P Fahey (IRE)	2nd Naas Gd2 nov hdl (1m7½f) (0)
20	3-51 **Saint Roi** D	5 10-13	137^{-8}	11-2f	W Mullins (IRE)	won Tramore mdn hdl (2m) (0)
19	-5692 **Ch'tibello** D	8 11-5	146^{-3}	12-1	D Skelton	2nd Aintree class 2 hcap hdl (2m4f) (0)
18	-1023 **Mohaayed** D	6 10-8	139^{-4}	33-1	D Skelton	3rd Gd1 Christmas Hurdle (0)
17	1142- **Arctic Fire** D	8 11-12	158^{-4}	20-1	W Mullins (IRE)	Seasonal debutant (0)
16	44-12 **Superb Story** D	5 10-12	138^T	8-1	D Skelton	2nd Cheltenham Gd3 hcap hdl (2m½f) (0)
15	F580P **Wicklow Brave** D	6 11-4	138^{-1}	25-1	W Mullins (IRE)	11th Newbury Gd3 hcap hdl (2m½f) (1)
14	8-141 **Lac Fontana** CD	5 10-11	139^{-3}	11-1	P Nicholls	won Cheltenham class 2 hcap hdl (2m1f) (0)

WINS-RUNS: 5yo 4-72, 6yo 3-65, 7yo 0-60, 8yo 3-29, 9yo 0-15, 10yo 0-8, 11yo 0-1 **FAVOURITES:** +£0.25

FATE OF FAVOURITES: P046041010 **POSITION OF WINNER IN MARKET:** 5030061010

Key trends
- At least one top-three finish in last two starts, 8/10
- Aged five or six, 7/10
- Officially rated 134-141, 7/10
- Carried no more than 11st 1lb, 7/10 (two of the exceptions trained by Willie Mullins)
- No previous festival form, 7/10
- Ran no more than nine times over hurdles, 6/10

Other factors
- There have been eight winning novices since 1996
- Ireland has won five of the last ten runnings, including four for Willie Mullins. Dan Skelton has had the last four British-trained winners

2.50 Albert Bartlett Novices' Hurdle ITV/RTV
● 3m   ● Grade 1   ● £135,000

This is the most difficult of the Grade 1 novices to solve and big-priced winners are the norm, even for those who go on to reach great heights such as Gold Cup hero Minella Indo and Stayers' Hurdle winner Penhill. Two of the key form races look to be the Grade 1 Lawlor's of Naas in January (won by Willie Mullins' Readin Tommy Wrong from stablemates Ile Atlantique and Lecky Watson) and the 2m6½f Grade 1 at the Dublin Racing Festival, which had a Mullins one-two with Dancing City and Predators Gold. Mullins also has the fancied and unbeaten High Class Hero. The home team is not without hope – possibles include Challow winner Captain Teague (Paul Nicholls), Nicky Henderson's pair Shanagh Bob and Jingko Blue, Gidleigh Park (Harry Fry) and Johnnywho (Jonjo O'Neill).

Dancing City
7 ch g; Trainer Willie Mullins
Hurdles form (left-handed) 511, best RPR 152

Point winner who had some useful bumper form, most notably when splitting Ballyburn and Slade Steel at Punchestown in April. Hurdles debut at Navan in November was underwhelming as he could manage only fifth to Stellar Story, but he improved quickly to win his maiden next time and then made another huge jump to take the Grade 1 Nathaniel Lacy & Partners Solicitors Novice Hurdle at the Dublin Racing Festival. He was the fourth string of the Mullins quartet there and the outsider of the field at 16-1, but having been prominent all the way he found plenty after the last and there didn't seem to be any fluke about it. That looked a strong staying performance over the 2m6½f trip ("He didn't stop the whole way to the line," according to rider Danny Mullins) and, having been given an entry in the Baring Bingham, this is now his only remaining entry. Arguably has the best form.

Going preference Handles deep ground well but good bumper form was on quicker
Star rating ✪✪✪✪

High Class Hero
7 ch g; Trainer Willie Mullins
Hurdles form 1111, best RPR 147
Left-handed 1, best RPR 139
Right-handed 111, best RPR 147

Had three cracks at points, winning the third of them, but wasn't seen again for 18 months until winning his bumper at Listowel in June. Since then he has won all four of his hurdles starts, and been odds-on every time, with his best run being his third when he beat The Big Doyen by a comfortable seven lengths in October. The runner-up was only half a length behind subsequent Challow winner Captain Teague at Cheltenham afterwards, so there is some substance, although High Class Hero was kept low key for his warm-up, winning a bog-standard four-runner race at Thurles (2-7). Could brush up on his jumping.

Going preference Seems fine on most ground
Star rating ✪✪✪

Readin Tommy Wrong
6 b g; Trainer Willie Mullins
Hurdles form 11, best RPR 149
Left-handed 1, best RPR 149
Right-handed 1, best RPR 116

Second in a point in February 2022 before winning both bumpers last spring, then he managed to only scramble home on his hurdles debut at Cork in November. That meant he was the unconsidered one of Willie Mullins' four in the Grade 1 Lawlor's of Naas Novice Hurdle in January, but having been 33-1 overnight, he went off at just 16-1, and he stayed on to lead on the line from his much better fancied stablemae Ile Atlantique. Unlike Dancing City and High Class Hero, he still has the Baring Bingham as an option and his trainer seemed to favour it.

Going preference No obvious preference
Star rating ✪✪

Lecky Watson

6 ch g; Trainer Willie Mullins
Hurdles form 123, best RPR 138
Left-handed 23, best RPR 138
Right-handed 1, best RPR 119
Cheltenham form (bumper) 4, best RPR 134
At the festival 15 Mar 2023 In touch with leaders on outer, shaken up 2f out, ridden over 1f out, disputed lead when hampered inside final furlong, soon lost ground, no impression final 110yds, finished fourth, beaten five and a half lengths by A Dream To Share in Champion Bumper

Was all out to win a 2m7f maiden hurdle on his debut at Thurles in November and has actually shown much better form in defeat dropped back to 2m4f in two starts since. In the second of those he was beaten just half a length in the Grade 2 Navan Novice Hurdle by Slade Steel, who will be favourite for the Baring Bingham if Ballyburn doesn't run. Then he was third to Readin Tommy Wrong in the Grade 1 Lawlor's of Naas, but this time was beaten nearly eight lengths. The fact he has been to Cheltenham and run so well when unfancied (80-1 fourth in the bumper) has to be a plus, but he can also be keen and is very awkward at his hurdles sometimes, and that wouldn't bode well for a stamina test in a big field. Still in the Baring Bingham, but much shorter for this.

Going preference Acts on yielding and soft
Star rating ✪✪

Shanagh Bob

6 b g; Trainer Nicky Henderson
Hurdles form (left-handed) 11, best RPR 133
Cheltenham form 1, best RPR 133

Point winner who is 2-2 over hurdles for Nicky Henderson but is very much a work in progress. Ran green and looked in trouble turning for home at odds of 2-9 on his debut at Plumpton before finding another gear and winning comfortably in the end, and it's likely both track and trip were too short for him. Better was to come in the Grade 2 Albert Bartlett trial over 3m at Cheltenham in December, but he was again green enough and took a while to get on top, and an RPR of 133 is some way from the best of these. The

form has worked out, though, with the third and fourth winning since, the latter in the Doncaster trial. Some of the better winners of this had relatively light campaigns, while many others had their share of runs in points, bumpers and novice hurdles. They all knew their jobs, though, and unless Shanagh Bob has learned plenty since we last saw him, it's easy to see him getting lost out there.

Going preference No obvious preference
Star rating ✪✪

Captain Teague

6 ch g; Trainer Paul Nicholls
Hurdles form (left-handed) 121, best RPR 143
Cheltenham form (all) 32, best RPR 143
At the festival 15 Mar 2023 Prominent, pushed along and made challenge over 2f out, disputed lead when hung right and hampered rivals inside final furlong, soon ridden and hung left, stayed on inside final 110yds, finished third, beaten two and a half lengths by A Dream To Share in Champion Bumper

Finished an excellent 40-1 third to A Dream To Share and Fact To File in last season's Champion Bumper and hasn't done a lot wrong in three hurdles starts. Won the Grade 2 Persian War on his debut at Chepstow in October, although that was a weak affair for the grade, and he suffered defeat next time at Cheltenham when second in another Grade 2, albeit coming out best at the weights as he was conceding 5lb to length-and-a-half winner Minella Missile. Proved how tough he is with a battling victory by the same margin in the Challow Hurdle, giving trainer Paul Nicholls his fourth consecutive success in the race. Arguably still has a bit to find against the Irish in either the Baring Bingham or here, but equally arguable that he has better form than some of the British ahead of him in both markets. Trainer will let conditions decide the target, with drying ground pushing him towards 3m.

Going preference Seems versatile
Star rating ✪✪✪

Gidleigh Park

6 b g; Trainer Harry Fry
Hurdles form 111, best RPR 136
Left-handed 11, best RPR 136

Right-handed 1, best RPR 115
Cheltenham form 1, best RPR 136

Another British contender with the options of the Baring Bingham and Albert Bartlett, and he's shorter for the former. Unbeaten in four starts, the first of them a bumper, and impressed in standard novice company on first two runs at Exeter and Newbury. Didn't really improve when just edging home from the 132-rated Lucky Place and, while he's essentially a stayer who wouldn't have been suited by the steady gallop and sprint finish, his price for either race suggests his form is better than it is.

Going preference All runs on good to soft and soft
Star rating ◐

Jingko Blue
5 b g; Trainer Nicky Henderson
Hurdles form 211, best RPR 142
Left-handed 21, best RPR 122
Right-handed 1, best RPR 142

Point winner who has taken his time to show his true colours but is certainly getting there. Beaten into second at odds of 4-7 on his Warwick debut, he scrambled home by only a neck at Newbury next time, but given a handicap mark of just 124 he won very easily by six lengths in a Class 3 handicap at Sandown in early February. A minor handicap it may have been, but an RPR of 142 (he got put up a stone officially) is better, for instance, than Grade 2 winner Gidleigh Park has produced. Trainer said he would like to mind him a bit this season, though, so whether he turns up here or in the Baring Bingham must be doubtful.

Going preference Acts on good to soft
Star rating ◐◐

Johnnywho
7 br g; Trainer Jonjo O'Neill
Hurdles form 144, best RPR 136
Left-handed 44, best RPR 136
Right-handed 1, best RPR 127
Cheltenham form 4, best RPR 128

Unbeaten in first three runs, which included a point, a bumper and a novice hurdle, and barely came off the bridle each time. That meant he was still learning on the job when sent for the Grade 1 Challow Hurdle, and he was outpaced in the straight at Newbury before getting the message, finishing best of all but good enough only for a two-length fourth. Couldn't match that form next time behind Gidleigh Park, although a steady gallop and sprint finish was never going to suit a horse who shapes like an out-and-out stayer. That's not surprising given he's a half-brother to 3m5f chase winner Doing Fine and his dam won over 4m. Likely we haven't seen the best of him and, while he has the Baring Bingham entry, if he goes anywhere it will surely be here.

Going preference Early days, but best form on soft/heavy
Star rating ◐◐

Answer To Kayf
8 b g; Trainer Terence O'Brien
Hurdles form 81231, best RPR 131
Left-handed 81, best RPR 124
Right-handed 123, best RPR 131

Placed in a point and a bumper and has won two of last four hurdles starts after being well beaten in the first of them. Third to Loughlynn in Limerick Grade 2 over Christmas was a fair effort, and he beat the well-regarded Captain Cody (sixth in Champion Bumper) at Naas in the second week of February, prompting everyone to cut him to 16-1 or 20-1 for this. Hard to put a big figure on the form, though, and he's going to have to find a lot more.

Going preference Seems to like soft/heavy
Star rating ◐

Chigorin
6 br g; Trainer Henry de Bromhead
Hurdles form 31, best RPR 122
Left-handed 3, best RPR 115
Right-handed 1, best RPR 122

Third in sole point and looked a little short of pace when occupying the same position on hurdles debut at Naas in November. Improved to win upped to 2m7f in another maiden at Fairyhouse in December, but the form is still very ordinary.

Going preference Only runs on soft/heavy
Star rating ◐

Croke Park

6 b g; Trainer Gordon Elliott
Hurdles form 117, best RPR 136
Left-handed 17, best RPR 136
Right-handed 1, best RPR 126

Won the second of two points and finished second to the very useful You Oughta Know in a Kilbeggan bumper in May before turning to hurdles in the autumn and winning his first two outings. An 11-length maiden scorer at Clonmel, he went on to take the Grade 3 Monksfield at Navan in fair style with a strong-staying performance over 2m4f. A rise in class for the Grade 1 Lawlor's of Naas didn't go to plan, though, and he was weak in the market before finishing a 23-length last of the seven runners. That can't have been the best of him, but it leave him with questions to answer. Still in the Baring Bingham, but trainer expects him to come into his own over 3m.

Going preference Good bumper run on yielding, all other form on soft/heavy
Star rating ✪

Largy Hill

7 b g; Trainer Willie Mullins
Hurdles form 21, best RPR 122
Left-handed 2, best RPR 117
Right-handed 1, best RPR 122

Won one of four bumpers but was certainly a long way behind the best in that sphere, finishing a 24-length seventh to A Dream To Share at Leopardstown. Has shown plenty of promise over hurdles, though, first when finishing second of 16 over 2m4f at Navan and then when winning his maiden over 3m at Cork in January.

Going preference Most runs on soft/heavy
Star rating ✪✪

My Trump Card

6 b g; Trainer Gordon Elliott
Hurdles form 421, best RPR 133
Left-handed 41, best RPR 133
Right-handed 2, best RPR 131

Fourth on maiden hurdle debut to now Grade 1-winning novice chaser Grangeclare West at Navan in November 2022, but took in two Navan bumpers on first two starts this season, winning the second and showing a fair level of form. Beaten 4-9 favourite on his next foray into maiden hurdle company at Fairyhouse in January, but went one better when scoring back at Navan later that month. Needs to step up in a big way, and Gordon Elliott sees him as a chaser of the future, but said he might let him take his chance.

Going preference All form on soft/heavy
Star rating ✪

Chapeau De Soleil

6 br g; Trainer Willie Mullins
Hurdles form 16, best RPR 127
Left-handed 6, best RPR 127
Right-handed 1, best RPR 126
Cheltenham form (bumper) 0, best RPR 123
At the festival 15 Mar 2023 In rear, slightly hampered over 2f out, pushed along and hung left over 1f out, stayed on inside final furlong, never on terms, finished tenth, beaten 14 lengths by A Dream To Share in Champion Bumper

Had his problems and was a beaten odds-on favourite on his bumper debut last season. Was still considered good enough to run in the Champion Bumper, though, and ran with a fair amount of credit to finish a 14-length tenth considering he was nearly brought down a couple of furlongs out. Won his maiden at Clonmel in fair fashion in December, but then made no show in the Lawlor's of Naas, finishing sixth of the seven runners and never looking likely to get involved after a bad mistake at the third. Probably capable of better, but this is a big ask on what he has shown.

Going preference Point win on yielding, all other runs on soft/heavy
Star rating ✪

Great Pepper

6 b g; Trainer James Moffatt
Hurdles form (left-handed) 11, best RPR 123

Pulled up in his first point in November 2022, but won his next two last year and has since made it 2-2 over hurdles. Wins in a maiden at Hexham and a novice under a penalty at Kelso (2m6½f) are hardly standout form, but he did it well on the second occasion and shaped as though a stiffer test would bring out more.

Going preference All form on soft/heavy
Star rating ✪

ALBERT BARTLETT NOVICES' HURDLE RESULTS AND TRENDS

	FORM	WINNER	AGE & WGT	Adj RPR	SP	TRAINER	BEST RPR LAST 12 MONTHS (RUNS SINCE)
23	12	**Stay Away Fay** BF	6 11-7	144-15	18-1	P Nicholls	2nd Doncaster Gd2 nov hdl (3m½f) (0)
22	111	**The Nice Guy**	7 11-8	147-10	18-1	W Mullins (IRE)	won Naas mdn hdl (2m3f) (0)
21	2120	**Vanillier**	6 11-5	153-3	14-1	G Cromwell (IRE)	2nd Limerick Gd2 nov hdl (2m7f) (1)
20	2211	**Monkfish** D	6 11-5	159-2	5-1	W Mullins (IRE)	won Thurles nov hdl (2m6½f) (0)
19	3-32	**Minella Indo**	6 11-5	147-13	50-1	H de Bromhead (IRE)	2nd Clonmel Gd3 nov hdl (3m) (0)
18	3113	**Kilbricken Storm** CD	7 11-5	152-11	33-1	C Tizzard	won Cheltenham Gd2 nov hdl (3m) (1)
17	11141	**Penhill** D	6 11-5	157-2	16-1	W Mullins (IRE)	won Limerick Gd2 nov hdl (3m) (0)
16	-1111	**Unowhatimeanharry** CD	8 11-5	154-9	11-1	H Fry	won Exeter class 2 hcap hdl (2m7f) (0)
15	11F12	**Martello Tower** D	7 11-7	151-6	14-1	M Mullins (IRE)	2nd Leopardstown Gd2 nov hdl (2m4f) (0)
14	-1253	**Very Wood**	5 11-7	143-18	33-1	N Meade (IRE)	3rd Naas Gd2 nov hdl (2m4f) (0)

WINS-RUNS: 5yo 1-27, 6yo 5-113, 7yo 3-32, 8yo 1-10 **FAVOURITES:** -£10.00

TRAINERS IN THIS RACE (w-pl-r): Willie Mullins 3-3-35, Gavin Cromwell 1-0-3, Henry de Bromhead 1-1-7, Paul Nicholls 1-0-5, Harry Fry 1-0-3, Ben Pauling 0-0-3, Dan Skelton 0-0-4, Alan King 0-0-2, Henry Daly 0-0-3, Gordon Elliott 0-4-12, John McConnell 0-2-3, Neil Mulholland 0-0-1, Nicky Henderson 0-2-12, Paul Nolan 0-2-2, Rebecca Curtis 0-0-6, Tom Lacey 0-0-1

FATE OF FAVOURITES: F0PU3244P0 **POSITION OF WINNER IN MARKET:** 9767003968

The Jukebox Man

6 b g; Trainer Willie Mullins
Hurdles form (left-handed) 113, best RPR 136
Left-handed 3, best RPR 136
Right-handed 11, best RPR 124

Point winner who was second to Gidleigh Park on bumper debut (six lengths) before winning one of his own at Ffos Las last spring. He then won his first two hurdles outings at Ffos Las as in November and December before taking a big step up in class and finishing an honourable 20-1 third to Captain Teague in the Grade 1 Challow at Newbury. Plenty of stamina in the family, and has better form than many ahead of him in the betting, but trainer says he relishes deep ground, so will need a wet spring to go there with any hope.

Going preference Point win on yielding, all other runs on soft/heavy
Star rating ✪

OTHERS TO CONSIDER

The Willie Mullins-trained **Mercurey** was a 50-1 shot at the time of writing and hadn't run beyond 2m. However, the 146 RPR he ran when last seen would put him only behind the first three in the betting and he'd be a fascinating contender if connections think he'll stay. There are others who have achieved a level of form better than some who are shorter in the betting, with the pick arguably being **Stellar Story**,

Key trends
- Aged six or seven, 8/10
- Adjusted RPR of at least 147, 8/10
- Two to six runs over hurdles, 7/10
- Rated within 11lb of RPR top-rated, 7/10
- Won over at least 2m4½f, 6/10
- Top-three finish in a Graded hurdle last time out, 6/10 (only one won)

Other factors
- Only four winners had won a Graded hurdle
- None of the last ten winners were RPR top-rated

although he has a lot to find with Dancing City on Leopardstown running.

VERDICT
This is always the hardest novice to solve, with a full field pretty much guaranteed and so many of the runners having no form over the trip. JOHNNYWHO has ground to make up on a couple of British rivals but looks guaranteed to improve dramatically for the step up in trip. I would also be highly tempted by Jingko Blue if he runs. Pick of the Irish might well be form horse Dancing City, but I can't back anything in single figures.

3.30 Boodles Cheltenham Gold Cup ITV/RTV
● 3m2½f ● Grade 1 ● £625,000

Galopin Des Champs improved his already high level by half a stone on Racing Post Ratings with a supremely dominant performance in last year's Gold Cup. Willie Mullins' superstar earned an elite RPR of 184 with his seven-length victory over Bravemansgame and after a couple of blips he matched it this season in his brilliant Savills Chase win at Christmas. Having followed up in the Irish Gold Cup, he is emphatically the one to beat again. Martin Brassil's Fastorslow, who beat the favourite twice in those blips, looks his biggest rival again as he tries this race for the first time, but now he has to turn around a four-and-a-half-length defeat in the Irish Gold Cup. There are other new challengers for this crown in the brilliant but sometimes moody Shishkin (Nicky Henderson), Gerri Colombe (Gordon Elliott), who had been on the rise until his distant second in the Savills, the recovered and resurgent L'Homme Presse (Venetia Williams) and the popular King George winner Hewick (Shark Hanlon).

Galopin Des Champs
8 bl g; Trainer Willie Mullins
Chase form 11F11112311, best RPR 184
Left-handed 11F1111, best RPR 184
Right-handed 1123, best RPR 177
Cheltenham form (all) 1F1, best RPR 184
At the festival 19 Mar 2021 Led, tracked leaders when headed after 2nd, led approaching last, ridden and kept on strongly run-in, readily, won Martin Pipe Conditional Jockeys' Handicap Hurdle by two and a quarter lengths from Langer Dan
17 Mar 2022 Led, 5 lengths ahead 2nd, not fluent 6th, mistake 9th, going easily 3 out, pushed along and went clear when good jump 2 out, 12 lengths ahead when fell last in Turners Novices' Chase won by Bob Olinger
17 Mar 2023 Held up in rear, not fluent 5th, headway 16th, in touch with leaders 17th, mistake 3 out, going easily when switched right before 2 out, soon went second, led last, ridden and kept on strongly run-in, won going away by seven lengths from Bravemansgame in Gold Cup

Would be a three-time festival winner if he hadn't fallen with the race at his mercy in the 2022 Turners, but the 2021 Martin Pipe Conditional Jockeys' Handicap hurdle winner made amends in a big way last season to provide Willie Mullins with his third Gold Cup success in the last five seasons. Galopin Des Champs had brushed off his Turners fall with a very easy win at Fairyhouse before signing off for his novice season, and he was back with a bang on his first start in open company when toying with his rivals in the John Durkan at Punchestown, his closest pursuer being the 13-lengths distant Fakir D'Oudairies, a four-time Grade 1 winner. An eight-length victory over the previous season's National Hunt Chase winner Stattler in the Irish Gold Cup confirmed 3m was no problem, and then it was on to the Gold Cup at Cheltenham, where Galopin Des Champs was always travelling and, despite a couple of sloppy jumps, stormed up the hill for a seven-length success from Bravemansgame, himself a 14-length King George winner the time before. Then came a couple of setbacks that set tongues wagging. It's not that unusual for a Gold Cup winner to feel the effects of their efforts later that season, and that appeared to be the case when he had his colours lowered by Fastorslow, who on his previous outing had just failed to win the Ultima, but was still rated 26lb inferior to his victim in the Punchestown Gold Cup. That was easy enough to write off, but on his reappearance this season he was again beaten by Fastorslow, this time in the John Durkan, in which even Appreciate It managed to hold him for second. Something clearly wasn't right and it led some to suggest his effort in the Gold Cup had somehow broken him and that he wouldn't be the same horse again. That couldn't have proved further from the mark, however. With new prominent tactics in the Savills Chase at Leopardstown, Galopin

Des Champs was back to his spellbinding best, measuring his fences well, cruising into the lead entering the straight and barely needing to be nudged out to beat a good field by 23 lengths and more, Gerri Colombe being the one to chase him home. His trainer let him loose in the Irish Gold Cup as well, and this time he gained his revenge over Fastorslow, winning by four and a half lengths. He wasn't quite as impressive as the time before, but that was understandable, and connections can go to Cheltenham knowing they have the measure of their biggest rival. For his Cheltenham and second Irish Gold Cup successes, Galopin Des Champs earned a Racing Post Rating of 184, and only the greats Kauto Star and Sprinter Sacre have bettered that in the last 15 years. Other than his Turners fall, he hasn't lost a race on a left-handed track since he was a 100-1 shot in a 2m novice hurdle at the Dublin Racing Festival in 2021, and it won't be a surprise if that's still true come 3.40pm on March 15.

Going preference Has never run on faster than good to soft/yielding
Star rating ✪✪✪✪

Fastorslow

8 b g; Trainer Martin Brassil
Chase form 1552112, best RPR 175
Left-handed 1522, best RPR 171
Right-handed 511, best RPR 175
Cheltenham form (all) 22, best RPR 165
At the festival 16 Mar 2022 In touch with leaders, went fourth 3 out, soon pushed along, ridden home turn, made strong challenge run-in, disputed lead final 110yds, kept on well but headed final strides, finished second, beaten a short head by Commander Of Fleet in Coral Cup 14 Mar 2023 Raced wide, midfield, headway going easily after 3 out, pushed along and briefly led last, soon edged left, ridden and every chance inside final 110yds, just held, finished second, beaten a neck by Corach Rambler in Ultima Handicap Chase

Just inched out of the Coral Cup by a short head on his first visit to Cheltenham in 2022, and after being highly tried in open Grade 1 company over fences on his first two starts last season (having won a chase in France in 2019, he wasn't a novice), he headed back there for a crack at the Ultima off a mark of 150. There he ran another blinder, but just

came up short again, this time going down by a neck to Corach Rambler, who was completing a double in the race and went on to land the Grand National next time out. Fastorslow was then thrown back into Grade 1 company in the Punchestown Gold Cup the following month against none other than the Gold Cup one-two of Galopin Des Champs and Bravemansgame and produced the mother of all shocks, hitting the front on the run-in and powering two and a quarter lengths clear from Galopin Des Champs, with a nose back to Bravemansgame. It was easy enough to assume that it had been an off day for the Gold Cup winner after such a big run at Cheltenham, but then Fastorslow did it again at Punchestown on his reappearance this season, being pushed out for a ready half-length win in the John Durkan from Appreciate It with Galopin Des Champs a length and a quarter further away. It looked to many as though we were seeing a changing of the guard, but Galopin Des Champs went a long way to changing minds when he won the Savills in such devastating fashion, and he confirmed he was still top dog with a four-and-a-half-length win from Fastorslow in the Irish Gold Cup in February. The runner-up was only a length down at the last, though, and the winner had the run of the race from the front throughout and is unlikely to get such an easy time in a bigger field in March. That said, Martin Brassil's eight-year-old is still going to have to up his game, but he's rightfully seen as the one most likely to.

Going preference Has run only on yielding and soft
Star rating ✪✪✪✪

Shishkin

10 b g; Trainer Nicky Henderson
Chase form 1111111P3121RU1, best RPR 179
Left-handed 111P211, best RPR 175
Right-handed 111131RU, best RPR 179
Cheltenham form (all) 11P2, best RPR 175
At the festival 10 Mar 2020 Mid-division, mistake 3rd and soon squeezed up, not clear run top of the hill and switched to outer, headway after next, left 5th when lucky to avoid faller and hampered 2 out, challenged last, led narrowly final 100yds, ridden out, won Supreme

Novices' Hurdle by a head from Abacadabras 16 Mar 2021 Chased leaders, good jump to lead 3 out, nudged along and went clear before 2 out, 6 lengths ahead last, easily, impressive, won Arkle Chase by 12 lengths from Eldorado Allen 16 Mar 2022 Didn't jump with fluency, slowly into stride, in rear, pushed along briefly just after 1st, switched right on outer after 5th, mistake and pushed along 6th, slow jump and pulled up quickly just after 8th in Champion Chase won by Energumene 16 Mar 2023 Slowly into stride, cajoled along early, towards rear, in touch with leaders when jumped left 4th, not fluent 4 out, bad mistake 3 out, soon cajoled along, hung left then switched right approaching last, stayed on and went second towards finish, finished second, beaten two and three-quarter lengths by Envoi Allen in Ryanair Chase

Dual festival winner over 2m (Supreme Novices' Hurdle and Arkle) who has had his share of ups and downs, including when pulled up not long past halfway when never travelling as an odds-on shot for the 2022 Champion Chase. He again looked sluggish when he could manage only a 15-length third to Edwardstone in that year's Tingle Creek and, while he was sent for a wind operation afterwards, the decided course of action was a step up in trip. That worked a treat and Shishkin went to Ascot, scene of the best run of his life (his victory over Energumene in the Clarence House Chase) and thrashed the talented Pic D'Orhy by 16 lengths, recording an RPR just 1lb shy of his best. He had to be a short-priced favourite for the Ryanair after that, but he again didn't jump at all well, and it was only his courage and will to win that hauled him into second place on the line, where he was a neck in front of Hitman but two and three-quarter lengths behind Envoi Allen. His season finished with a further step up in trip and he put himself into the 2024 Gold Cup picture when staying on well to beat Ahoy Senor at that one's favourite stomping ground in the Bowl at Aintree. This season has been a strange one as, set to be tried in first-time cheekpieces in the 1965 Chase at Ascot, Shishkin planted himself at the start and refused to race in what should have been his King George warm-up. A plan was then hatched for him to run in the rescheduled Fighting Fifth Hurdle at Sandown as a prep and he was declared for it overnight, but in the end

didn't run with the ground being deemed too soft. On it was to the King George then, and in it Shishkin proved he didn't need a prep run as he looked sure to win until suffering dreadful misfortune when stumbling after the second-last and unseating Nico de Boinville. He needed a little cajoling to get started, but was soon chasing leader Frodon and took over seven out. The previous year's winner Bravemansgame had narrowed the gap to just under a length going to the third-last, but it was a length and a half again at the next when disaster struck, and given how Bravemansgame and Allaho let themselves be caught by Hewick, it's hard to come to any other conclusion than that he would have won. He at least put a win on board when taking the Denman Chase at Newbury, and though he wasn't always fluent at his fences, correcting to his left as he often does nowadays, the result was never really in doubt, although he only beat Hitman, who wouldn't be the strongest stayer at the trip and did briefly look a danger. Shishkin is very much an out-and-out stayer now, and he certainly has the ability to be involved, but whether Cheltenham is his course nowadays is another matter as he has jumped poorly in the Champion Chase and Ryanair since his two festival wins. This Gold Cup is a considerably warmer race than last year's Ryanair, and he couldn't get away with it then. Add the fact no ten-year-old has won since Cool Dawn in 1998 and he looks short enough. He'd be one of the better ten-year-olds to try since then, but even better ones than him – Kauto Star and Denman – have come up short at that age.

Going preference Handles any ground
Star rating ✪✪✪

Gerri Colombe

8 b g; Trainer Gordon Elliott
Chase form 1112112, best RPR 168
Left-handed 212, best RPR 166
Right-handed 1111, best RPR 168
Cheltenham form 2, best RPR 163
At the festival 15 Mar 2023 Prominent, not fluent 9th, pushed along and outpaced after 3 out, ridden after 2 out, 4 lengths third last, rallied and went second final 110yds, kept on strongly, just failed, finished second, beaten a short head by The Real Whacker in Brown Advisory Novices' Chase

One of the new kids on the block, albeit at the same age as Galopin Des Champs and Fastorslow, Gerri Colombe started the season as one of the second favourites behind the defending champion, but he has a little bit to prove now. The winner of a point and his first seven races under rules, including two Grade 1 novice chases at around 2m4f, he didn't step up to 3m until running in the Brown Advisory last season, yet somewhat surprisingly was a little outpaced after the third-last. Still four lengths down on The Real Whacker at the last, he flew up the run-in, but the line came just too soon and he was beaten a short head. He bagged his third Grade 1 of the season with a very easy win in the Mildmay Novices' Chase at Aintree, although bar him it was a dreadful race by Grade 1 standards, and he arguably put up better form on his return at Down Royal in the Ladbrokes Champion Chase. There he again looked tapped for toe as the pace quickened, as he was pressing leader Conflated three out but had lost second two out, but he put his head down after the last and managed to collar course specialist and three-time Cheltenham Festival winner Envoi Allen (going for his fifth straight win at the meeting) to win by a neck. It was hard to put a massive figure on the run, but a steady pace wouldn't have suited, and Gerri Colombe again showed he could battle. He was, however, comprehensively outclassed when a 23-length second to Galopin Des Champs in the Savills, and the question is whether he was simply below form then or that's as good as he is as his RPR of 163 wasn't a mile off his best. Indeed, he has yet to run a 170 RPR. At the final forfeit stage before the five-day declarations, there were nine horses with better figures than him over the last 12 months, three of them 50-1 shots. As the fourth favourite, he's underpriced on form but the potential is there.

Going preference Acts on good to soft and heavy, yet to run on good
Star rating ✪✪

L'Homme Presse

9 b g; Trainer Venetia Williams
Chase form 1111131U12, best RPR 175

Left-handed 11311, best RPR 175
Right-handed 111U2, best RPR 173
Cheltenham form 11, best RPR 166
At the festival 16 Mar 2022 Travelled strongly, jumped well, tracked leader, led and made rest from 7th, 3 lengths ahead 2 out, ridden after last, kept on well, won Brown Advisory Novices' Chase by three and a half lengths from Ahoy Senor

No more than an average hurdler, L'Homme Presse won the first five chases of his life in impressive fashion during the 2021-22 season, including the Brown Advisory on his first run at 3m, when he beat Ahoy Senor by three and a half lengths and was very strong at the line. Clearly over the top when an 18-length third to Ahoy Senor at Aintree after that, he made a surprising reappearance under top weight in the Rehearsal Chase at Newcastle last season, but didn't let 12st or the concession of 26lb to the runner-up (who won the Rowland Meyrick off 4lb higher next time) bother him as he won very easily by a length. That performance was enough to make him favourite for the King George at Kempton, but not for the first time on a right-handed track he kept edging to his left and he paid for the concession of the ground in the straight with Bravemansgame taking his measure at the second-last. He'd have been a clear second had he not unseated at the last, so it was hardly a disastrous run and the return to Cheltenham promised to suit. Unfortunately he suffered an injury afterwards and missed just over a year, but he did make a really encouraging comeback when beating Protektorat in the Fleur de Lys Chase at Lingfield in January. There he was a bit slow to warm up (hit the first with his head!) and had to be cajoled along after leaving the back straight for the final time, but he soon got the message, threw in a big leap at the last and, while the runner-up briefly looked like closing up on him again, he was going away at the line. Venetia Williams was desperate to get another run into him, so he reappeared over a shorter trip in the Betfair Chase at Ascot, where he was a little disappointing in third, his tendency to edge left at his fences not helping. The yard was struggling for winners at the time and Williams said she was delighted with his five-and-a-half-length second to Pic D'Orhy. He was pushed out in the betting by some bookmakers, but it's easy to see where Williams was coming form, as L'Homme Presse ran well enough considering the trip, track and ground were against him. He certainly didn't bounce following his return at Lingfield and he'll surely be way more effective back at Cheltenham.

Going preference Acts on any ground, most effective on soft

Star rating ✪✪✪

Hewick

9 b g; Trainer Shark Hanlon
Chase form 12P21P11UF101, best RPR 173
Left-handed 21PUF, best RPR 168
Right-handed 1P211101, best RPR 173
Cheltenham form F, best RPR 168
At the festival 17 Mar 2023 Raced in second, left in lead 17th, not fluent 5 out, headed and ridden before 2 out where fell heavily in Gold Cup won by Galopin Des Champs

Little legend of a horse who cost only €850 but has now won in excess of £600k. The winner of the Galway Plate in July 2022 and the American Grand National (a 2m5f hurdle) that October, his next start was as a 40-1 outsider in the Gold Cup on soft ground that he doesn't care for. He still ran a cracker, though, having been prominent throughout and, after being left in the lead following the fall of Ahoy Senor, he led until headed just before two out, after which he took a very heavy fall. Hewick soon shrugged that off, though, as a month later he turned out at Sandown on the final day of the British season to win the Oaksey Chase by four lengths from First Flow. Fourth a month later in the French Champion Hurdle (3m1½f) on very soft ground, he was then tailed off in the Galway Plate, but the versatile then eight-year-old had a break and returned to score the biggest win of his life in the

King George at Kempton, beating the previous year's winner Bravemansgame by a length and a half with Allaho a head away in third. Quite how he won it takes some explaining, as he was being pushed along as early as the seventh, and was last and apparently going nowhere by the 13th, the only surprise being that his in-running price didn't go higher than the 550 he traded at. Gavin Sheehan, riding him for the first time, never gave up but Hewick was a ten-length fifth when he ploughed through the third-last and still at least six lengths down two out. Up ahead, though, Shishkin stumbled on landing and unseated Nico de Boinvile and knocked eventual runner-up Bravemansgame out of his stride, costing him a couple of lengths. It should have been Allaho's to win, but he started to tie up approaching the last and Hewick, who hadn't quite taken off when Allaho landed over

Galopin Des Champs: recorded an RPR of 184 for last year's brilliant seven-length victory

the final fence, pounced halfway up the run-in to win going away. It was as dramatic as any top-class race could be. It was also a career-best from Hewick, who heads into the Gold Cup a much shorter price than he was 12 months ago. He still needs to improve again, and it's unlikely events will conspire in his favour in such a way ever again, but he has defied the odds all his life, so who knows?

Going preference The faster the better
Star rating ✪✪

Bravemansgame
9 b g; Trainer Paul Nicholls
Chase form 111141123222, best RPR 177
Left-handed 11141222, best RPR 175
Right-handed 1132, best RPR 177
Cheltenham form (all) 32, best RPR 175
At the festival 17 Mar 2021 Pressed leader, led after 2nd, headed and pushed along 2 out, soon rallied and every chance, lost ground approaching last, ridden and lost second run-in, weakened inside final 110yds, finished third, beaten 12 lengths by Bob Olinger in Ballymore Novices' Hurdle
17 Mar 2023 Keen to post, prominent, ridden to lead 2 out, headed last, weakened final 110yds, finished second, beaten seven lengths by Galopin Des Champs in Gold Cup

Top-class performer at his best who won the Charlie Hall on his return last season and then put up the performance of his life to take the King George by 14 lengths, but hasn't managed to get his head in front in five starts since. He had stamina questions to answer in last season's Gold Cup and it's hard to say he didn't stay as he finished second and was six and a half lengths clear of the third, but he couldn't quite pack the finish of Galopin Des Champs. He got within a nose of Galopin Des Champs in the Punchestown Gold Cup, but that was only good enough for third as Fastorslow trumped the pair of them, and since then it has been a run of three seconds. He looked set to cruise to a second Charlie Hall victory in October, but reached for the last and lost momentum. That allowed Gentlemansgame, whose rider had been hard at work since two out, another chance and it was gratefully taken for a length-and-three-quarter win. An original plan to go straight to the King George was then shelved when trainer Paul Nicholls saw how weak the valuable Grade 1 Betfair Chase would be, but this time Bravemansgame couldn't live with course specialist Royale Pagaille and went down by six and a half lengths. He was still fancied for the King George the following month at Kempton, where unlike a year earlier when he was kept to the outside all the way despite the attentions of a left-jumping L'Homme Presse, he started off on the inner. His jumping was sketchy, though, before it improved markedly when Harry Cobden moved him out to give him more space. He was bang in contention turning for home, but looked held by Shishkin when that one stumbled and unseated two out. Bravemansgame almost certainly would have won had he not been impeded by that stumble as he arguably lost more ground than he was beaten by, and he has better form than some of those ahead of him in the Gold Cup betting. He needs to prove he's still up to last season's level, though.

Going preference Handles soft well but a bit of decent ground on Gold Cup day wouldn't go amiss
Star rating ✪✪✪

Gentlemansgame
8 gr g; Trainer Mouse Morris
Chase form 121, best RPR 165
Left-handed 11, best RPR 165
Right-handed 2, best RPR 155

Classy enough hurdler who finished third to Klassical Dream in the Champion Stayers Hurdle at Punchestown in April 2022, but has seen the racecourse only three times since. On his debut in a novice chase that December he jumped like an old hand and was a convincing eight-length winner from subsequent Irish Grand National hero I Am Maximus, but it was a full nine months before we saw him again in a Grade 2 at Gowran. He shaped well when a length-and-a-half runner-up to Easy Game and finished ahead of Envoi Allen, but it was hardly a run that screamed Gold Cup contender. He was entitled to be rusty, though, and was better next time at Wetherby in the Charlie Hall, where he beat odds-on favourite Bravemansgame by a length and three-quarters, although he was helped by the tiring favourite reaching for the last and losing a bit of momentum. He was getting

6lb as well, so still has plenty to find, and he hasn't been seen since. There will be novices who have run in this with more experience than he has.

Going preference Seems versatile enough
Star rating ✪✪✪

Corach Rambler
10 b g; Trainer Lucinda Russell
Chase form 3114U1541153, best RPR 162
Left-handed 114141153, best RPR 162
Right-handed 3U5, best RPR 135
Cheltenham form 111, best RPR 162
At the festival 15 Mar 2022 Slowly into stride, bit short of room soon after start, held up in rear, still plenty to do 3 out, pushed along and good headway before 2 out, ridden and went third approaching last, led inside final 110yds, won going away by two and three-quarter lengths from Gericault Roque in Ultima Handicap Chase
14 Mar 2023 Towards rear on inner, steady headway halfway, switched left and in touch with leaders after 3 out, pushed along and led run-in, idled towards finish, just did enough, won Ultima Handicap Chase by a neck from Fastorslow

High-class handicapper who made it back-to-back wins in the Ultima when edging out Fastorslow (who conceded 4lb) by a neck last March, and went on to score a famous victory in the Grand National the following month. That's his end destination again, but connections are keen to have a crack at this first, although it has to be said he has mountains to climb on form, particularly this season's. We probably shouldn't read too much into what he has done this term, though, as he tends to start the season sluggishly and did just that when only fifth of six on his return at Kelso in October. There was more to like about his finishing effort when he was third to Royale Pagaille in the Betfair Chase at Haydock, but he was still beaten just over 15 lengths. Still, he has proved in the past that he's a much better horse in the spring, and there's every chance there's a better run in him. A lot of the main protagonists in this Gold Cup like to race up with the pace, and it's a certainty that some of them will crack in the latter stages, while he'll be ridden cold out the back, so don't be surprised if he picks his way through some of them to grab a decent share

GOLD CUP RESULTS AND TRENDS

	FORM	WINNER	AGE & WGT	Adj RPR	SP	TRAINER	BEST RPR LAST 12 MONTHS (RUNS SINCE)
23	F1-11	Galopin Des Champs C	7 11-10	181⁻⁶	7-5f	W Mullins (IRE)	won Gd1 Fairyhouse nov ch (2m4f) (2)
22	12-12	A Plus Tard C, D, BF	8 11-10	184ᵀ	3-1f	H de Bromhead (IRE)	won Gd1 Betfair Chase (3m1½f) (1)
21	-11F4	Minella Indo C, BF	8 11-10	174⁻⁸	9-1	H de Bromhead (IRE)	won Wexford Gd3 chase (2m7f) (3)
20	11-21	Al Boum Photo CD	8 11-10	182⁻¹	10-3f	W Mullins (IRE)	won Cheltenham Gold Cup (3m2½f) (2)
19	F10-1	Al Boum Photo	7 11-10	173⁻⁹	12-1	W Mullins (IRE)	won Tramore Listed chase (2m5½f) (0)
18	113-1	Native River D	8 11-10	177ᵀ	5-1	C Tizzard	won Newbury Gd2 chase (2m7½f) (0)
17	-3211	Sizing John	7 11-10	172⁻¹²	7-1	J Harrington (IRE)	won Gd1 Irish Gold Cup (3m½f) (0)
16	111F1	Don Cossack	9 11-10	185ᵀ	9-4f	G Elliott (IRE)	won Gd1 Punchestown Gold Cup (3m1f) (4)
15	3/111	Coneygree C	8 11-10	173⁻⁹	7-1	M Bradstock	won Newbury Gd2 chase (2m7½f) (0)
14	1-876	Lord Windermere C	8 11-10	161⁻²⁴	20-1	J Culloty (IRE)	7th Gd1 Lexus Chase (3m) (1)

WINS-RUNS: 6yo 0-2, 7yo 3-21, 8yo 6-44, 9yo 1-41, 10yo 0-15, 11yo 0-6, 12yo 0-1 **FAVOURITES:** £3.98

TRAINERS IN THIS RACE (w-pl-r): Willie Mullins 3-5-26, Henry de Bromhead 2-2-10, Gordon Elliott 1-1-7, Nicky Henderson 0-2-9, Dan Skelton 0-1-2, Paul Nicholls 0-1-9, Venetia Williams 0-0-8, John Joseph Hanlon 0-0-1, Lucinda Russell 0-0-1

FATE OF FAVOURITES: 5014201311 **POSITION OF WINNER IN MARKET:** 7214361411

of the prize-money. It's very hard to see him winning, though.

Going preference Has won on good and soft, but probably wants a proper stamina test at this distance, so soft is preferable

Star rating ⭐⭐

OTHERS TO CONSIDER

It's hard to see what else can get involved. Willie Mullins says he's still tempted by the race for **Monkfish**, but that one hasn't run over fences for nearly three years and is shorter in the betting for the Stayers' Hurdle. **The Real Whacker** doesn't seem to have gone on from last season's novice campaign, which brought victory in the Brown Advisory, and it's hard to fathom the entry for **Jungle Boogie** after he was all out to record an RPR of just 152 on New Year's Day. Gary Moore has said **Nassalam** is unlikely to have a crack at this before the main target of the Grand National, and **Ahoy Senor**, **Protektorat** and **Conflated**, all previous Gold Cup runners, look more likely to go for the Ryanair this year.

VERDICT

*The performance of **GALOPIN DES CHAMPS** last year was that of a superior Gold Cup winner and, having rediscovered his form after a couple of defeats at Punchestown, he has to rank as much the likeliest winner again, while his Irish Gold Cup victim **Fastorslow** is much the likeliest runner-up. I'd*

Key trends

- Aged between seven and nine, 10/10
- Grade 1 chase winner, 9/10
- No more than 13 starts over fences, 9/10
- Adjusted RPR of at least 172, 9/10
- Won over at least 3m, 9/10
- Ran no more than four times that season, 9/10
- Within 9lb of RPR top-rated, 8/10
- Won a Graded chase that season, 8/10
- Won or placed previously at the festival, 8/10

Other factors

- In 2015, Coneygree became the first winner not to have run at a previous festival since Imperial Call in 1996. He was also the first novice to win since Captain Christy in 1974
- Four of the last ten winners had run in the King George or Savills Chase (formerly Lexus) that season

*be negative about the chances of **Shishkin** (jumping at Cheltenham) and **Gerri Colombe** (form) and wouldn't be that surprised if **Corach Rambler** once again proved his liking for the course and sneaked into a place late on.*

4.10 St James's Place Festival Hunters' Chase ITV/RTV
● 3m2½f ● Amateur riders ● £50,000

There has been an even split of British and Irish successes over the past decade after the score was levelled last year by 66-1 shot Premier Magic from trainer-rider Bradley Gibbs's Herefordshire yard.

Nine horses since 1956 have won the race twice – three of them (Salsify, On The Fringe and Pacha Du Polder) in recent years – and Premier Magic will be the latest to attempt the double.

He was ten last year when he continued the recent run of success for older runners, being the ninth in a row aged in double figures. Before the recent upward trend, 14 of the previous 19 winners had been nine or younger.

ONES TO WATCH Premier Magic will be faced by a renewed challenge from Ireland, led by top handler David Christie's **Ferns Lock**. The seven-year-old missed last year's festival but has improved in the meantime and warmed up with an impressive win at Thurles. Emmet Mullins' **Its On The Line**, runner-up last year, is set to return after a narrow prep win over **Billaway**, the 2022 winner for Willie Mullins.

HUNTERS' CHASE RESULTS AND TRENDS

	FORM	WINNER	AGE & WGT	Adj RPR	SP	TRAINER	BEST RPR LAST 12 MONTHS (RUNS SINCE)
23	P1-11	**Premier Magic**	10 12-0	129-18	66-1	B Gibbs	Pulled up Foxhunter Chase (3m2½f) (0)
22	5-211	**Billaway**	10 12-0	147T	13-8f	W Mullins (IRE)	2nd Foxhunter Chase (3m2½f) (4)
21	21-12	**Porlock Bay**	10 12-0	135-20	16-1	W Biddick	2nd Wincanton class 6 hunter chs (3m1f) (0)
20	-U117	**It Came To Pass**	10 12-0	126-29	66-1	E O'Sullivan (IRE)	won Cork hunter chase (3m) (2)
19	12-11	**Hazel Hill**	11 12-0	151-4	7-2f	P Rowley	won Warwick class 6 hunter chase (3m) (0)
18	114-3	**Pacha Du Polder** CD, BF	11 12-0	145-5	25-1	P Nicholls	won Foxhunter Chase (3m2½f) (2)
17	-3341	**Pacha Du Polder** CD	10 12-0	143-8	16-1	P Nicholls	3rd Uttoxeter Listed hcap ch (3m2f) (2)
16	11-17	**On The Fringe** CD, BF	11 12-0	148T	13-8f	E Bolger (IRE)	won Aintree Fox Hunters Chase (2m5f) (2)
15	-1122	**On The Fringe**	10 12-0	144T	6-1	E Bolger (IRE)	1st Punchestown hunter chase (2m7f) (4)
14	-6213	**Tammys Hill** BF	9 12-0	139-9	15-2	L Lennon (IRE)	2nd Down Royal hunter chase (2m7f) (2)

WINS-RUNS: 6yo 0-4, 7yo 0-13, 8yo 0-25, 9yo 1-41, 10yo 6-47, 11yo 3-49, 12yo 0-32, 13yo 0-10, 14yo 0-3 **FAVOURITES:** -£0.25

TRAINERS IN THIS RACE (w-pl-r): Paul Nicholls 2-1-14, Willie Mullins 1-2-4, Bradley Gibbs 1-0-2, Emmet Mullins 0-1-1, David Christie 0-1-3, Declan Queally 0-0-4, Gordon Elliott 0-1-4

FATE OF FAVOURITES: 5314812210 **POSITION OF WINNER IN MARKET:** 4216010910

Key trends
● Aged ten or 11, 9/10

● Won over at least 3m, 8/10

● Top-three finish last time out, 8/10

● Adjusted RPR of at least 139, 7/10

● Rated within 9lb of RPR top-rated, 7/10 (exceptions 18lb to 29lb off top)

Other factors
● The record of the previous year's winner is 141P7F

● There have been three back-to-back winners since 2012 – Salsify (2012-13), On The Fringe (2015-16) and Pacha Du Polder (2017-18). The last one before them was Double Silk in 1993-94.

● Five winners had competed at a previous festival

● Those aged 12 or older are winless in the last ten years. The 13-year-old Earthmover (2004) is the only winner from that bracket since 1990

4.50 **Mrs Paddy Power Mares' Chase**   RTV
● *2m4½f* ● *Grade 2* ● *£120,000*

Willie Mullins won the first two runnings but had to settle for second last year with 13-8 favourite Allegorie De Vassy, who was beaten two and a half lengths by the Colm Murphy-trained Impervious, her main rival at 15-8.

In fact, Mullins has had the beaten favourite in every running now and the one who looks set to carry that mantle this year is Dinoblue, who has been running well in open top-level company and is top on Racing Post Ratings. She led home a Mullins 1-2-3-4 in a Grade 1 at Christmas and then finished a respectable second to top-class stablemate El Fabiolo in the Dublin Chase.

Next on RPRs and in the ante-post market is Allegorie De Vassy, who looks set to attempt to go one better than last year.

Gavin Cromwell could be represented by Limerick Lace *(below)* and Brides Hill, while Gordon Elliott also has a couple of decent contenders in Riviere D'Etel, who was still travelling comfortably when falling three out in last year's race, and last-time-out Grade 2 winner Harmonya Maker.

MARES' CHASE RESULTS

	FORM WINNER	AGE & WGT	OR	SP	TRAINER	BEST RPR LAST 12 MONTHS (RUNS SINCE)
23	5-111 **Impervious** D	7 11-5	168-3	15-8	C Murphy (IRE)	won Punchestown Gd3 nov ch (2m3½f) (0)
22	1-321 **Elimay** D	8 11-2	171ᵀ	9-4	W Mullins (IRE)	2nd Mares' Chase Gd2 (2m4½f) (4)
21	5-111 **Colreevy** D	8 11-7	166-2	9-4	W Mullins (IRE)	won Thurles Gd2 nov ch (2m4f) (0)

WINS-RUNS: 6yo 0-3, 7yo 1-6, 8yo 2-10, 9yo 0-7, 10yo 0-2 **FAVOURITES:** -£3.00

TRAINERS IN THIS RACE (w-pl-r): Willie Mullins 2-2-9, Gordon Elliott 0-0-2, Gavin Cromwell 0-0-1, Henry de Bromhead 0-0-1, Venetia Williams 0-2-2

FATE OF FAVOURITES: 252 **POSITION OF WINNER IN MARKET:** 222

5.30 Martin Pipe Conditional Jockeys' Hcap Hurdle RTV
● 2m4½f ● £75,000

LAST YEAR'S WINNER Iroko was a first festival winner for joint-trainers Oliver Greenall and Josh Guerriero at 6-1, leading home a JP McManus one-two ahead of the Nicky Henderson-trained 14-1 shot No Ordinary Joe.

WEIGHT AND RATINGS Runners rated between 133 and 139 have won nine of the 15 runnings but four of the last six winners were rated 142-145.

AGE Five- and six-year-olds have won 13 of the 15 runnings.

TRAINERS Ten of the last 13 runnings were won by Willie Mullins, Paul Nicholls, Gordon Elliott or Joseph O'Brien.

BETTING Ten of the 15 winners have been sent off at double-figure odds and Sir Des Champs in 2011 is the only successful favourite.

ONES TO WATCH **Sa Majeste** is a Willie Mullins-trained possible for last year's winning owner. Gigginstown's likely types include Mullins' **Quai De Bourbon** and the Gordon Elliott-trained pair **Cleatus Poolaw** and **Stellar Story**.

MARTIN PIPE HANDICAP HURDLE RESULTS AND TRENDS

	FORM	WINNER	AGE & WGT	OR	SP	TRAINER	BEST RPR LAST 12 MONTHS (RUNS SINCE)
23	44-11	Iroko D	5 11-5	138ᵀ	6-1	O Greenall/J Guerriero	won Wetherby cl3 hcap hdl (2m3½f) (0)
22	11471	Banbridge D	6 11-3	137⁻⁷	12-1	J O'Brien (IRE)	won Navan nov hdl (2m) (0)
21	12P6	Galopin Des Champs	5 11-9	142⁻⁸	8-1	W Mullins (IRE)	6th Leopardstown Gd1 nov hdl (2m) (0)
20	52231	Indefatigable CD	7 11-9	145⁻³	25-1	P Webber	won Warwick Listed hdl (2m5f) (0)
19	30-52	Early Doors	6 11-10	145⁻³	5-1	J O'Brien (IRE)	2nd Leopardstown Gd1 hdl (3m) (0)
18	32161	Blow By Blow D	7 11-10	144⁻¹	11-1	G Elliott (IRE)	won Thurles Gd3 nov hdl (2m4f) (0)
17	23213	Champagne Classic D	6 11-3	138⁻⁹	12-1	G Elliott (IRE)	won Thurles mdn hdl (2m6½f) (1)
16	4-235	Ibis Du Rheu	5 11-7	139⁻⁴	14-1	P Nicholls	3rd Lanzarote Handicap Hurdle (2m5f) (1)
15	-5123	Killultagh Vic D	6 11-1	135⁻⁵	7-1	W Mullins (IRE)	3rd Leopardstown Gd2 nov hdl (2m4f) (0)
14	2-211	Don Poli	5 11-5	143⁻⁴	12-1	W Mullins (IRE)	won Clonmel Gd3 nov hdl (3m) (0)

WINS-RUNS: 5yo 4-59, 6yo 4-85, 7yo 2-41, 8yo 0-25, 9yo 0-10, 10yo 0-7, 11yo 0-1 **FAVOURITES:** -£10.00

FATE OF FAVOURITES: 0300020085 **POSITION OF WINNER IN MARKET:** 6267620563

Key trends

● Top-three finish in at least one of last two starts, 9/10

● No more than eight hurdle runs, 9/10

● Officially rated 137-145, 9/10

● Aged five or six, 8/10

● Had won that season, 8/10

● Rated within 5lb of RPR top-rated, 7/10

Other factors

● Willie Mullins (three) Gordon Elliott (two) and Joseph O'Brien (two) account for the seven Irish-trained winners, three of whom were owned by Gigginstown

● The six winners from 2012 to 2017 carried between 11st 1lb and 11st 7lb. Four of the last six shouldered 11st 9lb or 11st 10lb

● Willie Mullins trained the last two winners rated lower than 137 (Killultagh Vic in 2015 and Sir Des Champs in 2011)